ARK OF THE COVENANT & HOLY GRAIL

THE SYMBOLISM BEHIND THE MYSTERY

Henrietta Bernstein

DeVorss Publications
Camarillo, California

ISBN10: 087516-833-7
ISBN13: 978-0-87516-833-3
Library of Congress Control Number: 2007924013

FIRST DEVORSS EDITION, 1998
FIRST PRINTING REVISED EDITION, 2007

DeVorss & Company, Publisher
P.O. Box 1389
Camarillo CA 93011-1389
www.devorss.com

Printed in the United States of America

ACKNOWLEDGMENTS

Thank you, Manly and Marie Hall, for starting me on this quest and introducing me to Francis Bacon and the Shakespeare group; Victoria Ransom, for the unselfish time you spent with me; and for all the information I gathered from your companion "Grandmother"—a very special thanks; I am grateful to Hanna Levinson for clarifying many concepts in her insightful editing and giving me her time so generously; Georgia Lambert, whose brilliant lectures given at the Philosophical Research Society were so informative and from which I learned a great deal; thanks to my special friend William Dotson, a great mathematician, who helped me work through the mathematics and sacred geometry of Washington, D.C.; also, I feel especially grateful to Cheri Mariotto for the material she shared with me on the Statue of Liberty and the Statue of Christ in Brazil, and to Fred Cole, a very dear friend who helped me on many occasions and especially with the material about the tunnels under Bruton Churchyard in Williamsburg, Virginia, and the symbols of Athena throughout Washington, D.C.; thank you, Alan Bernstein, for your valuable support and advice with the mathematics of Phi, part of sacred geometry—your talent and willingness to help are very much appreciated; a special thanks to Elinore Detiger for providing the trip to Bruton Church in England, which exposed another clue about Christ and Glastonbury. To the editors at DeVorss & Co. I would like to express my gratitude for the valuable help they have given me with the publishing of this book. Some other very exceptional people whom I thank for offering their assistance: Art Kunkin, Anna Bernstein, Heide Rose, Edin and Esther Shapiro, Elisa Rothstein, Glen Craney, Simi Dabah and Carol Okuda. A great deal of gratitude to my husband, whom I applaud for being so patient for the five years when I could think of nothing else but the material of this book.

iii

EXODUS CHAP. XXXI.
Moyses receiveth the two Tables.

EXODUS 31. Verse 18.

The Lord gave unto Moses, when he had made an end of communing with him upon mount Sinai, two tables of testimony etc.

—from an old Bible

Moses Receiving the Tables of the Law

DEDICATION TO MOSES
AND THE EMERALD TABLET

Moses, priest of Osiris, the Egyptian initiate, was truly the or-
ganizer of monotheism. Through Moses the principle of one God
entered the course of history. The prophet of Sinai clearly had
before him distant vistas which extended beyond the destinies of
his people. The word "Israel" signifies all humanity, and the establishment of one universal religion or the oneness of all people is the true mission of Israel. Few Jews other than its greatest
prophets understood this, and this was the tremendous work of
Moses.

I dedicated my first book, *Cabalah Primer*, to Moses because
I felt his closeness while writing. But, as they say in America,
"Baby, you've come a long way!" I now realize that what Moses
brought down from Mount Sinai was The Ten Commandments,
which he gave to all the people, and the blueprint for the entire
scheme of the universe, coded in Cabalah and sacred geometry,
which he gave only to the highest initiates to hold in strictest
secrecy. This blueprint was the Ark of the Covenant, the connecting link of all civilizations—the link that makes them one.

Again, it is Moses who has inspired me, but this time he is
pointing to the Emerald Tablet on which the Ark of the Covenant
is inscribed.

CONTENTS

INTRODUCTION

 short while ago I began a journey that led me to a rare discovery about the Oneness of all things. I am writing this book to share with you this incredible story that has changed my life forever.

Like most things, becoming good friends with the distinguished philosopher and highly esteemed Mason Manly P. Hall and his wife Marie was not accidental. I think we were divinely brought together so that my destiny of telling these "Mysteries" could be fulfilled. My background with the Halls (as well as my background in Cabalah and sacred geometry with the great Cabalist William Eisen) was also not accidental. Without all these infusions into my life, this book could not have been written. As my dear friend Marie Hall has often said to me: "Men made secrets, and then God thought better and made women to break open all secrets." With this in mind, I will start at the beginning and tell how I became involved with Buried Vaults, the Ark of the Covenant, the Holy Grail, and America's Secret Destiny.

In 1984, I teamed up with a partner and we decided to do a conference on electric magnetic energy and the earth. The conference was held on a ranch in the Topanga Canyon area of California, which has spectacular energy. We invited many scientists from throughout the United States to participate. The conference was a great success; I don't think anyone who attended will ever forget it.

One of our speakers was Marie Bauer Hall, who revealed to us an amazing discovery she had made, in 1938, in the Bruton Churchyard in Williamsburg, Virginia. The subject of Marie's lecture was the discussion of a mystery about which the most excellent minds of Europe and America had concerned themselves for the past three centuries—a secret vault in Williamsburg, Virginia. Marie explained that the vault was buried in 1676 by Francis Bacon's group, exactly one century before the signing of the American Declaration of Independence in 1776. Marie was convinced that the Virginia Vault held the records for the foundation of a Universal Commonwealth.

A few days after the Electric Magnetic Conference, I received an invitation from Marie and her husband, Manly, inviting me and all the scientists from our conference to their home for Marie's eighty-first birthday. This was a real treat for all of us, and it is where my journey begins. Not only was Marie Bauer Hall a spectacular person, but she was married to a well-known philosopher of our time, Manly Palmer Hall, a renowned authority on philosophy, comparative religion, and the esoteric doctrines of antiquity. With knowledge, insight, and obvious love for his fellow human beings, he authored more than 200 books, essays and articles on the Ancient Mysteries and their meaning. In the course of six decades, he delivered more than 8,000 lectures in the United States and abroad, teaching the ancient theories of education as taught in the Mystery Schools—truly the first universities. For many years I had attended lectures in Los Angeles at The Philosophical Research Society, founded by Manly Palmer Hall, but this was to be my first meeting with him personally.

Of particular interest to me was the enormous respect Mr. Hall received from the Masons. He was given a 33rd degree Honorary, Scottish Rite, one year after he joined the Masonic Lodge. He was often called "Masonry's Greatest Philosopher." His great knowledge and the books he wrote were based on the Ancient Mysteries, both Western and Eastern, and there was no one more knowledgeable about the real meaning of Masonry. After joining the Masons he received "the Knight Grand Cross" of the

Supreme Council, an honor given to few Masons in the world and the highest award any Mason can receive.

After Marie's birthday party, I had another invitation to the Halls' house for a quiet Sunday afternoon. This began a regular routine of Sunday afternoons, where we would sit around the dining room table of their home and have wonderful discussions about the Bruton Vault in Williamsburg, Virginia, and all the subjects related to vaults and the founding of America. I began to realize there were many vaults all over the world. But only recently did I realize they contained copies of the Ark of the Covenant. In the years that followed, I often had an opportunity to spend time in Mr. Hall's rare manuscript vault at the Philosophical Research Society library and saw many rare treasures. It was my impression at the time that in this collection some of the books of the Alexandrian Library could have survived. Those were certainly special days.

This book weaves a story of the "Mysteries" which have to do with the mysterious Ark of the Covenant—its locations, contents and meaning; with the powerful concealed secrets of the Royal family of Christ; and with the Alchemical Marriage, which leads the individual into becoming a vessel or chalice to hold the "Holy Spirit," and in doing so, becoming the Grail.

The Mysteries also revealed the formation of a Utopia, planned at least a thousand years before it would come into being, where people could live with liberty, justice, and freedom for all. It was a united commonwealth on Earth to be known as the Republic of America. The stories of the Holy Grail were developed by the Masons and secret societies of antiquity as cloaked allegories about these Mysteries.

The Masons were the connecting link of various societies that we have not totally understood. Many of these societies were called by other names but were Masonic in origin. They were the caretakers of these Mysteries and were honor-bound to keep the secrets known to them. Among these societies were the Catharists, the Guilds, the Knights Templars, the Troubadours, the Druids, King Arthur and his Knights, and the Rosicrucians. These and many others were all part of the same Philosophical

Order protecting the same Mysteries for thousands of years.

Mr. Hall was one of the very few who knew these Mysteries and was given the privilege by the Masons to write about them; however, he always presented the material in a guarded and veiled manner. I learned a great deal from him—I did not invent the story that follows. Though Mr. Hall has now passed to the other side, I feel he would look favorably upon this book with its disclosures of information so important to the world today.

ARK OF THE COVENANT
& HOLY GRAIL

CHAPTER 1

THE INVISIBLE AND VISIBLE MASONS

The Invisible Masons

ne of the greatest sources for tracing the true story of the Ark of the Covenant and the Holy Grail is through the early writings of the Masons. This ancient organization has been holding and protecting these Mysteries for eons of time.

There exists indisputable evidence indicating that there are initiated philosophers possessing a superior knowledge of divine and natural laws. Also sufficient proof exists that these initiates were the agents of a World Fraternity of Adepts that had existed before the time of Atlantis. This fraternity has been called the Philosophic Empire and the Invisible Government of the World. References to this sovereign body of ancient teachers occur in sacred writings, philosophical literature, and the mystical traditions of all races and nations.

When tracing Masonry, I found it inspiring to realize that these Adepts, or inner-group Masons, have been responsible for civilization unfolding according to a predetermined plan, and not by accident. The architects of this plan have been the philosophic elect, the shepherds of the herds of human souls. During enlightened ages, Adepts appeared as teachers, seers, prophets, and social reformers.

1

Masonry is a fraternity within a fraternity—an outer organization concealing an inner brotherhood of the elect. Before it is possible to intelligently discuss the origin of Masonry it is necessary to establish the existence of two separate yet interdependent orders, the one visible and the other invisible.

Regarding the "Invisible Society," Manly Hall conveyed a remarkable theory, which only he could have been aware of because of his rank in the Masonic organization: "This theory asserts that the Rosicrucians actually possessed all the supernatural powers with which they were credited; that they were in reality citizens of two worlds; that, while they had physical bodies for expression on the material plane, they were also capable, through the instructions they received from the Brotherhood, of functioning in a mysterious ethereal body not subject to the limitations of time or distance. By means of this 'astral form' they were able to function in the invisible realm of Nature, and in this realm, beyond reach of the profane, their temple was located.

"According to this viewpoint, the true Rosicrucian Brotherhood consisted of a limited number of highly developed adepts, or initiates of the higher degrees being no longer subject to the laws of mortality; candidates were accepted into the Order only after long periods of probation; adepts possessed the secret of the Philosopher's Stone and knew the process of transmuting base metals into gold, but taught that these were only allegorical terms concealing the true mystery of human regeneration through the transmutation of the 'base-elements' of man's lower nature into 'gold,' of intellectual and spiritual realization. According to this theory, those who have sought to record the events of importance in connection with the Rosicrucian controversy have invariably failed because they approached their subject from a purely physical or materialistic angle."[1] Mr. Hall is describing for us the inner group or Adept group of the Philosophic Empire, those who organized and guided the formation of the present Freemasonry organizations.

The "Invisible Society" is a secret fraternity, an Invisible Government of the world whose members are dedicated to the service of a mysterious inner plan, to bring society to a higher consciousness. Those who have written the history of their Masonic craft have not included in their writings the story of that truly secret *inner* society which is to the body of Freemasonry what the heart is to the body of a human being. In each generation only a few are accepted into the inner sanctuary as invisible Adepts of the work. There is little doubt that their sainted names will be remembered in the future, together with the prophets of the ancient world. They are represented by great individuals such as Cervantes, Cagliostro, St. Germain, Andreae, Bacon, More, Raleigh, Washington and Franklin.

The history of the Masonic order as we know it is one of altruism and noble enterprises. The inner-group history is one of persecution, heroic martyrdom and silent conquest. This book covers the story of the inner history of Masonry, the side not yet revealed.

In several early Masonic manuscripts, for example those by Harleian, Sloan, Lansdowne, and Edinburgh-Kilwinning, it is stated that the craft of initiated builders (Masons) existed before the Deluge of Atlantis, and that its members were employed in the building of the Tower of Babel.

Albert Pike, who was the Grand Commander of the Ancient and Accepted Scottish Rite of Freemasonry, at the end of the nineteenth century wrote a book titled *Morals and Dogma*, which is considered a great historical document of Masonry. He confirmed the antiquity of Masonry by stating: "But, by whatever name it was known in this or the other country, Masonry existed as it now exists, the same in spirit and at heart, not only when Solomon builded the Temple, but centuries before—before even the first colonies emigrated into Southern India, Persia and Egypt, from the cradle of the human race."[2]

Secret societies have existed among all peoples since the beginning of recorded history. Secret orders existed among African tribes, the Eskimos, and in the East Indies and Northern Asia. The American Indians, the Chinese, Hindus and Arabs are known to have fraternal organizations. All of these secret societies have worked to create a background necessary for the establishment of an "Enlightened Society" in all nations of the world.

The rise of the Catholic Church broke up the pattern of the pagan world and brought persecution to these societies, driving the secret groups into greater disguise and cover. Persecution, however, could not completely destroy these groups; instead it scattered the members and in this way spread the very doctrines which it tried to eliminate. Between the thirteenth and seventeenth centuries, these persecuted wanderers drew to themselves other liberals in many lands and spread the seeds of spiritual liberty, helping to inspire the American, French and Russian revolutions. These secret societies were continually threatened by church and state, which wanted them destroyed because of the secrets and powers they held.

Among those for whom early Masonic historians claimed Masonic membership were, to name a few, Abraham, Noah, Moses, Solomon, Ptolemy, Pythagoras, and Julius Caesar.

Manly Hall's book *America's Assignment with Destiny* expands a little further on the Masonic Master Plan: "The explorers who opened the New World operated from a *master plan* and were agents of rediscovery rather than discoverers." An example of this is the discovery of America by Columbus, an Initiate and part of the Great Plan. "Prevailing historical accounts which deal with the discovery and colonization of the Western Hemisphere must some day be completely revised. . . . Time will reveal that the continent now known as America was actually discovered and, to a considerable degree, explored more than a thousand years before the Christian Era. The true story is in the keeping of the Mystery Schools, and passed from them to the Secret Societies of the medieval world. The Esoteric Orders of Europe, Asia and the Near East were in at least irregular communication with the priesthoods of the more advanced Amerindian nations."[3]

The discovery of America began with a long series of pre-discoveries. From about A.D. 500, people such as the Chinese, Venetians, Arabs, Norsemen, and French are known to have visited North America. An epitaph was found in Mexico to the memory of the Welsh Prince Madoc commemorating his voyage of exploration.

In a small but well-researched book, *New Truths about Columbus*, Grace A. Fendler further expands on the Great Plan, showing Columbus as an agent of rediscovery: "There is strong evidence that Columbus' own authentic discovery of America took place at some time previous to his voyage under the Spanish flag. In the famous Capitulations, or the Contracts between Columbus and the Spanish Sovereigns, Columbus undertakes to annex to the Crown certain Islands and Land declaring he has already discovered them. The second Papal Bull of 1493 takes official cognizance of Islands and continental lands found and to be found."[4]

The Visible Masons

The "Lesser" Mysteries of the Masons reveal the steps necessary for humans to master their personality and to attune to the cycles of the earth. The "Higher" Mysteries focus on opening the heart and attaining union with God. As this teaching is done within the individual, it then begins to move outward in service. It must begin internally. The Square must be prepared before the Triangle is possible.

Over the centuries the secret meaning of the Masonic compass and square has been lost. The square is used for obtaining the measurements of earth and represents the female polarity. The

compass is used for the measurements of heaven and represents the male polarity. Masonic oaths are taken on the compass and square, which rest on top of a Bible.

Masonry has been a science of morality, veiled in allegory and illustrated by symbols. It has been imperative for it to keep many secrets, so the veiled symbols that appeared to the outside world as one thing actually represented quite another to the initiated.

The purpose of Masonry was and is to teach the doctrine of one God, the dignity of the human soul, and the resurrection of man to eternal life, and to lead the people to see the reflection of the Deity in the beauty, magnificence, and splendor of the universe. True Masonry seeks to unite God and humankind by raising its initiates to that level of consciousness where the initate can understand the workings of the Great Architect of the Universe.

Religion teaches us the outer mysteries—the exoteric—but Masonry is the great repository for the inner teachings—the esoteric.

CHAPTER 2

THE ARK OF THE COVENANT:
ITS PURPOSE AND CONTENTS

ne of the most important mysteries that the inner group of Masons kept from the time of Noah was their knowledge of the Ark of the Covenant. This is the story of the Ark of the Covenant, what it is, its purpose and where it has been all these thousands of years. The Ark is something quite unusual; it is not easily explained. Unfortunately we are bucking the tide of Cecil B. De Mille's movie version of Moses in *The Ten Commandments* and Steven Spielberg's *Raiders of the Lost Ark*.

Most people have the impression that Masonry began about the time of Solomon's Temple because so many of the Masonic symbols go back to that time; however, this is untrue. There are several early Masonic manuscripts, as noted previously, such as those of Harleian, Sloan, Edinburgh-Kilwinning and Lansdowne, which state that the craft of initiated builders existed before the Deluge of Atlantis.[1] When you examine the following Masonic symbols you can see both a picture of Noah's Ark and the Ark of the Covenant. *Noah's Ark is the Ark of the Covenant.*

The philosophic power of Freemasonry lies in its symbols, a priceless heritage from the Mystery schools of antiquity. The distinguished Masonic scholar General Albert Pike, in his book *Morals and Dogma*, emphasizes the importance of the symbolism

7

—from *Freemasonry*, by W. Kirk MacNulty

Irish Silver Salver (18 inches in diameter) by J. and G. Angel, London, 1845. Grand Lodge of A. F. and A., Masons of Ireland.

—from *Freemasonry*, by W. Kirk MacNulty
Masonic Print, 1809

of Masonry. He writes that its symbolism and its spirit of brotherhood are its essence. Pike also conveys that Freemasonry is more ancient than any of the world's leading religions.[2]

The ancient Mysteries are often hidden in an allegorical manner or demonstrated with symbols. It is necessary to study the symbols of Masonry to begin to understand that *Noah's Ark is actually the Ark of the Covenant* delivered to our civilization from Atlantis. There is evidence that when Atlantis was about to sink in the Deluge, some of the high priests who were forewarned took their most treasured possession, the Ark of the Covenant, and journeyed to other parts of the world, which included Egypt. Noah, a priest of Atlantis, was the courier for the Ark of the Covenant to be taken to Egypt. There the Atlanteans established a great philosophic and literary center, which would later profoundly influence the religions and sciences of countless races and peoples.

The great mystic H. P. Blavatsky, in her book *The Secret Doctrine*, reasons that the Ark of Noah is depicted as a ship because it represents the *navis*, being the symbol of the female generative principle, as symbolized in the heavens by the moon and on earth by the womb. This vessel and bearer of the seeds of life is then fructified by the male principle, the Sun. She describes the animals of the Ark as shut-up human passions. They represent various ordeals of initiation in the Mysteries which were instituted among many nations in commemoration of this allegory.[3]

Manly Hall explains the esoteric or philosophical meaning of Noah and his Ark in his book *Old Testament Wisdom*: "In most of the ancient writings, Noah's ark did not actually or literally mean a boat. Its name signified rather some peculiar form of enclosure, a superior place to which men could go for refuge, and the idea of a boat floating on the waters of the universal night was a poetic form developed by later theologians as a symbol of the ship of salvation. Philosophically speaking, the ark symbolizes a spiritual sphere or over-state, above the material world, which survived the disintegration of the physical universe. Briefly, then, the ark of Noah, with its three decks, represents the three parts of the divine world, or the archetypal region. The Ark, as its symbolism develops, is evidently a miniature of the universe."[4]

The Hebrew *Talmud* states that Noah took into the Ark three hundred and sixty-five kinds of reptiles, and thirty-two major divisions of animals. The serpent was often used as a symbol of the year, like the Aztec calendar-stone. Therefore the three hundred and sixty-five reptiles could represent the days of the year. The thirty-two major divisions of the animals correspond to the thirty-two paths of wisdom used in the Cabalah, which consist of the ten Sephiroths from the symbol of the "Tree of Life" and the twenty-two adjoining paths or letters of the Hebrew alphabet. From this information we begin to realize the allegorical symbols used to describe Noah and his Ark.

Purpose of the Ark of the Covenant

In the *Zohar*, a Hebrew holy book which is a commentary on the Five Books of Moses, recorded in A.D. 1290, there are fifty pages devoted to the Ark of the Covenant. The instructions in the *Zohar* are the same as those in the Bible (Exodus 25:10). In the *Zohar* we read that Yahweh, the God of Israel, orders Moses to build a chest for the "Ancient of Days," (the Ark of the Covenant) giving precise details for construction of this remarkable chest and ordering that it and the "Ancient of Days" were to be taken on the journey through the desert by Moses from Egypt to Israel.

The chest of the "Ancient of Days," because of the sacred geometry of its construction also, along with the scrolls, carries great power. When the chest is opened a vortex of energy is activated. An example of this principle is to be found in the construction of the pyramids, which were built using the exact mathematics of the Ark. The ancients knew that the perfect pyramidal shape found in the sacred geometry of the ark opened vortexes of energy through all dimensions and, in a sense, helped facilitate evolution in the subtle bodies of humans.

The buildings that were built with sacred geometry and measurements from the Ark were a way of creating a physical instrument designed to open a vortex of energy, enabling one to penetrate the dimensions of space and time. By sitting in this vortex, it was possible to experience past, present and future as did the high priests, prophets and seers of ancient days. The scrolls or scripts of the Ark carry great energy because of their sacred words, even if they are not enclosed in the chest. It is necessary to understand that Arks can be built of any size, and because they are built according to the same sacred mathematics, they carry the same energy.

Certain early works on magical philosophy hint that the Ark of the Covenant was oracular in character because of specially prepared chambers in the interior of the chest. These chambers, by their shape and mathematical arrangement, were so attuned to the vibrations of the invisible world that they caught and amplified the voices of the ages imprinted upon, and externally existing in, the astral light.

There is a legend to the effect that any morally unclean individual who chanced to enter the Holy of Holies which housed the Ark of the Covenant would be destroyed by a bolt of divine fire from the Mercy Seat of the Ark. If the high priest had but one selfish thought while in the presence of Jehovah, he would be struck dead. As no man knows when an unworthy thought may flash through his mind, precautions had to be taken in case the high priest were to be struck dead while in the presence of Jehovah. Because other priests could not enter the sanctuary at the same time as their leader, who was to receive the commands of the Lord, they would tie a chain around one of his feet so that if he were struck down while behind the veil they could extricate his body.

In keeping with this thought, Erich Von Daniken tells of a well-known Jewish philosopher and mathematician, Lazarus Bendavid (1762–1832), who lived in Berlin and concluded that "The Ark of Moses contained a fairly complete system of electrical instruments and produced effects by them."[5] Lazarus Bendavid was an intelligent man and far ahead of his time. He knew that only a fixed, clearly defined group of high priests was allowed access to the Ark. Even then the priests could only visit it on occasion, since it was considered dangerous to do so.

"According to the Talmudists," Bendavid wrote, "mortal danger must have always been associated with visits to the Holy of Holies. The high priest always entered with a certain fear and thought it was a good day if he came back safe."[6] I think Lazarus Bendavid failed to realize that the mathematical construction of the Ark and the power of the written word are what produced the tremendous force of the electrical effects.

It is believed that copies of the Ark serve a positive function by their placement. People who really understand the grid can send messages with the Ark.

For example, there is a legend about Solomon's Temple in Jerusalem which states that the Ark of the Covenant was used as an amplifier. It is said that the Temple had a network of underground water channels spreading outward to all parts of the country. Through this vascular grid system, everything done in the Temple was amplified and broadcast. The influence of chants and rituals permeated the grid field of the earth and went through all parts of the country.

Because the Temple was the center where the Ark of the Covenant was housed and where the laws were proclaimed and rituals practiced, its energies were reproduced on the grids of the underwater channels elsewhere in the country. In the Temple the "light and energy" which came from the inner sanctum imparted health and fertility to the earth and the people surrounding the Temple and along the grid system. When the Temple was destroyed and the Ark of the Covenant removed from the Temple, the benefits of this "magic" from the Ark were lost.

The Ark of the Covenant can also be used for interstellar communications. The grid systems encapsulating the earth can be employed laterally between human beings and other species, but it is also an effective grid system vertically, through other dimensions, for interstellar communications. It is conceivable that we were once a sacred planet and were conscious of interdimensional connection to the rest of the universe.

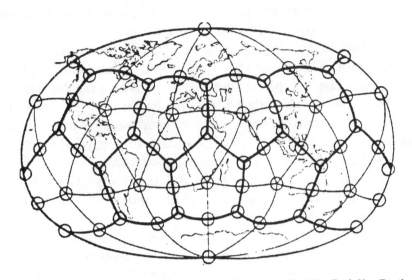

—from *Signs of the Gods?* by Erich Von Daniken

When Russian scholars transferred religious sites from all over the world to a globe, they thought it looked like a football made up of pentagons.

Within the esoteric community it is rumored that there are a few people today who know how to use the Ark of the Covenant, but that they avoid using it because they know that its incredibly powerful energy could cause a disruption in the earth's magnetic field. In the stories of Judaic history, Moses, when crossing the desert, seldom used the Ark because he knew that if it were used, some people would die and uncontrollable events would occur.

There are many theories about the purpose of this mysterious Ark of the Covenant. In the ancient texts I have researched, it was revealed that its primary purpose was to serve as a receptacle of all the knowledge of God's Laws and teachings. It can be likened to a vault of knowledge which facilitates the evolution of human consciousness.

It is necessary to understand that the Ark of the Covenant does not belong to the Jewish people exclusively. It did not come from the God of Abraham. The word *Israel* signifies not only the Jewish people, but all of humanity. The Jewish people became God's chosen people because Noah, after bringing the Ark to Egypt, became the father of the Jewish tribes. Naturally, the Jewish people thought the Ark belonged to their God and their lineage. This may disturb a lot of people, but the true nature of the Ark is not religious. People have created a religion about it because the Ark was more powerful than human beings and therefore God-like. Humanity must now raise itself up so that when we next use the Ark, we use it for what it really is—a new dimenison of growth permitting interstellar communication and travel.

The Contents of the Ark of the Covenant

The legend handed down regarding the origin of the Ark is that in ancient times the seeders of this planet from outer space came to give the Ark of the Covenant to Adam and then to the inhabitants of Atlantis. It was taken to Egypt and other parts of the world before the Atlantean continent was submerged. "There are many cabalistic writers such as Menahem di Recanti [A.D. 1290] who claim the secret doctrine is pre-Adamite."[7]

What the Priest Noah took from Atlantis to Egypt was a body of teachings recorded on a Tablet known as the Emerald Tablet or Ark of the Covenant. Once someone has this body of knowledge, even if the Ark itself were destroyed, another Ark could be constructed. The Emerald Tablet contains the records of the entire cosmology, past, present and future of this galaxy or solar system. This includes physics, sacred geometry, alchemy, geomancy, astrology, astronomy—the formula for time and space. It also contains the blueprint for the entire scheme of the universe—the microcosm and the macrocosm, the upper universe and the lower universe. This system carefully explains the deepest depths of the Divine Nature and shows the true tie that binds all things together. When we organize our view of reality according to these laws, we become one and forever united with God.

The High Priest of Atlantis, Hermes Trismegistus (also known as the Thrice Greatest), was able to translate the Emerald Tablet. It was to Hermes, known as the founder of Egypt, that Noah gave the Ark when he arrived in Egypt. Hermes wrote some forty-two books concerning the Ark. These are discussed along with more information about Hermes and the Emerald Tablet in chapter 8 of this book, "Alexandria and the Ark of the Covenant."

The sacred mathematics of the Ark of the Covenant contains, among other things, the mathematical calculations for the harmonic proportions of nature from which true architecture, music, poetry, and art are derived. When we say harmonic proportions we are describing the same proportions that are literally the building blocks of our universe. With these mathematical canons or formulae, it is possible to construct buildings where people can experience harmony not only in their society but within themselves. Examples of these structures are: Solomon's Temple; the Great Pyramids of Giza, China, Central America and Mexico; Stonehenge; and the Gothic Cathedrals.

The music, poetry, art and architecture created through these sacred dimensions are analogous to the basic structure of creation. By their very nature they induce us to raise our consciousness. Sacred geometry has the effect on humans of equalizing them with nature. This is the key to reconstructing our world as a planet of harmony.

Moses, who took the teachings of the Ark to Israel, was trained and initiated as a High Priest of the Egyptian Court. As part of his training, he must have studied and understood the Ark of the Covenant found in the Sanctuary of the Great Pyramid of Egypt. It is possible that when Moses left Egypt he took with him a copy of the Ark in the form of scrolls or scripts; or the information was carried within him.

After crossing the desert from Egypt to Israel, and talking to God on Mount Sinai, where he received the "Law" of the Ark, Moses wrote and concealed these great secrets in the *Five Books of Moses*, also known as the *Pentateuch* and the *Torah*.

When Moses instituted the mysteries of the Ark, he is said to have given the teachings to a chosen few. These teachings were never to be written, but given by word of mouth and transmitted from one generation to the next. They were delivered in the form of philosophical keys, by means of which allegories revealed their hidden significance. The philosophical keys were called by the Jews the *Cabalah (Kabbalah, Qabbalah)*.

Cabalah means the secret or hidden tradition, the unwritten law. According to early rabbis, in addition to containing the law, the *Cabalah* aided the deciphering of the abstruse principles of the mysteries contained in sacred writings like the *Bible, Zohar, Sepher Yetzirah, Apocalypse, Torah, Pentateuch, Ten Commandments,* and others. From these deciphered mysteries man could learn to understand the mystery of both the universe about him and the universe within him.

Albert Pike in his great Masonic book *Morals and Dogma* states: "The primary tradition of the single revelation has been preserved under the name of the 'Kabalah,' by the priesthood of Israel. The Kabalistic doctrine, which was also the dogma of the Magi and of Hermes, is contained in the Sepher Yetzirah and the Zohar and the Talmud. . . ."[8] Pike adds: "The Zohar, which is the Key to the Holy Books, opens also all the depths and light, all the obscurities of the Ancient Mythologies and of the sciences originally concealed in the Sanctuaries."[9] He also writes: "It was the dogmas of this Science that were engraven on the table of stone [the Emerald Tablet] by Hanock [Enoch] and Trismegistus. Moses purified and re-veiled them, for that is the meaning of the word *reveal*. He covered them with a new veil, when he made of the Holy Kabalah the exclusive heritage of the people of Israel and the inviolable Secret of the priests."[10]

H. P. Blavatsky, the founder of Theosophy, further confirms that the teachings of the Ark are given in the *Zohar*. She writes: ". . . .Moses de Leon [the recorder of the *Zohar* in A.D. 1290] has made the Zohar that which it has remained to this day, a running commentary on the Five Books [of Moses], or Pentateuch, with a few later additions made by Christian hands . . ."[11] Here we have the correlation that the *Zohar* teachings, the *Pentateuch* teachings and the teachings of the Ark are all related.

Another example of the wisdom of the Ark being concealed under the garment of Cabalah is in several Cabalistic and philosophical texts (including those of Manly P. Hall and Christian D. Ginsburg). According to certain Jewish mystics, Moses ascended Mount Sinai three times, remaining in the presence of God forty days each time. During the first forty days, the tables of the written law or the *Ten Commandments* were delivered to the prophet for all the people; this was called *the law*. During the second forty days, he received the *Mishna*, called *the soul of the law*, which was revealed to the rabbis and teachers. During the third forty days, he received what is known as *the Soul of the soul of the law*, when God instructed him in the mysteries of the Cabalah. Only the highest initiates among the Jews were instructed in its great secrets. Moses concealed in the first four books of the Pentateuch the secret instructions that God had given him, and for centuries students of Cabalah have sought them in the secret doctrine of Israel.

Again, in a very hidden manner, as is the custom of the Brotherhood, we learn that Cabalah is used for the teachings of the Ark. Commentaries in Cabalistic texts parallel statements in books written on the Ark, like the Pentateuch. Christian D. Ginsburg's book *Kabbalah* clearly states: "We have already seen that the Kabbalah claims a pre-Adamite existence, and asserts that its mysteries are covertly conveyed in the first four books of the Pentateuch."[12]

Because the *Torah* or *Pentateuch* contains the teachings of the Ark, when we study *Torah*, even on the simplest level, we link our minds and hearts with God's true purpose in creating the world. Our minds delight in the divine revelation which becomes available to us.

Because of the energies it carries, the Ark of the Covenant is like a time vault. You canot force it to activate. It can be compared to a person standing in front of a giant crystal. Such a person can only walk through the crystal if he or she has the same vibration; the energies of both the person and the crystal must be the same. Where this is the case, there is no material blockage; the two are in harmony and one passes through the other unimpeded.

If we are to draw a parallel with the Ark of the Covenant, we see that if one has the same vibration as the Ark, one can read it, touch it, see it and experience it. If one does not have the same vibrational rate, the Ark of the Covenant is then secured and cannot be accessed. Only those who are enlightened can access the Ark.

Let us use an example here which was discussed earlier: the energy and power of these scripts. Consider a priest who, as was the custom, ties a chain around his ankle before going into the Tabernacle, to ensure that he can be pulled out if he should die from the energy of the Ark. This would prevent the other priests having to enter the Tabernacle and thereby endangering their own lives. Remember, it is the combination of the Ark of the Covenant and its energies with the energy of an enlightened person that creates the polarity which begins the energy exchange.

I discovered that many Arks exist throughout the world; they were buried or seeded at various times and places throughout history. Certain adepts were given the responsibility of seeding these Arks during their particular epoch of history, so that the Arks of the Covenant could make a contribution to the evolution of humanity during their time. What follows in the next chapters is the tracing of some of these seedings in the Western tradition.

The figure of Hildegard's Vision of the Godhead on page 20 illustrates in a simple manner the teachings of the Ark of the Covenant. Here we find the Godhead with both a masculine and a feminine head. These represent the balance between the masculine and feminine forces that operate within each human being. It is said that when a person attains this masculine/feminine balance, enlightenment follows (see chapter 14).

The Godhead is connected to us by nature, represented by the stars and planets; these, in turn, are connected by grid lines of energy to the chakras and acupuncture systems of all beings and of the earth. The same canon of mathematics that determines the upper world also forms the lower world. The same light, sometimes referred to as magnetized electricity, forms these upper and lower worlds.

"The Sacred Books taught that we cannot understand matter without understanding Spirit, and that we cannot comprehend Spirit without understanding matter. Matter and Spirit are but opposite poles of the same universal substance. All through the

—from *Liber Divinorum Operum Simplicis Hominis*

Hildegard's Vision of the Godhead, Nature, and Man

Cabalah runs the axiom: that Malkuth is in Kether and Kether is in Malkuth; the same idea is repeated through the Gnostic teachings—the earth that is in heaven, the heaven that is in the earth."[13] Hildegard's illustration demonstrates the great teaching of the Ark of the Covenant: *as above, so below.*

CHAPTER 3

ATLANTIS AND THE ARK OF THE COVENANT

here are few topics that have inspired as many eso-
tericists as the fabled Atlantis which was destroyed
by tidal waves about 9,600 B.C. Atlantis lies at the
core of our traditions and enigmatic mysteries. The
basis of all that we understand about Atlantis comes from Plato,
who had been in Egypt and was initiated into the Egyptian Mysteries in the Great Pyramid. Plato claims he received his information from the Egyptian priesthood.

It was in the sacred structure of the Great Pyramid of Egypt
that the high priests taught the initiates. Moses, Sophocles,
Solon, Cicero, Pindar, Plato, Pythagoras and Christ were among
some of these high initiates. As an initiate, Plato wrote in veiled
and allegorical form a complete guide to the esoteric science. He
revealed in his teachings the story of Atlantis, which was found
on the "Pillars of Hermes" by the Egyptian Priests.

In notes appended to his translation of *Iamblicus, On the Mysteries*, Thomas Taylor refers to the ancient pillars as the pillars
of Hermes. He states that according to Ammianus Marcellinus,
these pillars were concealed prior to the deluge in certain caverns
not far from the Egyptian city of Thebes. Taylor suggests that a
first Hermes lived in antediluvian times and a second Hermes (the
conglomerate of writings by many authors of Alexandria) probably lived shortly after the beginning of the Christian Era. It was

the first Hermes who interpreted the ancient pillars, as Iamblicus informs us in his work on the Mysteries. These pillars are mentioned by Laertius in his *Life of Democritus*, by Dio Chrysostom in *Oration 49*, by Achilles Tatius in *Aratus*, and by others of the ancients.

According to Freemasonic tradition, Enoch, who was the High Priest of Atlantis, fearing that all knowledge of the sacred Mysteries would be lost at the time of the Great Deluge, erected two columns (pillars) to be delivered to Egypt by Hermes. Upon the one column, in appropriate allegorical symbols, Enoch engraved the secret teachings; and upon the other column he placed an inscription stating that a short distance away, in a subterranean vault, a priceless treasure would be discovered. In time, the location of the secret vault was lost.

The Greek legislator and initiate Solon, visiting Eygpt in the sixth century B.C., claimed to have examined these pillars in a subterranean temple near the banks of the Nile. Solon was taken by the High Priest through a long passageway of the temple, lighted only by torches, to a subterranean chamber. The light of the torches fell on two tall columns that appeared to be covered with curious writing in an unknown language.

The High Priest, pointing his rod at the pillars, explained their mystery to Solon: " 'These columns,' he said, 'were placed on the island beneath the ground thousands of years ago by a lost people which had vanished forever from the earth. The pillars were made of an unknown metal which neither rusted nor deteriorated with age.' " [It is implied that these columns were from the empire of the Golden Gate or Atlantis.] " 'From these ancient columns we have read the laws that were given in olden times for the government of nations. These laws are not made by men but are the will of Eternal Nature. Upon these laws enduring States must be built. To depart from these laws is to die. So perished the nations of the elder world.' "[1]

Because Solon was an initiate of the Great Pyramid of Egypt he could read the original writing from Enoch's pillars of the history of Atlantis. He coded and copied the information inscribed on the pillars and took that information back to Greece. Later he replicated it on the pillars that he built at Eleusis. These Pillars of Solon are said to have held the doors of Eleusis and contributed to making Eleusis a powerful spiritual center. It was known as the greatest spiritual teaching center of the Mysteries in Greece, and the priests and priestesses of Eleusis taught the Mysteries of Demeter, using the same initiation procedures given in the Great Pyramid of Egypt. Later, when the Persians invaded Greece, the Pillars of Solon were destroyed by Xerxes. Eleusis remained in existence from the 6th century B.C. to A.D. 395.

When Solon first returned to Greece from Egypt, he told his story in detail to his close friend Dropis, who told it to his son Critias. Critias communicated the story to his grandson of the same name who was to become a disciple of Socrates. In that manner, the story of the lost Atlantis came to be part of the Platonic dialogue of *Critias* as part of a conversation between the younger Critias and his master Socrates.

In John Michell's excellent study *The Dimensions of Paradise*, the author examines the geometry and proportions of Atlantis as given by Plato and concludes that Atlantis was an ideal political state based on the Pythagorean concept of numerical harmony.[2]

Rudolph Steiner, Theosophist and founder of the Anthroposophical movement, wrote in *Submerged Continents of Atlantis and Lemuria* that unlike the previous Lemurians, Atlanteans could remember mental images and had mastery of the mantric magic and the secrets of life-force. Steiner saw the fall of Atlantis as being due to an essential corruption in the etheric cleanliness of the oracular Mysteries, thus inviting an influx of depraved and destructive spirits into Atlantean culture. In Steiner's psychic remembrance of Atlantean culture, the only oracle to survive was that of the Christos, or Solar Logos. Following the great civilization's fall, the Oracle of the Christos was carried into remote Inner Asia for safekeeping. Was Steiner seeing the Ark of the Covenant? (*Christos* means *Spiritual Law*.)[3]

The history of Atlantis is the key to Greek mythology, states Ignatius Donnelly, in his book *Atlantis and the Antediluvian World*. He writes that there can be no question that the gods of Greece were human beings. Donnelly contends that the deities of the Greek pantheon were never looked upon as creators of the universe, but rather as rulers. He writes that the Garden of Eden from which humanity was driven is possibly an allusion to the earthly paradise supposedly located west of the Pillars of Hercules and destroyed by volcanic cataclysms (Atlantis).[4]

As far back as 1886, Dr. Augustus Le Plongeon, one of the most important writers on Mayan civilization, published his alphabetical key to Mayan hieroglyphics. When comparing this to the ancient Egyptian hieratic alphabet, he found that signs on the Pyramid of Xochicalo were both Mayan and Egyptian. His conclusion was that these decorative inscriptions indicated that the Mayan pyramid was a monumental structure erected to commemorate the submergence and destruction of the great Land of Mu (Plato's Atlantis). In his book *Queen Moo and the Eygptian Sphinx*, Le Plongeon gives five accounts of the same cataclysm, but the most important is in the known records in Mayan language. He writes that stories of the appalling event that gave rise to the story of a universal deluge are found in the sacred books of the Jews, Christians and the Muhammadans.[5]

Dr. W. P. Phelon, the honored scholar of the Hermetic brotherhood, demonstrated, in his book *Our Story of Atlantis*, that the priestcraft of antiquity possessed religious, philosophic, and scientific knowledge secured from Atlantis, whose submergence obliterated every visage of its participation in the drama of world progress. Atlantean sun worship has been perpetuated in the ritualism and ceremonialism of both Christianity and paganism.

The cross and the serpent were Atlantean emblems of divine wisdom. The Atlanteans wore the green and azure radiance of the plumed serpent. They were the progenitors of the Mayans and Quiches of Central America. The chief of the Atlantean order was the "feathered" snake. "Winged" or "plumed" serpent was also applied to Quetzalcoatl, the Central American initiate. A great pyramidal temple standing on a plateau, was said to be the center of the Atlantean wisdom-religion. It was from here that the Initiate-Priests of the Sacred Feather went forth, carrying their wisdom to the outermost parts of the world.

Mythologies of many nations have accounts of gods who

"came out of the sea." Some shamans of the American Indians tell of holy men dressed in bird feathers and beads who rose out of the blue waters and instructed them in their arts and crafts.

One of the legends of the Chaldeans is that Oannes, a partly amphibious creature, rose from the sea and taught the savage people along the shore to read and write, till the soil, study astronomy, establish government, and learn about the sacred Mysteries. In the Mayan legend of Quetzalcoatl, the Savior-God, after instructing the people, rides out to sea on a magic raft of serpents to escape the wrath of the fierce god Tezcatlipoca, who apparently embodied the primitive religious cult of Mexico which engaged in human sacrifice and adhered to the practice of war and destruction.

It seems that these demigods of a fabulous age who came out of the sea were Atlantean priests. All that primitive man remembered of the Atlanteans was the beauty of their golden ornaments, their wisdom, and the worship of their symbols—the cross and serpent. They came in ships, but this was soon forgotten, for the people considered even ships as supernatural.

Wherever the Atlanteans converted people to their creed, they erected pyramids and temples patterned after the great sanctuary in the City of the Golden Gates. Plato writes that the city of the Golden Gates was the capital of Atlantis, the one now preserved among numerous religions as the City of the Gods or the Holy City. This is the origin of the pyramids of Egypt, Mexico, Central America, the mounds of Normandy and Britain, and those of the American Indians, which are all parts of a similar culture.

During the Atlantean program of world colonization and conversion, the cataclysms which would ultimately sink Atlantis began. The Initiate-Priests of the Sacred Feather, who promised to come back to their missionary settlements, never returned. There remains only a story of gods who came from a place where there is now sea.

Before Atlantis sank, its spiritually illumined Initiates, who realized their land was doomed because it had departed from the

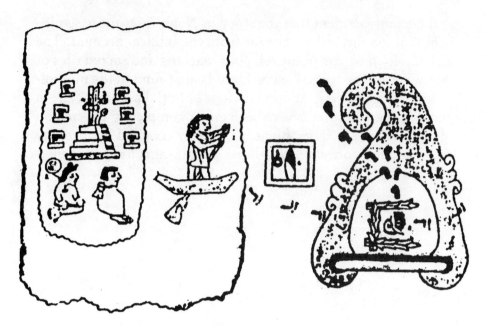

—Detail from an ancient Aztec manuscript, *Tira del a Peregrinacion Asteca*

This illustration shows the journey of the tribal ancestors from the lost continent of Atlantis. The footprints demonstrate the course followed by survivors from the lost continent.

"Path of Light," withdrew from the ill-fated continent carrying with them the sacred and secret doctrine of the Ark of the Covenant. These Atlanteans established themseves in Egypt and other parts of the earth where they would be safe, and they became the first "divine" rulers. In this way, the Atlantean secret teachings were preserved for later cultures. Many of the great cosmology myths forming the essence of the various sacred books of the world are based upon the Atlantean Mystery rituals.

The Priest Noah was chosen to carry the Emerald Tablet (Ark of the Covenant) from Atlantis to Egypt—you might say he was the "captain of the ship." Hermes, the High Priest who came from Atlantis to Egypt soon after Noah, became the successor to the High Priest Enoch of Atlantis. Hermes received the Emerald Tablet from Noah in Egypt and then founded Egypt.

It becomes evident that the story of Noah is far more significant than would at first appear from the biblical account. The Ark of Noah occurs in the religious teaching and sacred rites of many ancient peoples. Deluge legends are found in the mythologies of most ancient civilized nations of both East and West. In general, these accounts have been either completely rejected by modern science as fabrications, or entirely accepted by theology as actual. The concept of an allegorical meaning has been generally ignored.

CHAPTER 4

EGYPT AND THE ARK OF THE COVENANT

n the one-dollar bill of the United States is printed the Great Seal of the United States. It is unmistakably Masonic. It contains the all-seeing eye in a triangle above a thirteen-stepped, four-sided pyramid beneath which a scroll proclaims the advent of a new secular order, one of Masonry's long-standing goals. There is little doubt that the symbolism depicts the Great Pyramid of Giza.

To many, the most mysterious and awesome of the ancient monuments still existing in the world today is the Great Pyramid of Giza in the land of Egypt. The inquiring mind can easily ask whence came this great monument in stone which is sometimes

referred to as the miracle of the ages. Its very size is mind boggling. Peter Tompkins, in his most informative book, *Secrets of the Great Pyramid*, states that the Pyramid of Giza is composed of over 2,500,000 blocks of limestone and granite, each piece weighing from two to seventy tons. From its thirteen-acre base, this incredible structure soars gracefully into the desert sky to the height of a modern, forty-story office building. It contains some 210 steps or tiers as support for its great height.

If such a structure were attempted today, even with the aid of our "advanced" computer technologies, mechanized equipment, and engineering skills, it would tax our ingenuity to the utmost and, in most considered opinions, be impossible to duplicate. The original casing stones were cut with such precision that when fitted together, without the aid of cement, a razor blade could not be slipped between the joints.[1]

The design of the Great Pyramid of Giza expresses an intelligence far beyond that of our modern-day technologies. The geometry of its construction—its outer dimensions as well as the measurements and proportions of its inner passageways and chambers—demonstrates an incredible mathematical and astronomical knowledge. The very existence of this awesome structure, which modern science is almost embarrassed to reflect upon, seems to taunt humankind by saying, "Harken unto me. I exist. And even though the sands of time and the destructiveness of humankind have defaced my outer appearance, still I am. Wonder about me. Discover my secrets. Find out why I am."

The Sphinx, companion to the Great Pyramid—half human and half beast—seems to echo the same sentiment. In this chapter, I hope to bring more light to the question of why the pyramid and the sphinx exist.

The first question most of us wish to have answered is: How were these enormous stones raised into position? Imagine constructing a forty-story skyscraper without the use of modern equipment. Imagine it, if you can. Elevate more than two million blocks of granite and limestone, each piece weighing nearly as much as three Sherman tanks, into position to form a structure forty stories high. And let us not forget the precise manner in which they were placed.

Most historians think the pyramids were built by using slave labor. However, just imagine thousands and thousands of Egyptian slaves pulling on ropes and cables in order to drag these enormous stones up some tremendous ramp to their final resting place, flush against one another. The picture staggers the imagination. Perhaps in the dark ages of Egypt under the pharaohs this was the process, and small temples and obelisks were constructed in this manner. But the great pyramid of Giza dwarfed them by comparison.

Even though tremendous feats of strength and endurance were required to construct the smaller structures, it was technically possible. However, when we study and attempt to uncover the actual methods used in the larger and more incredible edifices, such as the Sphinx and the Great Pyramid, common sense demands that we search for an alternative solution. For example, how were these immense granite blocks quarried? Once quarried, how were they transported to the building sites? How was it possible to cut and then place the massive pieces so precisely?

Peter Tompkins suggests in his book *Secrets of the Great Pyramid*: ". . . that the Pyramid was designed by mysterious architects who had a deeper knowledge of the secrets of the universe than those who followed them."[2] The next paragraphs may provide us the answers to such questions as who these architects were and how they built the Great Pyramid.

The following material was taken from *Agasha Master of Wisdom*, by the brilliant mathematician William Eisen, who transcribed material transmitted through the mediumship of Richard Zenor by a teacher named Agasha. This suggests an alternative solution to how the Great Pyramid of Giza was constructed.

Eisen writes: "Some of the leaders [of Egypt, then called Austa] began to attune and recall the ancient Atlantean civilization; several of these souls recalled a great monument of spirituality that was constructed in the form of a pyramid. This pyramid had been erected many thousands of years earlier in the great city of

Atlantis that submerged so long ago. It had housed every record of that great Atlantean civilization, some of which dated back for thousands of years. It also contained information on the great cultures of the future and other prophecies of the tomorrows to come."

From the teacher Agasha we receive the answer as to how the Pyramid of Egypt was constructed: "How was it built, how was the pyramid actually erected? It was accomplished through learning the higher laws of alchemy as taught by the Ascended Atlantean Teachers, and this enabled them not only to bring into manifestation the Great Pyramid, but also to erect other temples, buildings, and works of art of great beauty. Thus, these great structures were constructed not only through hard effort, but also through the higher laws of alchemy, and through the anims [etheric part of the atom] and the forces of the other world, in order to assist and supplement the physical effort.

"It has always been a great mystery to mankind today as to how the ancient civilizations of the past were able to transport those huge blocks of stone in order to erect such a great temple as it stands there so nobly and high. These great stones were levitated into position and many of them were apported from various parts of the country through the powers of the special people or instruments who possessed great mediumistic powers. Much of the material was also precipitated as they do in spiritual centers.

"Many of the great stones were evidently first quarried in other parts of the country and then either apported or levitated to the pyramid site. It becomes apparent that the gold that was used in the great golden apex [as seen on America's dollar bill] which originally capped this great monument was either transmuted from baser metals or precipitated out of the atmosphere. Once the mortal mind can accept the reality of these spiritual and superphysical forces and powers, the erection of these ancient monuments becomes no longer a mystery."[3]

Another large question is, *why* was the Great Pyramid built? The answer is simple: the great pyramid was used for storage of the Ark of the Covenant brought to Egypt from Atlantis by

Noah. Most important, it was built as a temple of initiation for teaching the Mysteries of enlightenment.

The Great Pyramid was built using the sacred geometry of the Ark. The Pyramid's design is such that it represents, in stone, the laws of the universe and the true history of mankind. The ancient philosophers understood the structure of numbers to be analogous to the structure of creation. The pyramid is composed of the same mathematics of which the universe is built; the mathematical constants of Phi, Pi, E, and I. In other words, the Great Pyramid is a replica of the universe. William Eisen explains and outlines these mathematics in his book *The Essence of the Cabalah*. Pythagoras understood and taught these mathematics in his school in Greece. Plato, who was initiated in the Great Pyramid, only alluded to them in his writings.

When architecture, art, music and poetry are composed of these sacred mathematics, humankind and nature come into harmony. In this manner, a perfectly balanced society in harmony with the heavenly order is created where life can be experienced from a high level of integrity with extraordinary energy and intensity. For this reason, Plato, who understood the sacred mathematics, recommended, in *Laws*, the licensing of all craftsmen and artists, particularly musicians, who have a great influence on society. These musicians were to be required to compose their works in accordance with the harmony and proportions as specified in the code of music. Their compositions were to be designed to create harmony in the soul and consequently in humanity. The priests of ancient Egypt, says Plato, upheld these codes as their ultimate source of law for over ten thousand years and thereby preserved their civilization from corruption.

In ancient times, the temples built according to sacred geometry were used as meeting places where people assembled for religious purposes. The actual construction brought harmony and balance into their lives. The ancients would make pilgrimages to these sacred sites, where they would receive healings; and they would gather for ceremonies at special times of the year, such as the night of the full moon, and during the solstices and equinoxes. They would hold hands and weave about central figures, similar to the ancient maypole, to generate energy. We find that edifices such as Stonehenge, the Ruins at Zimbabwe, Rhodesia, Cuzco, Peru, and Uxmal in the Yucatan are constructed in such a manner as to draw in the light of the summer solstice and spring equinox sunsets.

In our soul memory we still meet that need today by attending our churches, temples and shrines; but in most cases, we have forgotten how to construct the buildings and create the music, art, and poetry using sacred geometry for the achievement of divine harmony and balance. Of course, there are still such buildings today, like the great cathedrals of Europe, which were built by the early Masons who understood the sacred math. In these soul-filled structures, which instill in us a sense of peace and harmony, we have the opportunity for great spiritual experiences.

Pythagoras healed with music composed of sacred geometry. The music of Mozart, the art of Leonardo da Vinci and others who understood the sacred geometry, help us to open our hearts. There are also more and more healers among us today who are working with the vibrations (or mathematics) of music and color to bring humans into balance.

The Great Pyramid is the symbolic key to introduce you to your Higher Self; it symbolizes the greater awakening. By first unlocking the consciousness within, we are enabled to awaken the soul. Other pyramids, temples, and monuments of this period —in China, South America, Central America and elsewhere— portray this same spiritual theme. The wisest of the ancient philosophers visited Egypt to be initiated by the priests of Thebes, Memphis, and Heliopolis into the sacred Mysteries. Thales, Solon, Pythagoras, and Plato journeyed from Greece to the delta of the Nile in quest of knowledge. Upon returning to their own country, these illumined men acknowledged the Egyptians to be the wisest of mortals and the Egyptian temples to be the repositories of the most sublime doctrines concerning the history of the gods and the regeneration of humankind.

The inner chamber and the passages within the Great Pyramid were constructed for the purpose of creating a great temple of initiation. It was here the disciples, or those taking the various degrees, had to traverse the labyrinth of passages, undoubtedly meeting with various obstacles on the way. With those obstacles overcome, they would eventually find themselves within one of the upper chambers, and in so doing, enter into even greater inner awareness.

From ancient manuscripts and their commentaries, we know that what today is known as the King's Chamber in the Pyramid of Giza was really used for the purpose of purification and enlightenment or, by its more familiar title, initiation. This is where the Emerald Tablet was stored. Powers generated within this chamber, which is located at the very heart of the pyramid, would enable the adept, or one who was ready for the higher initiation, to go into deep meditation and thus be able to raise his or her consciousness to an extremely high state. The other chambers or passageways also had their own individual functions and symbology. Yet the ultimate function of all of them was to raise the consciousness of humans to the realization of their own divine state.

H. P. Blavatsky, in *The Secret Doctrine*, writes about the "King's chamber" in the Great Pyramid as an Egyptian "Holy of Holies." Regarding the Mysteries of Initiation, the candidate, who symbolically represented the Solar God, had to descend into the Sarcophagus, and like the energizing ray of the sun, enter into the fertile womb of Nature.

The candidate emerged from the Sarcophagus the following morning, much as new life is resurrected after the change called death. In the Great Mysteries, the figurative "death" of the initiate lasted two days, after which he arose with the Sun on the third morning after a final night of the most severe trials. While the male initiate symbolizes the Sun, that life-giving power that "resurrects" every morning and imparts life to all, the Sarcophagus was symbolic of the female principle. Its form and shape changed with every country, provided it remained a vessel, a symbolic "navis," or boat-shaped vehicle, and a profound symbol of the seeds of life.

In addition to the halls, chambers and passages located within the main or central part of the Pyramid, occult tradition has long held that there are still other underground passageways connecting the Pyramid with the Sphinx and quite possibly with the two adjacent pyramids of Cephren and Mycerinus. The knowledge of the existence of these subterranean halls and passages has been lost by the outer world for many thousands of years; but, fortunately for mankind, it has been preserved on secret scrolls and manuscripts possessed by the archivists of some of the Mystery schools of the West and Tibet.

It seems that shortly after the Great Pyramid was constructed, the great Sphinx was also built. It is thought that one of the underground corridors of the great Sphinx leads directly to the main chamber within the Great Pyramid. Psychics predict that this knowledge will eventually be revealed.

New evidence regarding the time period when the great pyramid and the two smaller pyramids were built has been recently uncovered by the research of Graham Hancock and Robert Bauval, authors of *The Message of the Sphinx*. With the invention of computers, the procession of the stars can now be reconstructed with great accuracy. We can now view the skies as they looked in ancient times. Graham Hancock tells of going to the planetarium and having them preset skies of the dome of Egypt in 10,500 B.C. In this year, Leo rose in the east and the three great stars of Orion's Belt stretched along the meridian precisely along the path reflected by the Giza Pyramids. The three pyramids are a perfectly accurate sky map of the constellations of Leo and Orion in 10,500 B.C. In this manner the builders of the Pyramids of Giza demonstrated the time of the building of the Giza monuments. They also demonstrated the timing by building the Sphinx in the form of a Lion, the astrological sign of Leo.

Another confirmation of this timing was given by Edgar Cayce, the American psychic, who confirmed, before his death in 1947, that the Pyramids of Giza had been built between 10,450 and 10,390 B.C.[4]

In his book *Egypt the Cradle of Ancient Masonry*, Norman Frederick de Clifford gives us an inspiring and Masonic perspective of the Sphinx and the Pyramid, which are the embodiments of the masculine and feminine potencies in nature. De Clifford concludes that the Pyramid and the Sphinx were both built as houses of initiation. The initiations that occurred in these monuments led the initiates to the illumination of the heart. This was accompanied by an awakening of the soul or heart memory that reached back into reincarnational cycles of the past.

The Sphinx Initiation was also designed to develop other dormant powers belonging to the feminine aspect of spirit. It is only when the feminine dormant potency, which suffered a "fall" in early humanity, is redeemed and uplifted and brought into perfect balance with its complementary masculine polarity that humans arrive at a state of equilibrium and eventual illumination. This is part of the Mysteries of the Masons, called the "Alchemical Marriage."

—from *A History of Egypt*, by James Henry Breasted, 1912

The Great Sphinx of Gizeh.
In the background, the Pyramids of Khafre (Chephren right)
and Menkure (Mycerinus left).

CHAPTER 5

MOSES' EXODUS FROM EGYPT
WITH THE ARK OF THE COVENANT

he infant Moses was hidden by his mother in order to save him from the Pharaoh's decree that every Hebrew male child should be killed (Exod. 1:22). He was hidden within the reeds on a bank of the Nile, where he was found and adopted by the daughter of the Pharaoh of Egypt and thus became the grandson of the Pharaoh. Moses was instructed in all the learning of the Egyptians and afterward married the daughter of Yethru, a Priest of An. Strabo and Diodorus and Manetho (cited by Josephus) assert that Moses was himself an initiated Priest of Heliopolis. Before Moses started his journey into the desert, there were close relations between him and the priesthood; and he had successfully commanded, Josephus informs us, an army sent by the King against the Ethiopians. Simplicius asserts that Moses received from the Egyptians the doctrines which he taught to the Hebrews. Both Clemens of Alexandria and Philo say that he was a theologian and prophet, and interpreter of the Sacred Laws.

Moses was raised as a priest of Egypt trained in all the esoteric teachings. Tradition holds that Moses, in order to protect and at the same time interpret the cosmic law, used the Cabalah, which contains the philosophical keys by means of which the esoteric

38

allegories would reveal their significance. Although many Jewish and Christian scholars have realized that the Bible is a book of allegories, few have actually investigated the symbolism. When Moses instituted his Mysteries, he is said to have given to the chosen few initiates, the seventy elders, certain oral teachings which could never be written but were to be preserved from one generation to the next by word-of-mouth transmission. Later he took these teachings to compose the Torah.

The opening chapter of Exodus, one of the Five books of Moses (also called the *Pentateuch* or the *Torah*), is devoted to an account of the oppression of the Jews in Egypt. The wandering of the twelve tribes during their long struggle in the desert of hope and despair symbolizes the story of humanity's slow and painful search for truth, and the object of this search is described as the Promised Land. Here, in beautiful and peaceful Canaan, the land of milk and honey, the mortal quest ends in happiness, security, and the end of strife.

The twelve tribes of Israel represent the twelve signs of the zodiac, a universal symbol. The same zodiacal symbols have been used in countries as far apart as China and Iceland. The same patterns are repeated by the twelve Disciples of Christ and the twelve Knights of King Arthur.

It is written in the nineteenth chapter of Exodus that it was in the third month after the children of Israel had gone out of Egypt that they came to the wilderness at Sinai, and here the Commandments were given to Moses.

There are many teachings regarding the story of Moses and the Commandments. The *Pentateuch* tells us that while on the heights of Mount Sinai, Moses received the Ten Commandments from God. The two tablets bearing the characters of the Decalogue were traced by the very finger of Israel's God. These tablets were made from the divine sapphire, which God, after removing it from His own throne, had cast into the earth to become the foundation and generator of the worlds. Upon the two parts of this tablet were drawn, in black fire, the figures of the Law.

This same decade was known by the Pythagoreans under the form of the tetractys—a triangle of ten points which reveals to the initiate the whole workings of the cosmic scheme—ten being the number of perfection, the key to creation, and the proper symbol of God, man and the universe.

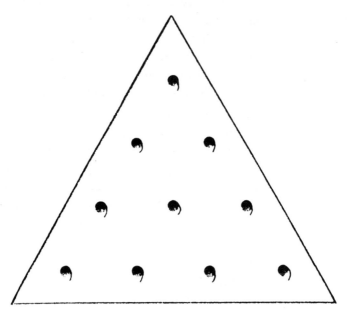

The Tetractys of the Pythagoreans

When Moses came down from Mount Sinai, he was appalled at the idolatry of the Israelites. Because he taught his people monotheism, the worship of only one God, Moses deemed the people unworthy to receive the sapphire tablets; therefore, he broke the tablets so that the mysteries of God should not be violated. In place of the original sapphire tablets, Moses substituted two of rough stone and into the surface he cut ten ancient letters. While the former tablets blazed forth eternal truths, the latter revealed only temporal truths. Through the destruction of the sapphire tablets, the ancient tradition of Israel returned again to heaven and only its shadow was left with the twelve tribes. The Ten Commandments are the summary of the mortal law, the complement of God's laws which are enclosed in the hermetic book of the Ark.

Moses, who was trained and initiated as a High Priest of the Egyptian court, would have wanted to protect the teachings of the Ark of the Covenant. Investigators suspect that he made copies of the Ark in the form of a book or scroll and that he left many copies along the way at various sites as he crossed the Sinai desert, over forty years, with the Ark. In those days it was not unusual to make copies because papyrus only lasted one lifetime and these divine teachings needed to be secured. Also, there were many wars at that time so it was necessary to secure sacred information in alternative locations.

When I read about the "Axis of Vision" in John Michell and Christine Rhone's well-researched book *Twelve Tribe Nations*,[1] it became evident why a certain ley line or earth current across Israel had been important in the history of Israel. There were sites along this natural corridor through the Holy Land where many visions and revelations had been given, according to information gathered in both testaments of the Bible.

Here Moses received the Law on Mount Sinai, the place of the Burning Bush. Here stands Bethlehem, the mother city of Israel, where King David and Jesus were born; Jerusalem, where King Solomon's Temple was built, and where the Ark was eventually deposited; Bethel, the sanctuary of the twelve tribes of Israel, where the Ark of the Covenant was consecrated for a time, where God told Jacob the land was given to him and his descendants, then foretold of the dispersal of the twelve tribes to all parts of the earth and their eventual return to the land of Israel; Shiloh, where the Ark of the Covenant rested for two hundred years after the Israelites entered the land of Canaan; Shechem, whose temple was built on the top of Mount Gerizim, on the same plan of sacred geometry as Solomon's Temple, by the Jewish sect of Samaritans who claimed it to be the holy city rather than Jerusalem.

Farther along the Axis is Mount Tabor, the place of Jesus' transfiguration, which has been used as a place of power by prophets and leaders for thousands of years; and Safed, which became an important Cabalistic Center in the Middle Ages (no doubt housing a copy of the Ark in the form of the Torah). Many of these sites are associated with the Ark of the Covenant. This could account for the extreme power responsible for the visions, revelations, and miracles produced on this axis.

"When the tribes crossed the Jordan from the east to begin their conquest and settlement of the Promised Land, they claimed possession of it in the name of Jehovah through certain geomantic rituals. Jordan's waters were miraculously rolled back, and where the bearers of the Ark stepped on to its west bank, a circle of 12 stones was erected (Joshua 4). The tribes were also instructed (Deuteronomy 27) to put up another circle of 12 stones on Mount Ebal which, with its neighbor Mount Gerizim, marks the geographical center of the Holy Land. The Stones were to be plastered and inscribed with the words of the Law."[2]

Paul Devereaux, author of *Places of Power*, studied the phenomenon of moving lights and apparitions associated with major arteries of the earth currents (ley lines). His experiments with magnetometers and other instruments proved that the sites of Stone Circles are anomalies in the earth's energy field. Also, the Stone Circles produced what Devereaux called "earth lights," and these places seem also to produce, for some people, a state of enhanced vision and other experiences.

The building of the Tabernacle that housed the Ark of the Covenant (described in Exodus 25–27) was revealed to Moses by God upon the peak of Sinai. Moses thought that he was to superintend the building; however, God said that this honor was reserved for Bezaleel, the son of Hur, for he was a man possessed of wisdom, insight, and understanding, and by these God himself had created the world. Bezaleel was from the noble tribe of Judah, but according to the divine will, another man was also chosen. It was Aholiab, of the tribe of Dan, which was without great reputation. God ordered this so that the great and lowly should be regarded equally in the works of the Lord.

The container of the Ark itself was an adaptation of the Egyptian Ark, even to the kneeling figures upon the lid. Bas-reliefs on the Temple of Philo in Egypt show Egyptian priests carrying the Ark, closely resembling the Ark of the Jews that was carried on the shoulders of slaves as described in Exodus.

This movable temple is a wonderfully appropriate symbol of an ideal spiritual institution. Truth does not abide in any one place, but moves about the earth and is entrusted in different times and under various situations to the noblest, wisest, and most virtuous of human beings. So states Josephus in his *History of the Jews*.

There were rabbis of ancient days who insisted that the Tabernacle is made in the likeness of humans. As humans are miniatures of the divine world, so the Tabernacle is representative of both the universe and humanity. Ancient commentaries declare that the great Tabernacle of the Lord is in the sun, and that in humans the heart corresponds to the sun.

When building the Tabernacle, Bezaleel recommended that the box for the Ark of the Covenant should be constructed first. In this way, there would be a resting place for the Ark of the Covenant, being a copy or scroll of the Emerald Tablet, which needed to be encased in a holder and later put in the "Holy of Holies."

The tent of the Tabernacle was made of three parts. There was an outer court consisting of a wall of curtains stretched between wooden uprights. Within this wall was an enclosure set aside for holiness. In the midst of this enclosure stood the Tabernacle itself—a tent-like structure divided into two rooms. The outer room was shaped like a double cube and called the Holy Place, and the structure of the inner room was of a single cube called the Holy of Holies, which contained only the Ark of the Covenant.

In the court of the Tabernacle stood the laver of purification, with mirrors on its sides. The mirrors were symbols of human vanity and egotism, which must be relinquished by those who seek a life of holiness.

In the Holy Place of the Tabernacle stood the table of shewbread, which signified the substance that was given to Israel for sustenance of the people while they wandered in the wilderness fed by manna, which came down from heaven. Also in the Holy Place was the Menorah, or seven-branched candlestick, which represented the seven planetary bodies, the seven days of creation, the seven races, the seven continents of earth.

In the Holy Place there also was the altar of burnt incense, which was fashioned of gold. Therefore, there were two altars: one outside the Tabernacle, made of brass, and one within, made of fine gold. Offerings were made upon the brazen altar outside the Tabernacle; but on the golden altar in the Holy Place only spices and sweet incense were offered, feeding the "higher" senses.

It is thought that the altar of burnt offerings represents earth; the laver of purification, water; the candlestick and the shewbread represent fire, the altar of burnt incense is air; and the Ark of the Covenant is the subtle ether over which hovers the Shekinah.

Curtained off from the sight of the priests, was the Holy of Holies, in the middle of which stood the Ark of the Covenant. The scrolls of the Ark of the Covenant were encased in three caskets. The outer one was of gold, and this held one of wood, which in turn contained one of gold. Because the Ark was a replica in miniature of the cosmos when it was carried about, it was covered with a fine cloth of blue, the color of the sky.

On the top of the Ark knelt two cherubs with the faces of boys. The face of each cherub measured a span, and their wings measured ten spans. Together they made up twenty-two spans, equal to the letters of the Hebrew alphabet. The space between the kneeling cherubs on the lid of the chest of the Ark was called the Mercy Seat. The chest of the Ark was fitted on either side with rings through which rods could be passed, and the Ark was then lifted onto the shoulders of men, so that it could be carried from place to place.

Moses added to the chest of the Ark the Staff of Aaron. Aaron's Staff was the rod he carried while traveling across the Sinai with Moses. The esoteric meaning of the rod or staff, when properly drawn, is the spinal column. When we observe the Caduceus used by the medical profession, we can see the staff as the spinal column with a snake traveling up each side of the column. In Hindu terminology, these snakes are called *Ida* and *Pingala*, or the masculine and feminine energy. Because of the thirty-three vertebrae in the spine, we find a similar thirty-three degrees in the Masonic tradition.

—from *Genisis*, by David Wood

The temple furniture showing the Mercy Seat being the lid of the Ark

The Masons have incorporated all that is in the Ark in their fraternities. Hermes, who received the Ark from Noah, was not only the messenger between God and humans, but the God of healing, and in pictures we often see him holding the Caduceus.

Albert G. Mackey, M.D., in his esteemed *Encyclopedia of Freemasonry*, relates that Aaron's Rod was the method used by Moses to determine which tribe should be invested with the priesthood. This story is detailed in the Book of Numbers (Ch. XVII). Moses directed that twelve rods, one for each tribe, should be laid in the Holy of Holies of the Tabernacle. The rod of Aaron represented the tribe of Levi. On the next day, these rods were brought out and exhibited to the people and, while the rest remained dry and withered, that of Aaron alone miraculously budded, blossomed and yielded fruit.

The seventeenth chapter of Numbers describes the budding of Aaron's rod. "And it came to pass, that on the morrow Moses went into the Tabernacle of witness; and, behold, the rod of

Aaron for the house of Levi was budded, and brought forth buds, and bloomed blossoms, and yielded almonds" (17:8).

It is said that a pot of manna was also added to the chest of the Ark. Manna represents spirit, truth or wisdom. It is the food which descends from heaven. For truly it is said that "Man doth not live by bread only, but by every word that proceedeth out of the mouth of the Lord doth man live" (Deuteronomy 8:3). In the New Testament, Christ, the personification of the divine wisdom, is made to say, "I am the living bread which came down from heaven: if any man eat of this bread, he shall live forever" (John 6:51). Therefore manna is not a precipitated dew, as some have suggested, but as the Greeks said, it is the food of the inner man, who lives not upon the fruits of the earth, but upon the fruits of the spirit.

The *Torah* ends with the death of Moses. On the lonely hill of Moab, Moses, the good man, was hidden away in God, and the people of Israel wept for thirty days, and then the mournings for Moses were over. He was the only figure in history to establish a nation founded and based wholly on the great universal "One Law."

When the migrations of Israelites were finished, and the Ark finally came to rest in the Holy of Holies of the temple, the pot of manna and the rod of Aaron had disappeared. According to one view of the *Aggadah* or *Haggadah* (Ber. 8b;BB 14b), the Ark of the Covenant, the Tablets of the Ten Commandments and the fragments of the original Sapphire Tablets, which were broken by Moses on the desert, remained.

When the Ark and its contents reached Jerusalem safely, King David was so happy that he danced for joy and leapt stark naked around the Ark (dancing around the ark symbolized the motion of the planets around the sun). Although David was proud of having the Ark, he did not agree to keep it in his palace, nor did he have a temple built for it. He placed it in a tabernacle. David's son and successor, King Solomon (965–926 B.C.), had the Ark placed in the Holy of Holies, a specially protected room in the temple, where it remained pure and protected during the following 300 years of wars and disasters in Israel.

Moses discovered that this "One Law," the Ark of the Covenant, was eternal and indestructible and governs all manifestations of life and the whole universe. "The Law," the one supreme power, is the connecting link which rules the plan of Cosmic Order.

CHAPTER 6

KING SOLOMON'S TEMPLE
AND THE ARK OF THE COVENANT

When I first visited Israel several years ago, I remember the bus stopped just before ascending the mount to Jerusalem and, at that moment, tears ran down my cheeks. My soul was remembering things past. One of my friends told me that when he first visited Israel, he instinctively bent down and kissed the ground as soon as he walked off the plane. I think Israel has many memories for all of us; I wonder if our memories go back to Moses, David, Solomon or Christ?

The youngest of the sons of David, Solomon was twelve years old when he became King over Israel. Though Solomon came to be remembered for his wealth and the magnificence of his court, these were really nothing when compared to the wisdom for which he has been better known. It is said that while Solomon was still a young man, God appeared to him in a dream at Gideon and he granted the new King any grace he desired.

Solomon chose wisdom because he was astute enough to know that if he possessed this, all else would come to him. God gave Solomon power over spirits and demons of the air; and animals obeyed him.

The Royal Arches of Enoch

An interesting legend associated with the story of the Hebrew Patriarch Enoch and the Temple of Solomon is the apocryphal account of the building of the "Royal Arches." It is believed that Enoch passed his early pastoral life in the neighborhood of Mount Moriah. After being enlightened by the divine knowledge which had been imparted to him, he fled to the solitude and secrecy of Mount Moriah and devoted himself to prayer and pious contemplation. We are informed that the Shekinah or sacred presence appeared to Enoch and gave him instructions which were to preserve the wisdom of the antediluvian world, the world before the great flood. This has been called the great Masonic "Legend of Enoch."

Enoch, inspired by the Divine and in commemoration of a wonderful vision, and aided by his son Methuselah, built a temple beneath the earth and dedicated it to God. The temple consisted of seven rooms, one above the other, each with an arched ceiling. It descended from one room to another, into the heart of the earth. Enoch placed in the lowest of the arched chambers a golden delta, or triangle, with the secret name of God inscribed on it. After the death of Enoch, the site of his temple was lost, and for centuries men searched for the secret rooms.

When Solomon decided to build his temple upon Mount Moriah, the workmen, while digging the foundation for the temple, uncovered the sealed vaults of Enoch. Solomon therefore built the temple upon the site of the mysterious structure contrived by Enoch.

In modern Freemasonry, a great deal of the symbolism of the "Royal Arches" of Enoch is preserved. The seven rooms, one above the other, represent the orbits of the planets. Therefore, we have a ziggurat inverted and descending into the earth. The golden triangle in the lowest room is a symbol of the divinity locked in the deepest parts of matter.

The story of the Royal Arches and the Golden delta is discussed in more detail by Albert Pike, the famous 33rd degree Mason, in his book *Morals and Dogma*.[1] Albert Pike quotes Albert G. Mackey, M.D. in his book confirming the Royal Arches. Mackey states in his *Encyclopedia of Freemasonry*: "There can be no doubt of the existence of immense vaults beneath the superstructure of the original Temple of Solomon. Prime, Robison and other writers who in recent times have described the topography of Jerusalem, speak of the eixstence of these structures, which they visited and, in some instances, carefully examined."[2]

When Solomon began the construction of his temple, he communicated with Hiram, King of Tyre, saying: "Thou knowest how that David my father could not build a house unto the name of the Lord his God for the wars which were about him on every side, until the Lord put them under the soles of his feet. But now the Lord my God hath given me rest on every side, so that there is neither adversary nor evil occurrent. And, behold, I propose to build an house unto the name of the Lord my God, as the Lord spake unto David my father, saying, Thy Son, whom I will set upon thy throne in thy room, he shall build an house unto my name." And it is stated: "And King Solomon sent and fetched Hiram out of Tyre." (1 Kings 7:13)

In addition to King Hiram, Solomon fetched Hiram the Artificer, called Hiram Abiff. The building of the temple was supervised by these three Grand Masters.

Da Costa, in his *Dionysian Artificers*, declares that Hiram Abiff of Tyre was an initiate priest of the Mysteries of Dionysius.[3]

The Dionysian Artificers

To understand Hiram, it is necessary to examine the Order of the Dionysian Artificers, which originated among the Greeks and Romans at some time before 1000 B.C. It was originally composed of skilled craftsmen, banded together in a guild to perpetuate the secrets of their crafts. Gradually the science of architecture dominated the policies of the society. According to legend, when Solomon, King of Israel, resolved to build his temple according to the will of his father, David, he sent to Tyre and engaged the services of a cunning workman, Hiram Abiff, a master of the Dionysian Artificers. The Dionysian Artificers called themselves sons of Solomon, and one of their symbols was the Seal of Solomon—

two interlaced triangles. The members of this society held the exclusive right in the Greek states to design the temples, houses of government, the theaters and buildings used for public games.

The Dionysian Artificers, who were part of the Masonic order, thought it possible by the combination of straight lines and curves to induce a change of mental attitude or emotion. They labored to produce a building in perfect harmony with the structure of the universe, and believed that because the building was in harmony with reality, it would endure throughout the span of mortal time. The architects deemed such a building to be an oracle because it was a duplication of the cosmos, much as the Ark was thought to have similar oracular qualities because of its sacred mathematics.

The Dionysians possessed a body of learning which included mathematical secrets as well as knowledge concerning universal dynamics; all of this was guided by a conviction concerning the perfecting of human society.

The greatness of this group and its knowledge of the sacred math was carried to other countries as well. As Grecian culture reached Rome, the Romans formed their own Dionysian society and named it the Collegia. The greatest of the Collegians was the architect Vitruvius, sometimes called the father of modern architecture. He was responsible for the superior sanitation systems of Rome and the great aqueducts. Vitruvius could produce certain changes in the tone and quality of the human voice by his placement of bronze vases about a room.

The Dionysian Artificer was capable of arranging the chambers through which the candidate of the Mysteries passed during initiation with their own special acoustics. In one chamber the priest's voice was made to sound so loud that his words caused the very room to vibrate. In another, the voice was softened to such a degree that it sounded like distant tinkling of bells. In some of the underground passageways the candidate seemed without power of speech. Even if he shouted, not even a whisper could be heard. But after advancing a few feet, he would find that even a sigh would be re-echoed many times.

Later the Dionysian movement went eastward to build the empire of Islam, with each stone in every mosque and palace bearing the mark of the master masons. The migration continued as far as India, where these same marks are to be seen on the buildings of the Mogul dynasty.

Early in Europe's development, the Dionysians became the guild of the cathedral-builders. They signed each stone with the secret symbols of their group, and into the carvings of churches they worked the old pagan figures and designs. In the ornate carvings of great old churches are frequently found representations of compasses, squares, rules, mallets, and other Masonic builders' tools.

Architecture was the chosen instrument for the perpetuation of the building of a perfect world. The structures built by the Dionysian Builders can be said to be "sermons in stone."

The Dionysian Builders, like all those who understood sacred geometry knew that *beauty is essential to the natural unfoldment of the human soul.* The Mysteries held that man, in part at least, was the product of his environment. Therefore, it was considered imperative that every person be surrounded by objects which would evoke the highest and noblest sentiments.

Structure of Solomon's Temple

The building of Solomon's Temple is described in the First Book of Kings, beginning with chapter 5 and continuing through chapter 9. It is believed the Bible story is historically true and describes the building of the temple, made from rock, wood, and ornamented with gold and precious stone. The architecture was thought to be Babylonian and Chaldean.

Construction of the temple started in the 480th year after the people of Israel had been released from Egypt. From the dimensions given in 1 Kings, Chapter 6, it is evident that the temple was not very large: the length was approximately 90 feet, the width was 30 feet, and the height 45 feet. Different methods of determining the Jewish cubit have been used, but in all probability, the dimensions given are approximately correct.

We can assume that assistance and favors were bestowed upon Solomon by God. It took seven years to build the temple, and

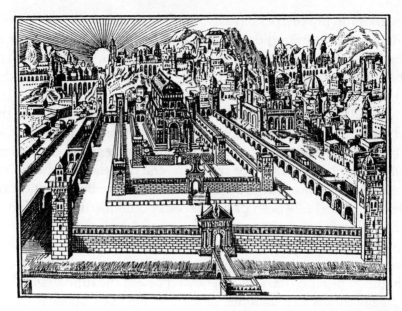

—Print engraved by Matthew Menan, 1695,
from *The Passover Haggadah*, Amsterdam.

The Temple of Solomon at Jerusalem

not a single workman died, nor fell sick. They were known to
have abounding good health. The tools used in their work did
not wear out nor become dull. There is a legend that after the
temple was dedicated, many of the workmen died and received
their wages in another and better world.

Josephus, the Jewish historian, was aware that the Tabernacle in the Wilderness and King Solomon's Temple were symbols
of the universe. Solomon's Temple was patterned after the Tabernacle. The sanctuary was divided into two parts—the Holy Place,
and the Most Holy of Holy Places, which was to receive the Ark
of the Covenant. When the temple was finished, in the month of
Bul, it stood closed for nearly a year because it was the will of
God that the dedication of His sacred temple should take place
in the month of the birth of Abraham. There is a story told that
when the Ark of the Covenant was to be brought into the Holy
of Holies of the temple, the door of the sacred chamber locked
and no one could open this door.

Solomon prayed passionately to God, but only when he said, "Remember the good deeds of David thy servant," the door of the Holy of Holies opened without human aid. Those who had thoughts about David being unholy were forced to acknowledge that God had forgiven him.

According to ancient rabbis, Solomon was an initiate of the Mystery Schools, and Solomon's Temple was actually a house of initiation. The palm-headed columns, pomegranates, the two pillars standing in front of the door, the Babylonian cherubim, and the mathematical proportions of the chambers all indicate the temple to have been patterned after the sanctuaries of Egypt and Atlantis.

Masons called the right and left pillars outside the Temple of Solomon respectively Jachin, which was light, and Boaz, the shadowy pillar of darkness. They represent the fundamental divine polarity which underlies all nature, the two opposites—male and female—whose union consitutes the symbolic great work of alchemy, the alchemical marriage. On these pillars were the same decad as on the two stones of the Ten Commandments. Without doubt, these pillars have as their prototype the stone pillars or obelisks that stand before the sanctuaries of Egypt and have the same symbolic importance.

H. P. Blavatsky explains the esoteric foundations of the temple in her writings when she states that: ". . . This will be made plain to the reader who reads the *Source of Measures* or *The Hebrew Egyptian Mysteries* and understands its undeniable, clear and mathematical proofs that the esoteric foundations, or the systems used in the building of the Great Pyramid, and the architectural measurements in the Temple of Solomon . . . Noah's Ark and the Ark of the Covenant are the same. . . ."[4]

King Solomon's Temple and the Great Pyramid of Egypt have an important role in the rituals of Masonry. Charles Leadbeater, known to us through Theosophy, writes in his book *Ancient Mystic Rites*: "The Jews applied what they knew of Egyptian systems to the temple of King Solomon, reflecting the wisdom of Egypt through the lens of their own fiery and poetical temperament, whence some portion of it gradually passed on the one hand into written and esoteric literature, on the other was handed down in the secret Lodges of Masonry. . . . The Jewish Mysteries are the source of our present traditions . . ."[5]

CHAPTER 7

ETHIOPIA AND THE ARK OF THE COVENANT

here are many legends associated with the visit of the Queen of Sheba to the court of Solomon. When the Queen of Sheba visited Solomon, it is said that she brought the King the same gifts which the Magi placed before Christ in the manger. Sheba is said to have come from Yemen, but the Ethiopians said she was of Meroe. In each story, the Queen of Sheba bore a son from Solomon; the Ethiopians claim that their royal house is descended from this union. When Sheba returned to her own country, twelve thousand Jews are said to have returned with her.

The *Book of the Glory of Kings, the Kebra Nagast*, originally written in the thirteenth century, was translated from the Ethiopic by E. Wallis Budge, the former keeper of Egyptian and Assyrian antiquities at the British Museum. This book contains what is thought to be the traditional history of the Queen of Sheba and her son Menelik, and discusses the transference of the Ark of the Covenant by Menelik from Jerusalem to Axum, Ethiopia, the new Zion. In the Ethiopic story, it was a merchant by the name of Tamrin from Jerusalem who told the Queen of Sheba about the wisdom of Solomon and the glory of his court. The Queen, who greatly admired wisdom and understanding then decided to visit the court of Solomon, whose fame had reached the most remote parts of the world. She arrived in Jerusalem while Solomon

56

was supervising the building of the Temple. Each day he mingled with the workmen and instructed and supervised all their constructions. Sheba, as she watched Solomon, was impressed by the perfection of his actions, words and thoughts.

As stated in the *Kebra Nagast*, the Queen remained for several months as a guest in King Solomon's court and he made her his wife. When the Queen knew that she was bearing a child, she returned to Ethiopia carrying a signet ring from Solomon. She gave birth to a son, Menelik, called "the son of the wise man." When Menelik grew older, he desired to visit his father in Jerusalem. The Queen gave him the signet ring and sent him to Solomon with the caravan of the merchant Tamrin. The boy closely resembled his father, so there could be no question as to his paternity. Solomon embraced Menelik and proclaimed him his son, recognizing him as a royal prince. After a lengthy visit, Menelik wanted to go back to his mother. He knew it was his destiny to rule in his own land and not over the kingdom of Israel.

It was then Menelik decided to take back to Ethiopia the Ark of the Covenant. Solomon, who was an exceedingly wise man and knew many prophets and seers, must have known of the fall of Jerusalem. Such an event would have been predicted and, in order to protect the Ark, he sent it to Ethiopia with his son. Menelik was aided by the merchant Tamrin and the sons of prominent Jewish families who desired to assist in the founding of a Jewish empire in Ethiopia.

In her great rejoicing at the arrival of this sacred treasure, Sheba abdicated in favor of her son Menelik, and he established in Ethiopia a kingdom modeled after Israel. The negus of Ethiopia is still referred to as the "Conquering Lion of Judah." This title was proudly carried by Haile Selassie even through the tribulations of the disastrous Italian invasion in 1935. The royal insignia of Ethiopia remains the crowned lion.

The Ark of the Covenant is alleged to be housed in the Holy of Holies of the most famous sanctuary in Ethiopia, the St. Mary of Zion Cathedral at Axum (sometimes spelled Aksum). Today in Axum, the most notable achievements of indigenous art are the deservedly famous Aksumite Obelisks, which have delicately executed ornamental designs. The monuments are pre-Christian; the largest standing today is 70 feet tall. Though broken through the force of its fall, the largest monolith found to date measured 110 feet when originally erected.

Obelisks are frequently near the arks or vaults. Often they carry part of the contents, so the treasure is not all in one place. Obelisks are considered powerful and magical and were interpreted in pagan or pre-Christian times as links between earth and heaven. They act as a needle in the earth's acupuncture system known as ley lines. When this needle is inserted on a vortex, where the ley lines cross, a center of power is created which is often associated with magic, creating an abundance of energetic life force and fertility. Therefore, the presence of obelisks always enhances the surrounding area. Obelisks that resemble the shape of a flame have caused these monuments to be consecrated to the Sun and to Fire; in pagan times the sun was worshipped as God. It is said that the etheric rays from the sun penetrating the earth via the monuments, can help raise consciousness and give the surrounding earth and its people healing energy and fertility.

In the introduction to his translation of the *Kebra Nagast*, published in the 1920s, Budge writes: "The object of the compiler and the later editors of the *Kebra Nagast* was to glorify Ethiopia by narrating the history of the coming of the 'spiritual and heavenly Zion,' the Tabernacle of the Law of the God of Israel, of her own free will, from Jerusalem to Ethiopia. The compilers or editors made it quite clear that the King of Ethiopia was descended from Solomon, the son of David, King of Israel, and through him from Abraham and the early Patriarchs."

Like Christ, the King of Ethiopia was also a son of God, and therefore both God and King to his people. The *Kebra Nagast* was written with the intention of making the people of Ethiopia believe that their country was specially chosen by God to be the new home of the spiritual Zion, of which his chosen people, the Jews, had become unworthy.

By allegorically reducing Solomon and Sheba to the basic elements of astrology, we have the two great orbs, the sun and the moon, which were thought of as the male and female principles of life by the wise old astrologers. These teachers realized that the moon shone with the reflected light of the sun; therefore, it was considered a magic mirror, a silvery disc of enchantment which captured the sun's power and held it by strange means.

Menelik is the union of spiritual and political authority by divine right. He is the child of the sun (male) and moon (female), whose union represents the principle of equilibrium in Nature (the Alchemical Marriage). He carried the Ark of the Covenant to Ethiopia and there established the true worship. The Ethiopians believed Menelik was the Messiah, one of the house of David upon whom the Lord looked with favor.

Several hundred years later the original Ark was taken out of Ethiopia by Alexander the Great when he conquered Ethiopia. At that time Ethiopia is said to have reconstructed the Ark, so we can say with a fair degree of certainty that there is an Ark in Ethiopia.

CHAPTER 8

ALEXANDRIA AND THE ARK OF THE COVENANT

he city of Alexandria, Egypt was founded by Alexander the Great in 332 B.C. Alexander assembled a group of skilled architects and artisans and built the city he envisioned to be the great wonder of the world. Two years later Alexander completed the conquest of all the known world, including the lands of Israel and Ethiopia. Ethiopia had made no secret of having the Ark of the Covenant. Because he had access to all in the land he had conquered, Alexander took the Ark of Solomon's Temple from Ethiopia and eventually returned it to the Temple in Jerusalem.

Although the story is clouded, it is speculated that Alexander brought the Ark to Alexandria where Aristotle, Alexander's teacher since an early age, and a group of Pythagoreans could help him decipher the Ark. As a consequence, and knowing the history of the Ark, he probably realized how inadequate he was to wield the power of the Ark; there also existed the possibility the Ark could kill him. The Ark was returned to its proper place in Solomon's Temple and no doubt Alexander felt this would put him in the good graces of the Deity.

The Libraries and Museums of Alexandria

After Alexander died, the expansion of Alexandria passed to the Greek pharaohs of Egypt. The first of these, Ptolemy Soter, was responsible for carrying out the original scheme, later carried on by his successor, Ptolemy Philadelphus. During the time of these two kings, the Bruchium, the most famous museum, was completed. When Ptolemy Philadelphus died, the collection of manuscripts housed in the Bruchium exceeded 100,000. Callimachus, Ptolemy Philadelphus' successor, classified and labeled the collection. The library contained more than 750,000 items when Julius Caesar conquered the city.

Ptolemy Soter had been a general in the armies of Alexander and during his years of military life he learned how to discipline himself and his army. Later rulers, unable to maintain order among the followers of Alexander, asked Rome for assistance. The assistance was given, but Rome's assistance ended with the Roman conquest of the city in 48 B.C. When Caesar besieged Alexandria, the Bruchium was accidentally destroyed. Following is an illustration of a silver coin minted by Ptolemy Soter. Note the similarity of the eagle to that appearing on American coins.

—from George Ebers' *Egypt: Descriptive, Historical, and Picturesque*, Vol. I

Coinage

After the destruction of the Bruchium, restoration was undertaken by Mark Antony, who presented Alexandria with the Pergamene library, consisting of approximately 200,000 manuscripts. Among the many famous scholars who studied the Alexandrian collection were Strabo, Archimedes, and Euclid.

H. P. Blavatsky, who was well informed about Coptic Christianity, wrote that from her friends she gathered some details concerning the fate of the great Alexandrian library. She states that several hours elapsed between the burning of the fleet in the harbor of Alexandria by Julius Caesar and the spreading of the fire to the city. In this interval, librarians and servants attached to the Bruchium saved the most valuable of the scrolls. The parchments themselves had been fireproofed, and even after the fire, many scrolls were found intact, although their bindings had been destroyed. Many other works were saved because they had been moved to the house of the principal librarian for reconditioning. Also, because of a prophecy that the library would be destroyed, the most important records had been hidden in other places. There are Arabic accounts that they were hidden in a subterranean temple some distance from Alexandria long before the Roman invasion.[1]

The Serapeum was built by Ptolemy Soter about A.D. 400 to honor the Egyptian deity Serapis. It was a most extraordinary sanctuary and contained many works of art and the sacred records of Alexandria. The Serapeum library contained about 300,000 manuscripts, but was burned by the Caliph Omar in A.D. 641. Details of this burning can be found in Gibbon's *The Decline and Fall of the Roman Empire*.[2]

With the periodic destruction of libraries, temples, and schools, the old landmarks were destroyed. However, the beliefs of the Gnostics, Neoplatonists, Cabalists, and Hermetists survived, and endure even today.

Alexandria was a great center for all types of knowledge. Every alchemical tract that we know goes back to Alexandria. Astrology as we know it has its roots in Alexandria. It was a model city that showed what could be done with people of various nationalities working together, and it proved that more than one race and more than one religion could live together in peace.

Milton S. Terry, translator of *The Sibylline Oracles*, referred to the ancient Sibylline prophecies as being a large body of pseudepigraphal literature from the beginning of the Christian era (about 150 B.C. to A.D. 300). The prophecies consist of such works as the Book of Enoch, the Testaments of the Twelve Patriarchs, the Book of Jubilees, the Assumption of Moses, the Psalms of Solomon, the Ascension of Isaiah, and the Second Book of Estrous. This literature was produced in Alexandria in the time of the Ptolemies.[3]

Hermes Trismegistus

The most important name to be associated with Alexandria is the Egyptian deity Thoth who, combined with the Greek deity Hermes, produced the semi-mythological deity of Universal Wisdom or Thoth Hermes Trismegistus. In a sense, there were two Hermes. The first Hermes lived during the time of Atlantis, who came to Egypt after the flood at the command of Enoch, the High Priest of Atlantis, to found Egypt as a nation. Hermes, a High Priest and successor to Enoch, became the rightful overseer of the Ark of the Covenant which had been delivered to him by Noah in Egypt. It is said that Hermes translated the Ark of the Covenant.

The Second Hermes, Hermes of Alexandria, was actually a compilation of many teachers, their writings having been put together under the name Hermes Trismegistus. Allegorically, this deity was truly the embodiment of all learning. The group that adopted the name *Hermes* in Alexandria was of Greek and Egyptian background. During the Renaissance, many thought that the Greco-Egyptian Hermes was actually a divinely enlightened person, so efforts were made to create a pseudo-biography for him.

There is little doubt that the Hermetic dialogues were written and compiled in Alexandria. The teachings were scholarly, scientific, and projected the highest ethical and moral teachings of the Egyptian Mysteries. Because these teachings were similar to the

—from *Historia Decorum Fatidicorum*

Hermes Mercurius Trismegistus

This plate was cut in the early 17th century by Theodore de Bry. It is one of
the best examples of the appearance attributed to Hermes. Theodore de Bry
was part of the Guild system, and his name is often used to demonstrate the
connection to the Masonic organization.

secret rites of the Greeks, there was little conflict between the
Greek and Egyptian communities in Alexandria.

These works compiled in the early centuries A.D. contain little or no trace of Christian influence. With the decline of the
Mystery Schools, Hermetic philosophy lost its importance and
gradually faded out of Alexandrian culture. But there are traces
of the Hermetic doctrine that have survived in modern mysticism.

Forty-two Books of Hermes

Clement of Alexandria, the greatest Christian apologist, or reconciler of Christian and Pagan religions, of the second century, mentions the finding of forty-two books of Hermes. Clement states that "this treasure was the treasure of Jerusalem." Presumably, he meant that the forty-two books of Hermes contained all the information from the Emerald Tablet. Clement of Alexandria, in his book *Stromata* (one of the few books of pagan lore that have been preserved to this age), gives practically all the information we know concerning the original forty-two books of Hermes. The importance of these books is that they reveal the secular and spiritual powers of Egypt.

These books were lost during the burning of Alexandria. The Romans, and later the Christians, understood that until these books were eliminated, the Egyptians could never be brought into submission. In some unknown manner, the Knights Templars, who were an early order of Masonry, are said to have obtained possession of these forty-two books. It is speculated that the books are now safely housed in the Masonic library in England.

The Emerald Tablet of Hermes the Thrice Greatest Trismegistus

Albert Pike, in his *Morals and Dogma*, informs us: "The whole Hermetic Science is contained in the dogma of Hermes, engraved originally, it is said, on a tablet of emerald."

Pike goes on to say that: "All the Masters in Alchemy who have written of the Great Work [the Emerald Tablet], have employed symbolic and figurative expressions; being constrained to do so, as well to repel the profane from a work that would be dangerous for them, as to be well understood by Adepts, in revealing to them the whole world of analogies governed by the single and sovereign dogma of Hermes . . ."[4]

Dr. Sigismund Bacstrom was initiated into the Brotherhood of the Rose Cross on the Island of Mauritius. In his rare 18-volume collection of alchemical manuscripts, Dr. Bacstrom has a section dedicated to the translations and interpretations of the extraordinary Emerald Tablet also known as the *Tabula Smaragdina*.

The Emerald Tablet of Hermes

His translations and notes of the Emerald Tablet are the genuine translation from the original ancient Chaldee and can be reviewed in Manly P. Hall's *The Secret Teachings of All Ages*, pp. CLVII and CLVIII.[5]

The writing upon the gem includes a statement of analogy, which is the main key to the Emerald Tablet: that which is above is like unto that which is below, and that which is below is like unto that which is above.

Book of Thoth

Antoine Court de Gebelin, an Egyptologist and former Grand Master of the Masonic French Lodge of the Nine Sisters, first recognized the pack of tarot cards as a repository of Ancient Egyptian wisdom and the secret teachings of the Egyptian priests. Gebelin gives us evidence for the theory that the tarot was the lost *Book of Thoth*. Gebelin informs us that the Egyptian Priests hid the arcane knowledge left to them by the Hermetic teachings in symbolic illustrations so as to survive the ordeal of Christianity after the collapse of the pagan world. The *Book of Thoth* is, in reality, the mysterious Tarot of the Bohemians—the strange emblematic book of seventy-eight leaves (or cards) which has been in the possession of the gypsies since the time when they were driven from their ancient temple, the Serapeum.

Samuel Roberts, in his book *The Gypsies*, written in 1842, gives evidence of the Egyptian origin of tarot. A legend states that after the destruction and burning of the Serapeum, many priests banded together to preserve the secrets of the rites of Serapis. The Gypsies, the descendants of these priests, carried with them the most precious volumes saved from the burning library, including the Book of Thoth (the Tarot).

In H. P. Blavatsky's *Isis Unveiled*, an important comment is made about the *Book of Thoth*: "It was Ammonius who first taught that every religion was based on one and the same truth; which is the wisdom found in the *Book of Thoth* (Hermes Trismegistus), from which books Pythagoras and Plato had learned all their philosophy. And the doctrines of the former he affirmed to have been identical with the earliest teachings of the Brahmans—now embodied in the oldest *Veda*."⁶

Blavatsky, quoting Professor A. Wilder, states: "The name *Thoth*, means a college or assembly, and it is not altogether improbable that the books were so named as being the collected oracles and doctrines of the sacerdotal fraternity of Memphis. Rabbi Wise has suggested a similar hypothesis in relation to the divine utterances recorded in the Hebrew Scriptures. But the Indian writers assert that during the reign of King Kansa, the Yadus (Judaens?) or sacred tribe left India and migrated to the West, carrying the four *Vedas* with them. There was certainly a great resemblance between the philosophical doctrines and religious customs of the Egyptians and Eastern Buddhists; but whether the Hermetic books and the four *Vedas* were in any sense identical is not known."⁷

While Hermes was still living on earth, he gave his chosen successors the sacred *Book of Thoth*. This book contained the processes of regeneration. It also contained the key to Hermes' other writings. According to legend, the *Book of Thoth* was kept in a golden box in the inner sanctuary of the temple and only the highest initiate of the Hermetic Arcanum knew what was written in the sacred book. The *Book of Thoth* was lost to the ancient world with the decline of the Mysteries, but it is said its faithful initiates carried it into another land. Could this other land be the Masonic Library in England?

The tarot is an essential element in Rosicrucian symbolism. It is possibly the book of universal knowledge which the Rosicrucians claimed to possess. Many ancient writers knew that the tarot (the *Book of Thoth*) carries the message of the Ark of the Covenant.

Hermes is important to Masonic scholars; he was the author of the Masonic initiatory rituals, which were borrowed from the Mysteries (Ark of the Covenant). Many of the Masonic symbols are Hermetic in character. The name "Thrice Greatest" (Trismegistus) was given to Hermes because he was considered the greatest of all philosophers, priests, and kings. The last poem of

America's famous poet Henry Wadsworth Longfellow was a lyric ode to Hermes (See *Chambers Encyclopedia*).

The Divine Pymander

Hermetic writings suggest that the ministry of Hermes was preceded by a vision, as recorded in the *Pymander*. After the vision, Hermes' mission was to convert the world to the great truths. The teaching of Hermes seems to have been spoken directly to certain disciples, and it is said he went up and down the land, with his staff (the Caduceus) in hand, teaching the wisdom. He preached that people of the earth were born and made of the elements, but had the spirit of the Divine within. He asked people to realize that their home is not in the earth but in the Light. Hermes reminded people to forsake corruption forever and prepare to climb through the Seven Rings (rungs) to blend their souls with the eternal Light.

In his writing Hermes states that the orbits of the seven planets known to the ancients, formed a ladder connecting heaven with earth, and conversely, earth with heaven. This was known as the sacred ladder of seven rungs, the ladder of Jacob, and was also the ladder of golden cords by which Mohammed ascended to the footstool of God. Also, the planets are the seven seals of revelation which must be opened, and the powers that emanate from these planets are the seven cardinal virtues, and the misuse of these powers constitutes the seven deadly sins.

Frances Yates, in her book *Giordano Bruno and the Hermetic Tradition*, writes: "The *Pimander* (the first of the treatises in the *Corpus Hermeticum*, the collection of fifteen Hermetic dialogues: chap. 1 pp. xivii–1) gives an account of the creation of the world which is, in part, reminiscent of Genesis. Other treatises describe the ascent of the soul through the spheres of the planets to the divine realms above them, or give ecstatic descriptions of a process of regeneration by which the soul casts off the chains which bind it to the material world and becomes filled with divine powers and virtues."[8]

Hermetic books, as we know them today, are probably later

versions of older writings. The *Pymander*, which is one of the most important of the Hermetic books, seems to have been written after the 2nd century A.D. It is possible that the older works were fading from memory, and an effort was made to preserve the old wisdom from disappearing entirely under the pressure of early Christian influence. It has been written that *The Divine Pymander* is equal in composition and brilliance of doctrines to any of the sacred books of the world.

So we have the Adept Hermes, founder of the nation of Egypt, who received the Emerald Tablet, bringing the Pillars of Enoch from Atlantis and supervising the building of the Great Pyramid. It was Hermes, also, who created the plans and wrote the books, leaving them for others to discover and study. Then, much later in history, a priesthood was formed in Alexandria to study and publish teachings from these original texts, also done under the name of Hermes.

It is thought that there are now in the world several secret schools which initiate candidates into the Mysteries, but in nearly every instance their teachings are illumined by the torch of Hermes.

After the Moslem conquest of Alexandria took place, the importance of Alexandria as a center of learning diminished. Although Alexandria is now a flourishing and important city of modern Egypt, its amazing history has been all but forgotten.

CHAPTER 9

CHRIST AND THE ARK OF THE COVENANT

 hortly before 21 B.C. King Herod Antipas ordered construction to begin on the rebuilding of the Temple of Jerusalem, the center of Jewish faith. This same Temple was destroyed in A.D. 70 by the Romans. It was during this time that Jesus Christ lived.

Barbara Thiering, Ph.D., is a biblical and Dead Sea Scrolls scholar teaching at Sydney University. From the research in her book *Jesus and the Riddle of the Dead Sea Scrolls*, we learn about the tense emotions of the time. The Essenes, hearing of Herod Antipas' intentions shortly before 21 B.C. to rebuild the whole Temple, offered thanks to God and at that time wrote the Temple Scroll (which was found in conjunction with the Dead Sea Scrolls). Barbara Thiering conveys from her research that the Essenes knew that God had a plan, which He gave on Mount Sinai long ago, as to how the temple should be built. The Essenes felt the plan would be accepted because God was in charge.

Herod was concerned that the return of the Essene priests would bring out the old conservatives who would oppose him. So Herod rejected the plan.

The Essenes found it a disaster that their prophecy of the temple given by God, and the re-establishment of their order in Jerusalem, had failed. They knew there must be a king and he must be of the bloodline of David, answerable only to the priests; not an upstart like Herod.[1]

The story most people know about Jesus is told in the New Testament. The New Testament, like much of the Old Testament, is in many places a greatly altered version of the original accounts on which it is based. In the well-researched book *Messianic Legacy*, the fact is mentioned that Pope Leo X is on record as declaring: "It has served us well, this myth of Christ."

Many of the changes and deletions to the New Testament were made by special church councils. The editing process began as early as A.D. 325 during the first Council of Nicaea, and continued well into the 12th century. The second church council of Constantinople in A.D. 553 deleted from the Bible Jesus' references to reincarnation, which was an important concept to Jesus and his early followers.

Later, the Lateran Councils of the 12th century added a tenet to the Bible that was never taught by Jesus: the concept of the "Holy Trinity." Jesus' divinity was decided by a vote at the Council of Nicaea some three centuries after Jesus had lived. This same Council also voted to change the Sabbath from Saturday to Sunday. They appropriated one of the most holy holidays—the winter solstice—and claimed it as the day that Christ was born. The Council of Nicaea also voted that Mary was a virgin. Christianity, as it is known today, was derived not from the time of Jesus, but from the Council of Nicea in A.D. 325.

The Roman Christian church did not simply limit itself to changing a few ideas; it also rejected entire books, especially those considered to be too Jewish in origin. The Church destroyed many documents and records which might serve to contradict the radical changes made to Christian doctrine by these councils. Fortunately, the original writings which did survive this destructive process still offer valuable clues and insights into the life of Jesus.

Many of the writings rejected by the church councils found their way into a book known as the *Apocrypha*, meaning hidden writings. The *Apocrypha* consists of writings which were judged by the church to be of dubious origin or quality. Other Apocryphal works were omitted simply because they contradicted the official church version of Jesus' life on several crucial points. These are details which, if carefully researched, would offer a somewhat different outlook on the life of Jesus from the one presented in the Bible.

In the chapter on Mystic Christianity in Manly P. Hall's *The Secret Teachings of All Ages*, Mr. Hall makes some very informative statements about Jesus Christ and the Masons: "The facts concerning His [Jesus'] identity and mission are among the priceless mysteries preserved to this day in the secret vaults beneath the 'Houses of the Brethren.'" Here Mr. Hall is undoubtedly talking about the Masonic library in England. He goes on to say: "To a few of the Knights Templars, who were initiated into the arcana of the Druses, Nazarenes, Essenes, Johannites, and other sects still inhabiting the remote and inaccessible fastnesses of the Holy Land, part of the strange story was told. The knowledge of the Templars concerning the early history of Christianity was undoubtedly one of the main reasons for their persecution and final annihilation. The discrepancies in the writings of the early Church Fathers not only are irreconcilable, but demonstrate beyond question that even during the first five centuries after Christ these learned men had for the basis of their writings little more substantial than folklore and hearsay. . . .

"About A.D. 180 St. Irenaeus, Bishop of Lyons, one of the most eminent of the ante-Nicene theologians, wrote *Against Heresies*, an attack on the doctrines of the Gnostics. In this work Irenaeus declared upon the authority of the Apostles themselves that Jesus lived to old age." Mr. Hall then quotes from Irenaeus: " 'They, however, that they may establish their false opinion regarding that which is written, 'to proclaim the acceptable year of the Lord,' maintain that He preached for one year only, and then suffered in the twelfth month. [In speaking thus], they are forgetful of their own disadvantage, destroying His whole work, and robbing Him of that age which is both more necessary and more honourable than any other; that more advanced age, I mean, during which also as a teacher He excelled all others. For how could He have had His disciples, if He did not teach? And how could He have taught, unless He had reached the age of a Master? For when He came to be baptised, He had not yet completed His thirtieth year, but was beginning to be about thirty years of age (for thus Luke, who has mentioned His years, has expressed it: 'Now Jesus was, as it were, beginning to be thirty years old,' when He came to receive baptism); and (according to these men), He preached only one year reckoning from His baptism. On completing His thirtieth year He suffered, being in fact still a young man, and who had by no means attained to advanced age. Now, that the first stage of early life embraces thirty years, and that this extends onward to the fortieth year, every one will admit; but from the fortieth and fiftieth year a man begins to decline towards old age, *which Our Lord possessed while He still fulfilled the office of a Teacher, even as the Gospel and all the elders testify;* those who were conversant in Asia with John, the disciple of the Lord (affirming) that John conveyed to them that information. And He remained among them up to the time of Trajan. Some of them, moreover, saw not only John, but the other apostles also, and heard the very same account from them, and bear testimony as to the (validity of the) statement. Whom then should we rather believe? Whether such men as these, or Ptolemaeus, who never saw the apostles, and who never even in his dreams attained to the slightest trace of an apostle?' "[2]

In the same section, Mr. Hall makes these candid statements: "Of all the early Fathers, Irenaeus, writing within eighty years after the death of St. John the Evangelist, should have reasonably accurate information. If the disciples themselves related that Jesus lived to advanced age in the body, why has the mysterious number 33 been arbitrarily chosen to symbolize the duration of His life? Were the incidents in the life of Jesus purposely altered so that His actions would fit more closely into the pattern established by the numerous Savior-Gods who preceded Him?"[3]

The Essenes

Christian Ginsburg, a well-known Cabalist of the nineteenth century, in his book *The Essenes* comments that the Essenes, a select inner brotherhood within the Tribes of Israel, lived according to the Law that Moses had handed down to them, the same Law that had been passed down to the Egyptians from the Atlantean Enoch. They were knowledgeable of the Pythagorean teachings and were part of the Pythagorean school. The Essenes practiced the pure life, linking the Angelic realm with the nature realm. Most of the writing about the true story of Christ's life is said to have been kept by the Essene Brotherhood.[4]

The Essenes' activities were of a constructive nature. Many of them were builders and potters and artisans of crafts requiring a coordination of hands and mind.

Regarding the Masonic connection, in Albert Mackey's book, *History of Freemasonry*, published in 1898, we find he confirms that the Essenes' organization was a branch of a brotherhood in Palestine; that it had systems of degrees and used a symbolic apron, and in many ways was the precursor of the Masons and the Rosicrucians. There were many artificers among their members.

H. Spencer Lewis, Imperator of the worldwide Rosicrucian Order, wrote in his book *The Mystical Life of Jesus* that material taken from the Rosicrucian archives tells that for several centuries before the Christian Era, the Essene Brotherhood maintained two principal centers—one in Egypt and the other in Palestine (Israel) in Engaddi near the Dead Sea. The branch in Palestine, because of the despotism of the rulers of the country and the jealousy of the priesthood, was forced to moved to Mount Carmel in order to be in greater solitude. At Mount Carmel the principal activity of the Brotherhood seemed to be the translation of ancient manuscripts and the preservation of the records of their teachings.[5]

Edouard Schuré, the distinguished French writer and mystic, also associates Jesus with the Essene Order. Earlier writers, too, have long suspected that the references in the Bible to Jesus the Nazarene have been mistranslated and should have read *Jesus the Nazarite*, that is, Jesus of the Order or Society of Nazarites. The Nazarites and Essenes were either branches of the same brotherhood or closely associated orders, imposing similar vows and obligations and expounding similar mystical philosophies.

With the discovery of the Dead Sea Scrolls, a great deal of information on the Essenes was made available for the first time.

It is generally supposed that they were the custodians of the true knowledge of Jesus and were also those who initiated and educated him.

The Essenes were known as one of the better-educated classes of Jews. One of their main interests was the reinterpretation of the Mosaic Law according to certain secret spiritual keys (cabalah) preserved by them from the time of the establishing of their Order. Because the Essenes were cabalists and astrologers, they were also conversant with the timing of prediction and were awaiting the event of the Messiah promised by the early prophets. Unlike the holy Messiah awaited by the Essenes, the Messiah expected by the Jewish people was largely a political figure, possibly like King David or King Solomon, whose intent would be to redeem Israel from the Roman yoke.

Bibles in use today are based on ninth-century manuscripts; scholars who are comparing them to the Dead Sea Scrolls of the first century are now raising many questions. The Dead Sea Scrolls, in the opinion of many scholars, have cast further light on the origins of Christianity. Manuscripts dating from 100–200 B.C. reveal a striking resemblance between the Essene sects of Judaism and early Christianity.

The Essenes were destroyed by the Romans in the first century A.D., but before their dispersal they collected their precious library of important records and teachings of the prophets, dating from 100 B.C. or earlier, and put them into jars, to be hidden in the caves of Qumran. Although the sect itself was destroyed, the scrolls were saved from decay by the fortunate climatic conditions prevalent in the Holy Land.

It was the Essenes who provided the religious and social background into which Jesus was born; their goal, years before Jesus' birth, was the preparation of a proper community where the Messiah could be born and raised. Ironically, the Greek translation of *Jesus* is *Messiah* and the word *Essene* is *expectancy*. The Essenes were a dedicated people who lived plainly and existed to nurture this great soul into the world. Eventually they were able to create a family and a mother so pure that she could provide the vehicle through which such a great Soul as Jesus was able to incarnate. Their existence is not recorded in the Old Testament or the New. They were known through the works and writings of Pliny, Philo, Joesphus and now the Dead Sea Scrolls.

Edmond Bordeaux Szekely, in his book *From Enoch to the Dead Sea Scrolls*, comments that "Records of the Essene way of life have come down to us from writings of their contemporaries. Pliny the Roman naturalist, Philo the Alexandrian philosopher, Josephus the Jewish hsitorian and soldier, Solanius and others spoke of them variously as 'a race by themselves, more remarkable than any other in the world,' 'the oldest of the initiates, receiving their teaching from Central Asia,' 'teaching perpetuated through an immense space of ages,' 'constant and unalterable holiness.'

"Some of the outer teaching is preserved in Aramaic text in the Vatican in Rome. Some in Slavic text was found in the possession of the Hapsburgs in Austria and said to have been brought out of Asia in the thirteenth century by Nestorian priests fleeing the hordes of Genghis Khan."

Mr. Szekely suggests that echoes of the teaching exist today in many forms, like the rituals of the Masons. He writes: "From its anitiquity, its persistence through the ages, it is evident the teaching could not have been the concept of any individual or any people, but is the interpretation, by a succession of great Teachers, of the Law of the universe, the basic Law, eternal and unchanging as the stars in their courses, the same now as two or three thousand years ago, and as applicable today as then."[6]

The Parents of Jesus: Mary and Joseph

In the Apocryphal writings, the story of Jesus begins with his maternal grandparents, Joachim and Anna. Joachim was said to be a man of piety. Joachim and Anna were happily married except for one problem: they had not been able to conceive any children.

One day Joachim was standing alone in the fields when an angel appeared. The angel told Joachim that an angel would cause Anna to become pregnant. The only stipulation was that the child be given to the Temple of Jerusalem to be raised by priests and angels. The child was Mary, mother of Jesus. She was raised by the Essenes. The Essenes in those days were outwardly Jewish, but it is thought they also studied the Zend Avesta of the Zoroastrian religion. Zoroastrianism is a Persian religion founded in the 6th century B.C. This would explain the visit of the three Persian wise men to the baby Jesus in Bethlehem.

In his book *The Great Initiates*, Edouard Schuré writes: "Mary, the wife of the carpenter Joseph, was a Galilean woman of noble birth and was related to the Essenes."[7]

Manly Hall, in *The Mystical Christ*, makes an intriguing statement: "Although Jesus was said to have been born miraculously, the genealogies were compiled to show that he descended from the royal line of David and was the rightful King of the Jews. Thus, he emerged in the dual role of priest-king ruling by authority of heaven and the traditions of men. . . . There is no profit to be gained by attempting to reconcile the immaculate conception with the genealogies. The mystic understands what is meant, and the meaning is true and clear."[8]

It was St. Paul (Romans 1:3) who spoke of "Jesus Christ our Lord, which was made of the seed of David according to the flesh." Jesus was born Jewish and his Mother Mary was of the House of David and went from the tribe of Israel to being an Essene. At the same time Mary was married to a Jew, Joseph, who was also from the House of David. Both of Jesus' parents were of royal blood.

The priests would have wanted to make sure the child would be born under the House of David. The learned rabbis and others, by the signs in the stars, knew that at this time there was to be born a great leader. It was common knowledge and well known in Babylon, Judea and Jerusalem that this generation of babies held someone special. Because King Herod knew of this prediction, he calculated that certain babies born in a certain period of time were a threat to his crown and ordered that they all be put to death. Herod's "Massacre of the Innocents" took place so that there could be no new leader in the role of Priest-King who might unify Israel and the Jewish people, thereby posing a threat to Herod and Rome.

When Jesus was twelve years old, it is known that he was ushered into the temple and directed by the rabbis to stand in front of the Ark, the ultimate lie detector test. It is written that if you are of the bloodline of David or Aaron and are enlightened, then you can touch the Ark and not die or get electrocuted.

Apparently Jesus passed the test, because it is implied that the rabbis returned and told Mary and Joseph to hide Jesus and to make sure of his education elsewhere. He was to be taken out of the country to protect him from the threat of Herod's massacre, which stipulated that the firstborn son of each Jewish family would be put to death.

H. P. Blavatsky, quoting from Hone's *The Arabic Gospel of the Infancy*, gives us a picture of what happened in the temple at that time: "And when he [Jesus] was twelve years old . . . a certain principal Rabbi asked him, 'Hast thou read books? . . . and a certain astronomy,' and the Lord Jesus explained to him . . . about the spheres . . . about the physics and metaphysics. Also things that reason of man had never discovered . . . The constitution of the body, how the soul operated upon the body, etc. . . . And at this the master was not surprised and he said: 'I believe this boy was born before Noah . . . he is more learned than any master!' "[9]

Again we find in Manly Hall's *The Mystical Christ* this version of Jesus entering the temple: "In the proper season, Jesus entered the synagogue and there discoursed with the Elders. He confounded them with insight and left them disturbed because they could not understand. These Elders were the faculties of the mind that had explored the Torah and even the Mishnah, but had not experienced the spiritual substance of the law. They were amazed at this gifted child, but were not prepared to accept him as soul power."[10]

Jesus' Silent Years

It is likely that Jesus began to understand more through John the Baptist, who was knowledgeable in rabbinical teachings. It may have been John who informed Jesus that he was "the one." When John took Jesus to the River Jordan and baptized him, it is said by the Gnostics that John was the instrument to activate the Christ Consciousness in Jesus. He must have known that Jesus was the Messiah.

The Gospels of Luke and Matthew explicitly state that Jesus was of royal blood—a genuine king, the lineal descendant of David and Solomon. Jesus had legitimate claim to the throne. Because he was of the royal blood-line, the threat to Jesus by Herod and Rome was very real. It is for this reason that Jesus was taken out of the country. Jesus was raised with rabbinic Law and also educated by the Essenes. He was later initiated into the most profound Mysteries. He was brought up to be a child of the universe and given a cosmic education.

When Jesus was taken out of the country, this began the period known as the "Lost Years." There are persistent rumors that Jesus visited and studied in Tibet, India, Egypt and Great Britain during this time. A coin has been discovered which was struck in His honor in India during the first century. Early Christian records were known to exist in Tibet and monks of a Buddhist monastery in Ceylon preserved a record which indicated that Jesus sojourned with them and learned their philosophy. It is said that in the Homis Monastery of Tibet there are manuscripts proving that Jesus joined a caravan bound for India, where he remained for some time, and then returned to Syria in his twenty-ninth year. The records concerning the youth of Jesus were no doubt suppressed or destroyed by the early church to prevent the new Christians from discovering that Christianity was rooted in the religions of the pagans.

There is evidence during this time that the uncle of Jesus, Joseph of Arimathea, took Jesus to England on one of his tin merchant boats. Joseph had been a tin merchant between Judea, Spain, Rome and Cornwall for many years; since he did business in England, he owned land there. It is said that in these early years in England Jesus studied with the Druids on the Isle of Avalon (Glastonbury).

After his sojourn on the Isle of Avalon, Jesus revealed himself to be an adept of the Celtic or Druid science. The most learned men of Europe came to this Druid center to learn the traditional

form of the Mysteries, and it is likely that the Druids initiated
Jesus into their Mysteries at this time. Edouard Schuré, in *Jesus,
The Last Great Initiate*, was of the opinion that Jesus then trav-
eled to Egypt where he was initiated into the highest level of the
Great White Brotherhood at the Great Pyramid of Giza.

On one occasion when I was at the Philosophical Research Society bookstore, I came across Mr. Hall's lecture notes for "The
Unrecorded Years in the Life of Christ," which included a great
deal of information concerning these years. He writes: ". . . by
circumstance or by connivance [the material of the lost years],
has been obscured and concealed.

"When the Crusaders were in the Near East they came upon
some of this material relating to the possibility of Jesus having
been in Egypt. This material was one of the causes for the inquisi-
tional destruction of the Knights Templars.

"The first school of Christianity in Alexandria was founded in
the first century. Therefore, there can be no doubt that the material available there can be authenticated.

"It is said that Cyril, the Bishop of Alexandria, was responsible for the destruction of most of the records. Why he destroyed
them is uncertain except perhaps that they would be regarded as
detrimental to the orthodoxy prevailing at the time. It was an effort to obscure any source of the life or teachings of Jesus that
could be in conflict with the rising power of the church. It is said,
but not confirmed, that there are very early manuscripts relating to Christianity in the Vatican."[11]

Christ was whisked off to other cultures and the experience of
comparative religions. It is said that when Jesus returned from
his travels, he gathered about him the disciples and instructed
them in the secret Mystery teachings which had been lost, in part,
from the doctrines of Israel. The selection of the twelve disciples
was an extension of the earlier symbolism of the twelve tribes of
Israel. Also, the selection of the twelve disciples was like the
Pythagorean dodecahedron (a twelve-faced symmetrical solid
which represented the universe), and the twelve houses of the
zodiac, again following a cosmic pattern. The ancients understood the principle of all things on earth being the same as those

in heaven, represented by the saying: "as above, so below." This same knowledge is symbolized by the "Star of David" with its interlaced triangles, one leading to heaven and the other into the earth.

Jesus was the conduit through which a tremendous evolution of new teaching was brought to humanity. He was a true revolutionary—*and represented a shifting to the feminine teachings.* Gone is the harsh teaching of an eye for an eye. Jesus taught the Torah, but a new version—with the feminine principle of unconditional love as its foundation.

When we talk about the feminine here we are talking about the feminine part of each of us, whether male or female. Jesus ushered in a new way of looking at all the holy teachings. Not just the holy teachings of the Jewish faith, but a universal faith. Jesus never intended to start another religion. Because of his training in different religions, his teaching must have seemed radical—not only to those of his own religion, but to others as well. It was a new philosophy for all people.

Crucifixion Conspiracy

At this time, John the Baptist and Jesus shared a common destiny—they were both to be martyred. Christ became part of a large conspiracy. In many of the ancient texts it is suggested that the different factions of the Jewish nation—the Pharisees, Sadducees and the Essenes—had been fractured. They desperately needed to be galvanized to work together in order to fight the Romans who had invaded Israel and taken over the country. Jesus soon drew about him followers and disciples who saw this teacher called Jesus not only as a man of God, but as the political liberator of their nation. There is evidence to the effect that a group of Jewish leaders made a plan to have the Rabbi Jesus Christ, the Messiah and King of the Jews, be placed on the cross but not killed by the Romans.

This would serve to galvanize all the factions of the Jewish nation, and then there would be a war to rid them of the Romans and reconstitute the State of Israel. At the same time, the idea of Christ and his bloodline could be kept alive and the Israelites brought out of bondage. The plan was for the overthrow of Roman rule and reconstitution of the House of David. As to the Romans, they needed to kill Jesus because he, being the legitimate heir to the throne of Israel, was a great threat to Herod and the Romans.

It is obvious that Christ did not come to earth to be martyred for the sake of war. He had not come to teach war but to teach love and peace. The plan to have Jesus fulfill the reconstituting of the State of Israel did not work. History reveals that it took World War II to accomplish the reestablishment of the State of Israel.

"Some accepted Jesus as the son of God, the promised Messiah, who was to redeem the faithful by his advent and ministry. Others were convinced that he was to become the redeemer of the Jewish nation and the restorer of its ruling house . . ."[12] (Manly P. Hall, *The Mystical Christ*).

Every king of Israel was regarded as a Messiah; the term was always applied to David and David's successors. All Jewish kings of the House of David were known as Messiah, or Christ. The way of referring to the High Priest was the "High Messiah." The Jewish people had expected the Messiah to remove them from the yoke of the Romans, as had been foretold by the early prophets. Because this did not happen with Jesus, the people were disappointed and questioned him as the promised Messiah.

John Allegro, author of *The Dead Sea Scrolls and the Christian Myth*, was an original member of the Dead Sea Scrolls team in Israel and is an Oxford-trained Hebrew scholar. He was the lone violator of the rule of secrecy adopted by his colleagues. He was convinced that the information in these texts would have a dramatic impact on Christianity, possibly undermining the whole basis of Christian beliefs. He long suspected that the members of the Dead Sea Scrolls team were engaged in a cover-up of sensitive information.

Mr. Allegro writes: "The scrolls from the caves confirmed much of the earlier information about the Essenes, but added a most important feature of their teaching concerning the expected

Messiah. This charismatic leader of the future, born of the lineage of the famous King David, would establish a new world order where the will of God reigned supreme. Such a blessed state could only come about after wars and bloody revolution, in which the 'Anointed' (Hebrew Messiah), in his role of warrior prince, would personally lead the forces of Light in their apocalyptic struggle against the powers of Darkness under the archfiend Belial, the devil. When the divine kingdom had been established, this Davidic leader would control its administration, while its spiritual direction would be undertaken by another Anointed, a priest, acting as intermediary between God and man in all matters relating to law and doctrine."[13] The scrolls indicate that the Essenes did expect a Messiah from the house of David to take Israel from the yoke of the Romans and re-establish the Davidic kingdom. As to the spiritual direction by another Anointed, Allegro does not shed much light on this statement.

During the Last Supper or Passover Seder, Jesus, realizing the end was near, would have wanted to put his house in order and communicate to his disciples his most secret teachings. This was the last meeting of the twelve who were to carry on after the passing of their Master. The only hints we have as to the nature of the secrets which Jesus imparted are to be found in the *Gnostic Gospels*, the *Pistis Sophia*, and the *Books of the Savior*. The orthodox churches have rejected the *Gnostic Gospels* and such words of Jesus as were recorded in the Apocryphal texts. It is said that at the Last Supper or Seder the disciples sang a hymn together followed, in the ancient Jewish custom, by the breaking of the unleavened bread and the passing of the cup. After this, according to one of the Apocryphal writings, Jesus and his Apostles celebrated with a ritualistic dance. (The *Gnostic Gospels* came from the Gnostics, a collective name given to a variety of religious teachings which existed before and after the early centuries of the Christian era.)

It was not planned that Christ should die on the cross. And it was known quite openly at the time that he did not die on the cross. When the Bible came to be written there was some confusion and omission, but very careful records were kept by the

Essenes, which have now surfaced as the Dead Sea Scrolls. Because this period of history was so precarious, this knowledge had to be suppressed. Though the vast majority of the population was illiterate, there were a number of obstacles that made it difficult to keep the truth intact. But the truth was kept, in fact carefully guarded, by the Essenes and, according to Manly P. Hall, ultimately passed down to the Masons and Rosicrucians.

Jesus allowed himself to be martyred. He was put on the cross by the Romans because he was very dangerous to Rome. The Romans wanted to see that the Jewish people were blamed for the crucifixion of Jesus. If it were known that the Romans engineered it, there would have been rioting in the streets, which would have bound together the different factions of the Jewish nation. That would galvanize the people and create a dangerous situation for the Romans. Why did the Holy Family of Jesus feel it had to leave Jerusalem if it were not perilous for them to stay? There was much trickery involved, and Jesus was taken away to be put on the cross. But, as we stated earlier, Jesus did not die on the cross.

From the authors Baigent, Leigh, and Lincoln in their excellent book, *Messianic Legacy*, another interesting piece of information is given: The historian Julius Africanus, who lived between A.D. 160–240, writes that "Herod, who had no drop of Israelish blood in his veins and was stung by the consciousness of his base origins, burnt the registers of their families . . . Herod as a usurper, deemed [Jesus' Bloodline of David] a threat to his legitimacy. Among other things, this would have engendered the tradition of Herod's Massacre of the Innocents. On the other hand, it has been argued that the burning of genealogies to which Julius Africanus refers was perpetrated not by Herod, but by the Romans after the revolt of 66 A.D. They, quite as much as Herod, would have been threatened by the survival of a legitimate royal bloodline around which the rebellious Jews might have rallied."[14]

The Talmud confirms that Joseph of Arimathea was the younger brother of Christ's mother. Because Jesus' father died while Jesus was very young, under both Roman and Hebrew law the next of kin automatically becomes the legal guardian of the family. This was Joseph of Arimathea. He was the uncle to Jesus and, as mentioned earlier, a very prosperous tin merchant and an influential member of the Sanhedrin. Because of his position, he was well acquainted with Pilate the Roman Procurator, and with Herod. There is little doubt that he would have had any problem bargaining with Herod, who was known to be easily corruptible and open to bribes.

The Crucifixion was to be a trick. Christ was not to die on the cross. The agreement was to have Christ taken down from the cross and given to Joseph and Nicodemus. After Christ was released from the cross, he was taken to the Essenes where he was nursed back to health and was soon joined by his disciples at Mt. Carmel. This is what the Bible has misidentified as the "ascension."

There is a first-rate piece of investigation done in the book *Holy Blood, Holy Grail*, by the authors Baigent et al of *Messianic Legacy*. They state that only the Fourth Gospel remains an eye-witness account of the Crucifixion. In the Fourth Gospel it is related that Jesus' feet were affixed to the cross, therefore relieving the pressure on his chest muscles—and his legs were not broken. In theory, he should have survived for two or three days. But he was on the cross for no more than a few hours before being pronounced dead. It is written in the Gospel of Mark that even Pilate was astonished by the rapidity with which death occurred (Mark 15:44).

In the *Koran* Jesus is referred to many times with appellations such as Messenger of God and Messiah. The *Koran* maintains that Jesus did not die on the cross. It states that they did not kill him nor did they crucify him, but they thought they did.

The Gospels were written during the years A.D. 65–100. *These Gospels were compiled for a Greek and Roman population for which they needed to be acceptable.* It was necessary to paint the Jews as villains. The Romans had just fought a costly and fierce war with the Jews. *The role of the Romans in the trial and crucifixion of Jesus had to be erased and whitewashed.* Therefore, Pilate is depicted in the Gospels as good and the Jews as the opposite. But, historically, this makes no sense at all. Since Jesus was arrested on the night of Passover, when he was having a

Seder, this is not possible. According to Judaic Law the Sanhedrin was forbidden to meet during the Passover and at night. The Law also forbade them to meet in private houses or anywhere outside the Temple.

The Gospels relate that Jesus' arrest and trial occurred on the night of the Passover. Not only that, but if the Sanhedrin wanted Jesus dead they would not need Pilate's approval. Why would the same multitude of people who gathered in great spirit to welcome Jesus on his entry into Jerusalem and invoke blessings on the son of David in any way want him dead?

It seems there are a great many attempts by the authors of the Gospels to transfer guilt to the Jewish people and remove the responsibility from the Romans. The fact remains that Jesus was tried in a Roman court and sentenced to execution by the Romans in a manner of execution used exclusively by Romans for enemies of Rome who committed crimes against the empire. And yet, in order to make Jesus Christ acceptable to Christianity in Rome, the truth had to be covered up. A new version of the events had to be created in the Gospels and, as we know, written many years after Christ.

John Dominic Crossan, professor of biblical studies at DePaul University in Chicago, as well as co-founder of the "Jesus Seminar," points out in his book *Who Killed Jesus?* that the traditional understanding of the Gospels as historical fact is not only wrong, but dangerous. Taking from the best of anthropological, sociological, and biblical research, he definitively demonstrates that it was the Roman government that tried and executed Jesus as a social agitator. Crossan's re-examination shows that the belief that the Jews killed Jesus is an early Christian myth, directed against rival Jewish groups, and must be eradicated from authentic Christian faith.

Crossan writes, "As long as Christians were the marginalized and disenfranchised ones, such passion fiction about Jewish responsibility and Roman innocence did nobody much harm. But once the Roman Empire became Christian, that fiction turned lethal. . . . Think, now, of those passion-resurrection stories as heard in a predominantly Christian world. Did these stories of ours send certain people out to kill?"[15] Crossan is revealing to us the roots of anti-Semitism.

Robert W. Funk is a Guggenheim Fellow, former senior Fullbright Scholar, distinguished biblical scholar, co-founder of the "Jesus Seminar," and author of many books. His latest book, *Honest to Jesus* (Harper San Francisco), comments on the conclusions of the "Jesus Seminar." Present at the Seminar were seventy-five active scholars who were able to examine 1,500 items in the course of six or seven years, attempting to isolate words they thought originated with Jesus, or at least that he spoke. The Jesus seminar concluded, on a case-by-case basis, that less than twenty percent of the words attributed to Jesus in the Gospels were actually spoken by him.

Members of the Seminar pretty much agreed that Jesus was an iconoclastic Jewish sage. He was a wisdom teacher of the Jewish tradition. He was a smasher of idols. He was subversive.

In an article reviewing his book, Mr. Funk states, regarding the conclusion of the Seminar: "He [Jesus] was also what I call a comic savant. He was a wise man who traded in humor to make his critical remarks more palatable to people. His rhetorical skills bordered on the magical. The combination of his style with the content of his discourse marked him as a social deviant in his time. That may be the reason his mother and brother thought him daft. It was certainly one of the reasons he was both feared and adored.

"Another important insight for me was that Jesus appears to have told his parables as though he was hearing them; that is, he did not regard himself so much as somebody who had a vision to pass on to others as he did as someone who was *having* a vision that he had to articulate for himself. He was overpowered by this vision. His teaching and his behavior can only be accounted for by the fact that he was being claimed by that vision —by the vision of an alternative reality, is the way I like to put it.

"But what would happen if 'the dangerous and subversive memories' of that solitary figure were really stripped of their interpretive overlay? Were that to happen, the gospel of Jesus would be liberated from the Jesus of the gospels and allowed to speak for itself. The creedal formulations of the second, third and fourth centuries would be de-dogmatized and Jesus would be permitted to emerge as a robust, real, larger-than-life figure in his own right. Moreover, current images of Jesus would be torn up by their long affective roots and their attachment to pet causes severed. The pale, anemic, iconic Jesus would suffer by comparison with the stark realism of the genuine article."[16]

H. Spencer Lewis, F.R.C., Ph.D., was the Imperator of the worldwide Rosicrucian Order, Fellow of the Essene Ashrama in India, and American Legate of the G.W.B. Monastery in Tibet. One of many books he wrote, *The Mystical Life of Jesus*, first published in 1919, was on the life of Jesus from data researched over many years, from the records of the Essenes, the Nazarenes and the Nazarites, as well as the complete records of the Great White Brotherhood in Tibet, India, and Egypt contained in the archives of the Rosicrucian Order.

Mr. Lewis made a number of comments relating to the crucifixion of Jesus: "The early drafts of the Apostles' Creed clearly show that the idea meant to be conveyed was that after the crucifixion, Jesus was temporarily placed in a tomb *among the dead*, and that He quickly rose from that place and out of that environment, and returned again to His place among the living."[17] He goes on to reinforce this statement: "The disappearance of Jesus from public sight, closing His public work and public mission as *the Christ*, was not the end of his existence on the earth plane in the *physical body*. This is definitely stated in so many ancient and reliable records that it is surprising that the Holy Fathers of the Christian church attempted to make His ascension a *physical fact*, and proclaim it the end of His earthly career. In many of the discussions of the Council of the church in the first centuries after Christ, there were *frank admissions* on the part of the greatest of the authorities that Jesus lived to be fifty, sixty, or even seventy years of age. . . ."[18]

Mr. Lewis also comments regarding the development of the Cross as a symbol of Christ. After the retirement of Jesus from public life He and His Apostles were assembled at a certain place in Jerusalem for the purpose of establishing the first congregation of the movement which was to be organized and known as the *Christine Church*. Mr. Lewis explains that Jesus Himself had no part in the foundation of this movement and that there is nothing in the records to show that Jesus agreed to this plan, or gave it consideration. After a year the *Christine Church* had developed so much that it was organized more extensively. Also at this time the cross, as a Christian symbol, was adopted; however, it was not adopted with a crucified body upon it, but a rose.

Regarding the cross, H. Spencer Lewis comments that his research suggested that the Essenes had always used the cross as a symbol. It first originated as a mystical symbol in the days of Akhnaton, Pharaoh of Egypt, who used it in the Mystery Schools as an emblem of the body of a man with arms outstretched, representing the sufferings and trials of earthly life. At that time, the cross had not been used for the purpose of crucifixion; it was purely an emblematic mystical symbol.

A rose was added to the cross as a second element. The rose was compared to the soul in man, because of its gradual unfoldment, beautiful perfume, and richness of color and manifestation of maturity. In later Christianity, the terms "the Rose," the "Rose of Sharon," the "Beautiful Rose," and the "Holy Rose" were used by many to represent the soul of Jesus on the cross *uncrucified*. Many centuries later the Holy Fathers of the church, in their high Councils, made the cross with the *crucified body* upon it the emblem of the Christine movement.

The emblem of the early Knights Templars was a red rose on a cross, adopted by them because of their affiliation with the Essenes. Also, the Rosicrucian emblem, the rose and the cross, goes back to early Christian mysticism.[19]

The Dead Sea Scrolls also give us a great deal of information about the true story of Christianity, but even the Dead Sea Scroll information was suppressed for many years. In 1903 Pope Leo XIII created the Pontifical Biblical Commission to administer and monitor all Catholic scholarship. The New Catholic Encyclopedia states that the Commission's function is to ensure that God's words will be shielded not only from any breath of error, but from every rash opinion.

Father Lagrange, one of the earliest members of the Pontifical Biblical Commission and founder of the École Biblique et Archeologique Française de Jerusalem, came to dominate the Dead Sea Scrolls scholarship. Need I say more? It seems obvious that the true account of Christianity has been suppressed to lend credence to the earlier stories created by the Roman Catholic Church. For further insight, I recommend Michael Baigent and Richard Leigh's book, *The Dead Sea Scrolls Deception*. Knowing the connection between the École Biblique in Israel, which has been involved in translating the Dead Sea Scrolls, and the Roman Catholic Church, which has a vested interest in their interpretation, one could reasonably question whether the material coming from the Israeli government on the Qumran scrolls is to be trusted. Presently, copies of the Scrolls are in the Huntington Library in Pasadena, California, and more information is in the process of being released.[20]

It is important to understand that Jesus never intended to be the founder of other religions; this was Paul's idea. Paul's teachings were quite close to Jesus' teachings. He taught that there is a Christ in each of us, that God put the same blood in all human beings, and therefore there is a oneness among all peoples.

Jesus' teachings were about love. They were about finding the love and joy within, as opposed to being in the dark and being fearful of divine judgment. It was a message of peace and liberation for all beings, a rallying cry for people to put aside their petty problems in the world and focus on the divine light that dwells within every human being. Jesus adhered to the Judaic law; he would never have worshipped a mortal person, and he makes this clear in the Gospels when he cautions his followers to acknowledge only God. It is Paul who makes Jesus into a God, and this is contrary to the true teachings of Jesus.

Paul legitimized his teachings by crediting them to Jesus. He had never personally known Jesus, but was taking Jesus' fundamental teachings and embellishing them, adding such things as the Virgin Birth and the Ascension. These were Paul's ideas, acquired from earlier pagan teachings of other saviors. He turned this new teaching into a cult, which eventually became canonized as a religion. It was not Jesus' idea to make a separate religion or church.

Jesus did not have his finger on the pulse of every disciple, and there were many differing interpretations of his teachings. It is likely that this was meant to be, because it seems difficult for humanity to dwell in too much light. Humanity has been moving, sometimes quickly and sometimes at a snail's pace, toward ultimate enlightenment and a level of consciousness where Jesus' teachings can be truly heard.

CHAPTER 10

FRANCE AND THE ARK OF THE COVENANT

hen the Romans captured Jerusalem they also had the Ark, but they probably did not know what they really owned or what it represented. Herod, who was of the land but ignorant of the rabbinical teachings, was chosen to rule Israel under the Romans. We assume the rabbis around Herod were wise enough to keep quiet about the workings of the Ark, and because Herod was so uneducated, the Ark was protected.

There is evidence in the ancient Grail writings that the Ark left Jerusalem with Joseph of Arimathea and Jesus after the feigned crucifixion. It would have been logical for Joseph as a rabbi and part of the Sanhedrin to tell the other rabbis and holy men that it was necessary to take the Ark out of the Temple to protect it from the Romans. The Ark was presumably hidden until the time that it would be safe to take it out of the country. It is likely that Joseph and Jesus took only the parchment scrolls and the instructions—all the information—but not the actual box itself. It is known that the box was later taken by the Knights Templars during the Crusades. The Templars took the box of the Ark and other treasures such as implements and relics of things built by Moses. They probably did not know exactly what they had—only that these treasures were of the House of David.

After the mock Crucifixion of Christ, Joseph of Arimathea, Christ, Mary Magdalene, Martha, Lazarus, the disciple Philip, and others left Israel for France in one of Joseph's boats. They took with them, from the Temple of Jerusalem, the Ark of the Covenant, which was the legacy of Christ, King of the House of David.

In the *Ecclesiastical Annals* ending in 1198, Cardinal Caesar Baronius (1538-1609), a learned historian and librarian to the Vatican, identified those who accompanied Joseph. Baronius quotes a manuscript from the year A.D. 35 in which is written: "The two Bethany sisters, Mary and Martha, their brother Lazarus, St. Eutropius, St. Salome, St. Cleon, St. Saturninus, St. Mary Magdalene, Marcella (the maid of the Bethany sisters), St. Maxim (or Maximin), St. Martial, St. Trophimus, Rostitutus the man who was born blind. Mary the mother of Jesus undoubtedly was not left behind." Cardinal Baronius further writes that the "Mother Mary goes on to Glastonbury with Joseph and his eleven other disciples." The Cardinal quotes the "Acts of Magdalene" for the record of the voyage to Marseilles, then known as Sarras, and the preaching of the Gospel in the south of France by the Bethany family. The original manuscript was compiled by Rabanus Maurus (766-856) and a copy is in the Magdalene College Library at Oxford, England.

Joseph returned from France to Jerusalem and was incarcerated for the crime of taking Jesus' body. Those close to Jesus were persecuted and Joseph, even with his status, was put in jail for a period of time. After his incarceration, Joseph once again returned to France and, together with Jesus, traveled to Glastonbury, England. (The following chapter chronicles the research regarding Joseph and Jesus in England.)

The disciples of Jesus went in different directions at this time. Some disciples went to Syria, some to Jaffa (Israel), some to Greece, Spain, Italy and France. Mark is known to have started the first Christian community in Alexandria (Egypt) where many original documents were thought to be preserved. If these documents were in fact preserved, they are probably now in the Masonic Library of London.

In her well-documented book *The Holy Grail*, Norma Lorre Goodrich has quoted an intriguing Grail story that takes place in Sarras, France. She writes: "One of the finest French texts of the Middle Ages puts Sarras there in glory as a first center of the 'New' culture from Jerusalem, which was center of the 'Old' or Hebrew culture. The French hero Perceval asked his grandfather, who was King of the Grail Castle, to tell him about Sarras where once reposed the Grail hallows: Lance, Grail, and Platter ('Tailloir'). His answer lies in the *Perceval Continuation* (Mons, MS, v. 33, 755 ff.) as edited by Armand Hoog.

" 'How does it happen,' asked Perceval, 'that we now have them here?'

" 'Very well, young friend, I will explain it to you,' said his aged grandparent, 'since I promised to do so. Joseph of Arimathea took the Grail to Sarras, you see, after Vespasian let him out of the prison where the Jews had put him. Joseph and his friends had preached in Jerusalem and baptized many people there. Forty-five of their converts accompanied them to the new Western world. There they carried the Grail.

" 'They arrived one day at the great city of Sarras where the local king was praying in the Temple of the Sun. He was hard put to win a war he was waging. Joseph promised him victory if he would paint a red cross upon his white shield. The King obliged and proved victorious. Joseph converted the people of Sarras to the New Law.

" 'Thereafter he journeyed into Great Britain where he built,' continued the Grail King, 'this very manor where I dwell. I am myself descended from Joseph of Arimathea, and so are you, Perceval. It was God's will that the Grail come here.' "[1]

In the above Grail story, the author is writing about the Ark of the Covenant (the Grail) being brought by God's will to Sarras, where Joseph of Arimathea converted the people to the New Law of the Ark, and thereafter took the Ark of the Covenant to Britain. The reference to Perceval being descended from Joseph of Arimathea, and to the manor in England where they lived, indicates the relationship of Joseph's group with the legendary King Arthur. The Red Cross on the White Shield is the symbol of the Knights Templars and the "Rosy Cross" of the Rosicrucians.

Mary Magdalene, the Adept

Barbara Thiering, a Dead Sea Scrolls scholar and author of *Jesus and the Riddle of the Dead Sea Scrolls*, has uncovered some provocative material, through her interpretation of the Scrolls, on the marriage of Jesus and Mary Magdalene. She suggests that Jesus needed to follow the rules of any dynastic order. He had to marry to continue his family line, and in his case it was all the more necessary in order to affirm his legitimacy in the line of David. One of the main purposes of the Essenes was to reserve the lines under King David of the three main priestly dynasties Zadok, Abiathar, and Levi (2 Sam. 20:25-26), and bring them back to power in the Jerusalem temple. The Dead Sea scroll numbered QM 17:2-3 shows the Essenes' loyalty to the old families. One of the dictates of the Law was to marry, be fruitful and multiply. At no point did Jesus preach celibacy; so there is no reason to believe he practiced it.

In the *Gospel of Philip* (G. Phil. 63:30-64:10), which has indications of being composed at an early date, it is written: "There were three who always walked with the Lord: Mary his mother, and his sister, and Magdalene, the one who was called his companion. His sister and his mother and his companion were each a Mary."

In a later passage, *The Gospel of Philip* says: "And the companion of the [Savior] was Mary Magdalene. He loved her more than all the disciples [and used to] kiss her often on her [mouth]. The rest of the disciples [were offended and] said to him: 'Why do you love her than all of us?' The Savior answered and said to them, 'Why do I not love you like her? When a blind man and one who sees are both together in darkness, they are no different from one another. When the light comes, then he who sees will see the light, and he who is blind will remain in darkness.'"

Dr. Thiering's book quotes the theologian William E. Phillips who considers Mary Magdalene "the supreme initiate" of Jesus and the teacher of the other Apostles. Phillips argues that Jesus did not believe in celibacy, and even that he may have been Mary Magdalene's husband. There are other statements to indicate the marriage of the disciples of Jesus such as in Hennecke's *New Testament Apocrypha*, Vol. II (p. 470). According to Paul's own statements, he himself had been married and at the time of his conversion was a widower. Clement of Alexandria, in his esteemed volume *Stromata*, writes: "Certainly there was no prohibition against marriage and paternity either in Jesus' immediate entourage or so called Early church."[2] According to Clement of Alexandria, the disciple Philip, as well as Simon Peter, had both married and sired families.

Dr. Thiering, who has derived a great deal of her information from her particular methods of interpreting the Dead Sea Scrolls, claims that the Scrolls indicate that Jesus had three children. For more intriguing disclosures about the history of the bloodline of Jesus, I suggest you read *Holy Blood and Holy Grail* by Baigent, Leigh and Lincoln. These authors show how the bloodlines of the "Holy Family" affected the Merovingian dynasty of Jewish Kings in Europe.

John Shelby Spong, an Episcopal Bishop, has recently written a book titled *Born of a Woman?* in which he proposes that the marriage feast at Cana, a well-known Gospel story, is about Jesus' own wedding. There are others who also believe this to be true.

This brings us to another part of our story, that concerning Mary Magdalene and the children of Christ who stayed in Sarras, where Mary Magdalene continued her teaching and retired to the Saint Baume sanctuary. Today, one of the most sought-after places of pilgrimage in the world is thought to be the burial site of the Magdalene. Sarras is in southern France; it has been suggested that Sarras, as spelled in Arthurian manuscripts, is Marseilles. This city was widely recognized as a spiritual ancestral home of the Celts and was built 600 years before Christ.

An excellent work by David Wood, *Genisis*, presents a description of Mary Magdalene as written by William Caston in his famous fifteenth-century translation of the influential Genoese work *Legenda Aurea* (Golden Legend), which was originally published in 1275. It provides clear evidence that Mary Magdalene was not a woman of the street but in actuality a woman of noble birth: "Mary Magdalene had her surname of Magdalo, a castle, and was born of right and noble lineage and parents, which were descended of the lineage of kings. And her father was named Cyrus, and her mother Eucharis. She with her brother Lazarus, and her sister Martha, possessed the castle of Magdalo, which is two miles from Nazareth, and Bethany, the castle which is nigh to Jerusalem, and also a great part of Jerusalem, which, all these things they parted among them. In such wise that Mary had the castle Magdalo whereof she had her name Magdalene. . . ."[3]

Because Jesus was "the Messiah," or of the bloodline of David, and the one destined to be the King of Israel, he could only have married another of royal blood in order for the Messiahs or Kings of Israel to be preserved. Royalty has always been acknowledged through the woman's bloodline. As Jesus' mother Mary had been of royal blood, so his wife would also need to be of the royal bloodline.

Among the now famous Nag Hammadi Scrolls found in Egypt in 1940, which date from A.D. 400, there is a "Gospel of Mary." This Nag Hammadi scroll was suppressed because it told of the history of Jesus, his mother, and his relationship to the Magdalene. In the "Gospel of Mary," in the "Dialogue of the Saviour," and in the "Gospel of Thomas," the Magdalene's prominent role is revealed as that of a disciple, a messenger of esoteric revelations and visionary. Mary Magdalene clearly assumes the role of the symbol of, or chief disciple and companion to, the Savior; his spouse, consort and partner. All of this vanished, only to reemerge in orthodox Christianity as "witness to the resurrection" and "apostle to the apostles," and even more significantly (especially when one looks at the history of Christianity and women in particular), as a "repentant whore."

The genealogies of the Royal families were kept in the Temple. In A.D. 66–74, during the Jewish revolution, the Herodian and Roman rulers destroyed the Jewish genealogies of the nobles in order to ensure that the kings of Israel could never again claim their legitimate rights to the country.

The Crucifixion and his near-death experience must have been extraordinarily demanding on Christ physically. No doubt He would have needed time to recover from such an ordeal. It is speculated that Christ was drugged to withstand the pain of crucifixion, but it was not foreseen that he would be speared on the cross. There were things that apparently Joseph could not prevent from happening. But Christ did not have to suffer the customary breaking of the legs.

It is assumed that Jesus stayed with his family in France for a period of time, left his family to go with Joseph of Arimathea to Glastonbury, after which he went back to Mt. Carmel, thought to be the home of the Essenes, to teach his disciples.

H. P. Blavatsky writes: "The Gnostics maintained that Jesus was a man overshadowed by the Christos or Messenger of Life, and that his despairing cry from the cross, 'Eloi, Eloi, lama shabahthani,' was wrung from him at the instant when he felt that this inspiring Presence had finally abandoned him, for—as some affirmed—his faith had also abandoned him when on the cross."[4] (Also affirmed in Matt. 27:46, Mark 15:35.)

Manly P. Hall quotes the Gnostics in this regard: "Christ was the personification of *Nous*, the Divine mind and emanated from the higher spiritual Aeons. Christ descended into the body of Jesus at the baptism and left it again before the Crucifixion. The Gnostics declared that the Christ was not crucified, as the Divine *Nous* could not suffer death, but that Simon the Cyrenean, offered his life instead and that the *Nous*, by means of its power caused Simon to resemble Jesus."[5]

After returning to France, Joseph of Arimathea and his disciples took the Ark to Glastonbury, England. William of Malmesbury, the early historian who stayed for a time with the monks of Glastonbury (1125), made careful examination of the records, especially their early chapters, and wrote a small treatise, "On the Antiquity of the Church of Glastonbury." He found the whole story in ancient writings—how the Holy Apostles had been scattered throughout the world; how St. Philip came to

France with a host of disciples and sent twelve of them into Britain to preach; and that in Britain, taught by revelation, they constructed a chapel which the *Son of God afterwards dedicated to the honor of His Mother.* It would seem that William of Malmesbury is indicating that Christ, "the Son of God," was in Glastonbury with Joseph and his disciples.

The Holy Repository, Rennes-le-Château

There is a quotation in Manly P. Hall's booklet *Legends of Glastonbury Abbey* that refers to the Holy Grail as being a book that was buried at Glastonbury. The Ark of the Covenant or "Holy Book" was taken to Glastonbury, but likely a copy was also left in the area of southern France at Rennes-le-Château. Legends lie deep in the history of this French community and even today one of the famous ones surrounding this town is of a buried treasure.

Treasure hunters in the area of Rennes-le-Château have discovered an immense geometric temple stretching for miles across the landscape. There are pentacles, circles and hexagons in the countryside marking key landmarks made of natural mountains. Two excellent books explain the awesome parameters of this natural pentagon. For more understanding of this area, I refer the interested reader to *The Holy Place* by Henry Lincoln and *Genisis* by David Wood.

The valley of Rennes-le-Château in southern France, often referred to as the Languedoc, has always had an aura of mystery about it. A great deal of the history of the Church of Rome was concerned with religious persecution, and the Languedoc received more than its share of this persecution. The Languedoc was the region of the Catharists and the Templars. Why did the Church of Rome need to obliterate these people? What were the Catharists and Templars protecting that so threatened the Church of Rome?

In 1828 the Abbe Gregoire stated, and others have agreed, that Christ delivered to St. John a "Secret Doctrine" which was later in the keeping of the Catharists and Templars. There is little doubt that what these groups had was the true history of Christianity. A history which, if known, would have greatly threatened the teachings and therefore the status and political power of the Church of Rome.

In the Village of Rennes-le-Château, there is evidence to suggest that the local priest, Berenger Sauniere, appointed in 1885 as parish priest of the Church of Rennes-le-Château, found a treasure of immense symbolic value. In 1887 Sauniere had extensive work carried out in his little, but very old, church of St. Mary Magdalene. While he was replacing the old altar inside the church, which stood on two stone pillars, one of which was found to be hollow, he found coded parchments.

Regarding the mystery of Rennes-la-Château, Lionel and Patricia Fanthorpe, authors of *Secrets of Rennes-le-Château*, have done a great deal of investigation. They tell of an interesting interview they had with Henri Buthion in 1970. Buthion owned the hotel where Berenger Sauniere lived almost a century before. Buthion stated that he had heard from an actual witness, who was there when Sauniere arrived at Rennes, that the little church was in a bad state of repair. Thanks to the generosity of a local benefactress, the priest was able to carry out the necessary restoration work on the altar. It was during this refurbishment that the coded parchment scrolls were discovered in or near one of the altar pillars. According to Buthion, the priest examined the documents for about two hours and then ordered his builders to stop work. About two weeks later, as the story goes, Sauniere went to visit the Abbe Grasseau at St. Paul de Fenouillere. It is known that Grasseau was in contact with hermetic centers in Paris. Buthion indicated there was little doubt that Sauniere found treasure of a sacred nature—something more valuable than gold or jewels. Henri Buthion stated that it must have been something absolutely beyond price.

Another interesting account in the Fanthorpe book was about a visit they had with Dr. Arthur Guirdham, the renowned authority on Catharism. (See the section on Catharists following in chapter 12.) They asked Dr. Guirdham what he thought the four heroic mountaineers from Montsegur (the hilltop castle of the Catharists), had carried down its precipitous sides under cover of darkness just before the Church of Rome attacked and murdered the Catharists. Guirdham told them he thought that it was books or esoteric manuscripts of some kind.

In 1899 Sauniere purchased parcels of land around the church and presbytery—all in the name of his housekeeper. Large building projects went on for the next few years, built with money from an unidentified and mysterious source. Interesting names were given to the buildings constructed by Sauniere—names such as the Villa Bethania and the Magdalene Tower.

Sauniere died on January 22, 1917. It was reported at the time that Father Riviere, who received Sauniere's last confession, was so shocked by the confession that he himself became ill and was unable to work for several months thereafter.

There is every indication that the priest Berenger Sauniere actually discovered information regarding the true history of the Holy Family contained in the coded parchments he had discovered and decoded. This would certainly prove a problem for a priest loyal to the Church. It has been suggested that Sauniere replaced the parchments in the pillar which now stands in the garden in front of the Church of Mary Magdalene. It is possible that the reason Father Riviere, the priest who took Sauniere's confession, was so upset was that he too had uncovered the true story of Christianity.

It is known that Mary Magdalene taught in the south of France, and there are many indications that she and her group traveled from Sarras to Rennes-le-Château. Because Mary was an initiate, she would have recognized and known about this holy site as a natural pentagon formed by the mountains. Here sacred geometry had been used to lay out a plan in the Rennes valley so that it could not be erased, a great geometrical figure which is indelibly marked on the ground of the forty-mile radius of what David Wood called the "Temple of Rennes-le-Château." This story in geometry would ensure that it could never be misunderstood—never misconstrued or misinterepted by the Church. The marking of this valley set up a "Holy of Holies," where the Magdalene could deposit the "Holy Repository" that she and Jesus brought from Jerusalem.

There are those of the opinion that in ancient times the first people who lived in the Rennes valley were Druids from Atlantis, pagan Celts and Goddess worshipers. They no doubt knew the geometry of the Ark and laid out the mountains of the valley in the shape of a pentagon. (A pentagon is part of the powerful mathematical principle of "Phi"—one of the mathematical principles that construct our universe, a part of sacred geometry.) It was likely already a megalithic site in Mary Magdalene's time. If we were to excavate the ruins there would probably be remnants of ancient standing stones. The structure of the mountains gives great energy to this area. You might say that metaphorically Mary Magdalene and her group of followers were looking for a place to erect a new Temple of Jerusalem and deposit the treasure they had brought from that Temple. So it is likely that Mary and her followers knew of this ancient site and traveled to it. It was also in the south of France, close to where they had landed in Sarras.

The "Holy Place" is a natural pentagon marked by five mountain tops with a church, castle, or rock outcrop on top of each. Three castles form a triangle on three of the mountain tops. These are the Knights Templars Château of Bezu, the Château of Blanchefort, and Rennes-le-Château. The Château of Blanchefort provides a link with the Templars as does the Château

Coat of Arms of Rennes-le-Château

of Bezu. Bertrand de Blanchefort, who excavated here and built the castle, was the Grand Master of the Templars from 1156 until 1169. There were also other Templar castles in the area.

Today the elements that define the Temple are the alignments between readily identifiable ancient structures such as churches and castles. The alignments of these structures cover no more than a few miles and can generally be confirmed by direct line of sight or by sightings from intervening high spots. There is no possibility that the many meaningful alignments of churches and castles in the Rennes-le-Château area are the result of pure accident or chance.

It was known by the Templars, the Prieures de Sion (who were the secret Order behind the Knights Templars and still exist today), that some of the treasures of the Temple of Jerusalem were in Rennes-le-Château and most likely discovered by the priest Berenger Sauniere. It is known that the present church in the village was built in 1059 and consecrated to the Magdalene. It stood on the foundation of a still older Visigoth structure dating from the sixth century. Sauniere drew attention to his knowledge of Mary Magdalene when he named the gothic library tower he built "Magdala." He also built the Villa Bethania around the area of the church. There is a labyrinth of Merovingian tombs below the church of Rennes. It is possible that the "Holy Repository" is now in this labyrinth, placed there by those who still wish to keep it hidden, possibly the Priory of Zion.

Jesus, Mary Magdalene and Joseph of Arimathea, along with some of the Apostles, founded the Nazarene Church in France which led to the Catharists, Knights Templars, Priors of Zion and many other groups in this area of southern France. This church followed the teachings of Christ and the customs of Judaism which included the Seder. They considered themselves to be the "Pure Ones." The southern part of France, often called the Languedoc, was really a country apart from the rest of what we know now as France—socially and politically. It even had its own language. The church founded here was not the Church of Rome but the Church of the Apostles.

CHAPTER 11

GLASTONBURY
AND THE ARK OF THE COVENANT

Christ in Glastonbury

he original Ark of the Covenant from Solomon's Temple did not remain in France for long because it could not be protected there. Joseph of Arimathea, who had traveled to England earlier and founded his tin business, was familiar with the area. He would have known that the Ark would be protected in Glastonbury. Here Druids had their schools and practiced their rituals and ceremonies. Down through the ages and the accompanying wars, Glastonbury had been miraculously protected and preserved. Christ, his Mother Mary, Joseph of Arimathea and his disciples brought the Ark to Glastonbury where they knew it would be safe.

Lionel Smithett Lewis, in *St. Joseph of Arimathea at Glastonbury*, writes: "All down the ages of warring heathendom the place [Glastonbury] was almost miraculously preserved. No wonder men called it 'The Secret of the Lord.' No wonder that here, from a ravaged country, for centuries men brought their treasured holy things for protection. No wonder that an oath by 'The Old Church' or 'Vetusta Exclesia' was the most sacred oath that men of this province could take."[1]

There is no doubt that there would have been written records about the fact of Christ being in Glastonbury. Unfortunately, the famous Abbey library, which held over a thousand years of Glastonbury history, burned in the twelfth century. No records have survived. The only thing we can hope to find is scattered references, and there are many. A few of these are the following:

The Rev. Lionel S. Lewis, Vicar of Glastonbury in the 1920s and 1930s, collected many of the old traditions still surviving among the people of Somerset about the sacred road followed by Christ and Joseph of Arimathea on their journey across Britain from the coast. According to some, they made their landing on the north Coast of Somerset and traveled by way of the river Brue, which later became Glastonbury Canal. Others say that the Holy Spirit touched Britain first at St. Michael's Mount in Cornwall and took the straight way to Glastonbury on the line (ley line) of St. Michael.

The same author tells us about Gildas, the wise Albanicus (425–512), who took refuge in Glastonbury Abbey after being driven by Saxon pirates from the island of Steepholme. Gildas became a monk there until he received permission to resume his anchorite life (of being a religious hermit) in an adjacent cell. Gildas is quoted as saying: "Christ the True Sun afforded His light, and knowledge of His precepts, to our island in the last years, as we know, of Tiberius Caesar."[2] *This was in* A.D. *37, four years after the crucifixion*, which were the last years of Tiberius Caesar.

The following passage by Frederick Bligh Bond, hired in 1907 to be the director of excavations for Glastonbury, expands upon this information. In the foreword of his book *The Mystery of Glaston*, Mr. Bond informs us of the following: "The Glastonbury tradition, which is our priceless national heritage, may be concisely stated thus: The Church in Britain was the earliest organized church in Western Europe. It was founded in the last year of Emperor Tiberius—about A.D. 37—by Joseph of Arimathea and a company of twelve, at a place now known as Glastonbury."[3] Mr. Bond confirms A.D. 37 as the year the church was founded. Also he informs us that Joseph was accompanied not by eleven, but a company of twelve, disciples. The possibility exists that the extra person was Christ.

Rev. Lionel Lewis gives us another piece of information about Christ in England. He quotes a letter written by St. Augustine to Pope Gregory: "In the Western confines of Britain there is a certain royal island of large extent, surrounded by water, abounding in all the beauties of nature and necessaries of life. In it the first Neophites of Catholic Law, God beforehand acquainting them, found a Church constructed by no human art, BUT DIVINELY CONSTRUCTED [or by the hands of Christ Himself] for the salvation of His people. The almighty has made it manifest by many miracles and mysterious visitations that He continues to watch over it as sacred to Himself and Mary the Mother of God." (p. 86). St. Augustine arrived in Glastonbury in A.D. 597 and found a powerful British Church in the western parts of the island. The island which St. Augustine referred to is obviously Glastonbury, and "the first Neophites of Catholic Law" no doubt refers to Joseph and his companions. His statement that the Church was dedicated to the Virgin Mary is also confirmed by William of Malmesbury (1090-1143).

In the great Register of Glastonbury of the Middle Ages occur two titles. *Domus Dei* and *Secretum Domini* or *The House of God* and *The Secret (or Retreat) of the Lord*. Regarding these titles, The Vicar of Glastonbury, Lionel Lewis, suggested to Rev. C. C. Dobson (former Vicar of St. Mary in the Castle Hastings) at the time of the writing of his book *Did Our Lord Visit Britain as They Say in Cornwall and Somerset?* that the later title has reference to the old tradition that Joseph buried there the Holy Grail. But Dobson suggests that "the two titles reflect the old tradition which we have seen survive even today that our Lord Himself stayed there. Do we know otherwise why it should be called the 'Home of God,' and the expression 'Secret of the Lord' is exactly the term we should find applied if Our Lord had made a private residence there."[4]

In his book Rev. Dobson suggests that some deeper cause for sanctity lay at Glastonbury; that it had been hallowed by the presence of the Lord Himself. Dobson points out that the Lord's stay at this place would have been strictly private, and passed unnoticed. Residents would only have taken note of Him as an earnest young man living a strange and mystic hermit's life. A few years after His departure, His memory would be forgotten. He no doubt did not announce His identity. Rev. Dobson also suggests that Jesus actually stayed some time in Glastonbury and constructed a building there using wattles.

A. H. Lewis, the namesake of Reverend Lionel Lewis, was Vicar of St. Martins, Scilly, and has done a major amount of research on Christ in Britain. He wrote a book titled *Christ in Cornwall* and later, in 1948, privately printed a pamphlet where he suggests that Jesus came to Britain twice at least—first as a child or youth on a visit with Joseph, and again as a man to reside for some years at or near Glastonbury. "At Talland I traced the beautiful story of the visit of 'a little boy and his uncle' (The Child Christ and Joseph) to Lammana (Looe Island in Talland Parish). This was the subject of my first booklet, *The Child Christ at Lammana*. At Falmouth I traced a more definite and rather different version of the Holy Visit. Here it was rather of a grown man (The Saviour) visiting with or without Joseph, most of the old mining districts of Cornwall. . . ."[5]

Lewis states further in this same pamphlet that Jesus came as a child with Joseph of Arimathea to Cornwall to the tinners. However, in other versions, notably those at Priddy and St. Just, he states that he finds no suggestion at all that they are about a child. Lewis expresses an indebtedness to the Rev. C. C. Dobson for the suggestion, which he now accepts, that Christ first visited British shores as a child and that he later sojourned there for a longer or shorter time as a man.

Rev. Dobson discovered similar legends in Somerset, accepted by the people of Priddy, that Jesus had passed over those hills on his way to Glastonbury. He also relates in his book the story of Jesus and St. Joseph of Arimathea coming to Summerland in a ship of Tarshish and staying in a place called Paradise. Glastonbury is the ancient paradise of Summerland; Somerset is often called Summerland, and there is an area called Paradise at the

West end of the town of Glastonbury. Rev. Dobson traced Jesus'
route from the Bristol channels at Burnham, where he found
another Paradise name, to the Isle of Avalon by way of the river
Brue, and concluded that Jesus had indeed visited Glastonbury.

"In folk memory these visits have been kept alive and passed
on from one generation to another, held dear by the older inhabitants by whom it is not considered a subject for glib and
skeptical discussion, nor for the prying of strangers out of mere
curiosity. The lips of the native residents are then sealed, but
among themselves in their own homes, they talk about the time
in the long ago when our Lord visited Glastonbury and the surrounding country and accepted hospitality in their homes. . . .
Even today there are homes in and around Glastonbury where
an extra place is always laid at table in the belief that one day he
will return."[6] This is from *Joseph of Arimathea* by Isabel Hill
Elder, whose booklet is published in Glastonbury and sold at the
Abbey's bookshop.

William of Malmesbury was a monk historian of the twelfth
Century, who studied in Glastonbury Abbey at a time when the
original manuscripts were still available (before the destruction
of the Abbey in 1539). He was known for being extremely careful not to repeat unsubstantiated legends. Therefore it is significant that in his later work on Glastonbury he strongly supports
the belief that Jesus did preach His precepts in Glastonbury.

The following passage taken from Malmesbury forms part of
the famous charter given to Glastonbury by King Ina in 708, and
records the belief then commonly held that Jesus lived and ministered in Glastonbury. The charter reads in part: "To the ancient
Church, situate in the place called Glastonbury which Church the
Great High Priest and Chiefest Minister, formerly through His
own Ministry and that of angels sanctified by many an unheard
of miracle to Himself and the ever Virgin Mary, as was formerly
revealed to St. David, do grant . . ."[7]

The quotation of Malmesbury was taken from E. Raymond
Capt in his well-researched book *The Traditions of Glastonbury.*
Capt further states in the same work: " 'The Great High Priest'
and 'Chiefest Minister' are clearly references to Christ, Himself,

and this would seem to affirm that He personally ministered there. This is certainly a confirmation of Gildas' statement that Christ afforded His light and a knowledge of his precepts. The ancient church referred to by King Ina was, of course, the little wattle church built perhaps by Joseph of Arimathea. Today the site is covered by the ruins of the 12th-century Church of St. Mary, known as Mary's or the Lady's Chapel." The reference to St. David in Malmesbury's quotation marks the occasion when St. David visited Glastonbury about 546. Malmesbury relates the story that St. David came to Glastonbury from Wales with seven bishops "of whom he was primate" to dedicate the Old Church to the Blessed Virgin Mary. On the night before the ceremony, Jesus appeared to St. David in a vision and said that he had already done so and David must not. "He himself had long before dedicated the church in honor of His mother and the sacrament ought not be profaned by human repetition. St. David then started to build another church 'lest they should seem to come out for naught.'"

One of the most unusual monuments having all the hallmarks of an ancient piece of masonry which survived the disastrous fire of 1184 is a weather-worn tablet outside the south wall of the present Chapel. The tablet bears two names: JESUS—MARIA. The question is often asked what it means and why it was put there.

As an interesting aside, on a recent trip to England I was taken by a dear friend to St. Mary's Bruton Parish Church in Bruton. The Church was very special and had a wonderful energy. It was built in Saxon times and is related to Bruton Church in Williamsburg, Virginia. There is even a picture of the Williamsburg Bruton Church hanging on one of the walls. In the chancel of Bruton Church in England is the crypt of Sir Charles Berkeley, who traveled to America in 1639 to be Governor of Virginia and was instrumental in the building of Bruton Church in Williamsburg, one of the earliest churches constructed in the United States. Here, I knew, was a Masonic connection. Then my attention was directed to a stained glass window in the church depicting an adult Christ surrounded by apple trees bearing fruit. Here the

Stone in South Wall of Mary's Chapel

Masons had dropped a little hint, a piece of information, about Christ and Glastonbury, historically known as the Isle of Apples.

There is a poem called "The Glastonbury Hymn," which is quoted by many authors who wrote books on Glastonbury, probably because its message touches us on a soul level. It was written by the famous poet and visionary William Blake, who was born in London in 1757. Blake had imbibed deeply of the wisdom of the Troubadours and often expressed a familiarity with the tenets of the Rosicrucians and Freemasons. In the poem it is clear that William Blake meant to convey his belief that Jesus Christ did come to England when he asks the question "was Jerusalem builded here?" And further: "Nor shall my sword sleep in my hand, Till I have built Jerusalem In England's green and pleasant land."

The Rev. C. C. Dobson, in *Did Our Lord Visit Britain as They*

Say in Cornwall and Somerset? summarizes by stating that his study "has been based upon the existence of the tradition embodied in Blake's poem that our Lord in person visited our land [England]. This tradition has been shown to be intermingled with a mass of traditions connected with Joseph of Arimathea." Rev. Dobson goes on to say, "Probably most will admit that no adequate reason really exists why it may not be true. The mere possibility of its truth has in the writer's [Dobson's] view been ample warrent for its investigation, and that investigation reveals stronger basis than he, at any rate, believed existed . . ."[8]

THE GLASTONBURY HYMN

And did those feet in ancient time
Walk upon England's mountains green?
And was the Holy Lamb of God
On England's pleasant pastures seen?
And did the Countenance Divine
Shine forth upon our clouded hills?
And was Jerusalem builded here
Among those dark Satanic mills?
Bring me my bow of burning gold!
Bring me my arrows of desire!
Bring me my spear! O clouds unfold!
Bring me my Chariot of Fire!
I will not cease from mental fight,
Nor shall my sword sleep in my hand,
Till I have built Jerusalem
In England's green and pleasant land.

From all the information gathered it becomes evident that Christ as a man spent some time in Glastonbury.

History of Joseph of Arimathea and His Disciples

In Glastonbury live the legends not only of Christ, Joseph of Arimathea and his disciples, but also of the Celts, Druids, Christians, Merlin the Magician, King Arthur, his knights of the Round Table, and the quest for the Holy Grail. To begin the history of Joseph of Arimathea and his group, we will consider an early manuscript, one of the most important found to date. It is called *Grand-Saint-Graal* and relates how the early missionaries left Sarras in the area of Marseilles, France, and crossed the English Channel to Glastonbury. One meaning of the word "Saint Graal" is Blood Royal, which undoubtedly applies to the Holy Family of Christ. The abundant literature of the Grail quest dates from about the twelfth century onwards.

This particular Grail story recorded in Norma Goodrich's book *The Holy Grail* informs us that Joseph of Arimathea and his son Josephe brought the Chalice of the last supper with them from Jerusalem, and that they were ancestors of those great knights who formed the court of King Arthur. The author of *Grand Saint Graal* is anonymous. He writes in Old French and appears to be a person descended from one of those who knew Christ. From this writing we get a more definitive feeling of the trip from Sarras to Glastonbury and how the Ark of the Covenant came to arrive in Glastonbury:

"Joseph of Arimathea and his companions wandered away from Sarras until they came, after much journeying, to the seashore. That night the brave Galaaz was by the grace of God conceived.

"The next day Joseph and his company prayed before their sacred Hebrew Ark of the Covenant, kneeling before their Hebrew or Holy Grail, weeping and requesting that they be made strong to cross the sea into that promised land where they would multiply and become the best people.

"They plodded along the path to the very sand and edge of the sea. There they saw neither galley nor ship wherein to embark. They crowded moaning and weeping, praying to the Lord to assist them in their distress, to bring them over the sea. 'What are we to do?' They asked Joseph's son Josephe, their Bishop. They knew this was to be the last leg of long travels.

"Josephe replied that only some should go. Those who had kept the commandments would be paid according to their virtues. Those who were filled with holiness would pass over the sea.

"As it turned out, 250 were declared pure. As it happened also, they were the closest in blood to Joseph of Arimathea. The remaining 460 were sinners."

The author of *Grand Saint Graal* continues: "The night was both fair and still and the sea peaceable at her own will. Without any storm or other distress and the moon shone in all her brightness. . . .

"And it was Saturday certainly, before Easter Day most truly . . . when Josephe went to his father, kissed him and all the company good-bye, and prepared to depart. However, a voice warned him to halt.

"The first to go were the Grail Bearers. They departed on foot, bearing the Holy Vessel, without dread of the sea, and walked across water dry shod.

"When Josephe saw the Grail Bearers safely embarked, he offered his shirt before the others there and changed his clothes. Then he spread 'that Schirte' upon the sea as if it were dry land and bade his father set his feet aboard. After that, Josephe embarked the others by order of rank until there were 150 standing thereupon. Then Josephe blessed the 'Schirte' and the water they stood upon . . . two wicked men fell off and drowned.

"They made a safe crossing. Next morning they were in Britain. Josephe had held up the shirt all night by the sleeve. Thus, it moved easily in the water, fortunately, for the rest of their work was cut out for them. Britain was full of wicked folk, all Saracens.

"Josephe predicted the reign of King Arthur, whose adventures would last for twelve years.

"An angel had already told Josephe that the Grail meant something that did not displease but that pleased. One looking inside the Vessel, after first lifting off the lid, would be blinded. The Holy Lance would draw healing blood from a wound into the Grail. The blood could cure blindness. Therefore the Lance meant the commencement of the adventures at King Arthur's Court during which the true descendants of Josephe would be shown.

"Then great, terrifying wonders caused by the Grail would occur in Britain. There the Fisher King would be struck through the two thighs by the Lance and suffer ages of pain only to be cured by the one pure descendant who would persevere until all the wonders of the Holy Grail were revealed: that the Grail provides food endlessly, that the Sword could never be mended until Galahad by his touch alone mended it, that the Grail King Aleyn (Noble) was one of the Fisher Kings casting his net about for damned souls, that Joseph of Arimathea brought the Hebrew wonder, which was his Holy Grail, to Glastonbury where he was interred, that the Abbey where he was buried stood under the 'Cross of England,' that 'Corbenie' was the name of the castle built to house the Holy Grail, that 'Corbenie' was located in a foreign land where during services at this Grail Castle the Grail was placed on a silver plate. The priest there stood under the sound of a thousand voices [choristers?] and the beating of hundreds of birds' wings overhead. . . .

Signed:
Henry Lonelich"[9]

This early manuscript of Grail text reveals that the Holy Grail which Joseph of Arimathea and his company prayed before on their way to Britain was the sacred Hebrew Ark of the Covenant. The Ark of the Covenant had come to Britain. From this manuscript we are informed that the Grail originated in Jerusalem, meaning it was the Ark of the Covenant from the Temple of Jerusalem. The Grail Bearers, those who carried the Ark, were the first to board the vessel. This was because the Ark was their most precious and holy possession. *The Ark has now traveled from Jerusalem to Sarras to Glastonbury.* The author even associates a "blinding light" with the Grail which is often associated with the Ark of the Covenant and the manner in which the Ark heals.

Glastonbury, originally given the Saxon name of Glasstingabyrig, is also known by many other names, including the Isle of Glass, the Isle of Crystal, Avalon, and the Isle of Apples.

While many have never even heard of this little town in England, it has been the center of ancient Roman activity, ancient Goddess worship, and the genesis of European Christianity as well as the birthplace of the Arthurian epoch. Glastonbury lies on the main road from London to Exeter, in Somerset, near Bath, which might be more familiar due to the ancient Roman ruins which are such a popular tourist attraction. The river Brue winds in a serpentine course through Somerset, and at Glastonbury was formed an island in the stream, separated from the mainland in early times by marshes and streamlets.

On this island there were many apple trees, and in honor of this Island of Apple Trees, the strip of land came to be called the Isle of Avalon (apples), known to the Romans as Insula Avallonia. The town itself is best described as lying in the midst of orchards surrounded by water-meadows. Out of the water-meadows or marshes rises a hill achieving the elevation of 500 feet. This hill is called the Tor, or Tower Hill, and on its summit are the remains of St. Michael's oratory. It is in this majestic setting that Joseph of Arimathea and his dedicated followers would eventually settle.

After leaving Sarras or Marseilles, it is recorded that St. Joseph of Arimathea, with his son Josephe, ten others, and Mary, the mother of Jesus, went as missionaries to the remote land of Britain. It is said that these travelers were led by an invisible hand which brought them to a dark and dismal region, heavily forested, swampy and covered with a leaden sky heavy with fog.

At the time the group of missionaries arrived, Arviragus was the prince or chieftain of the district. Joseph of Arimathea is referred to as Joseph de Marmore of Arimathea, "Mar" being an Eastern term for lord. "More" signifies "great." Thus the title would mean the great Lord Joseph of Arimathea. Undoubtedly this title derived from Joseph's elevated status as "nobilis decurio," a title designated by Gildas and Rabanus.

Joseph's daughter Anna was already married to Prince Belinus, youngest brother to King Arviragus. Joseph was no stranger when he and his group arrived in Britain. The missionaries were entertained with great kindness in the Court of Arviragus. Arviragus listened with great respect to the doctrines which they had brought, and also to their plans for the establishment of a holy house. In the end, however, Arviragus declined to renounce his own faith or to follow the teachings of these mysterious people who had been banished from their own land. Nevertheless, he did permit them, with great liberality of mind, to settle in his dominion and was moved to grant them twelve hides of land, one for each member of the company. Each hide of land equaled about 160 acres. On this land, Joseph and his followers would settle and teach their doctrines according to their own convictions.

The tax-free land grant gave the recipients many British concessions, including right of citizenship and the same privileges accorded the Druidic hierarchy. This grant of twelve hides of land is recorded in the Domesday Book of 1086 (Domesday Survey, folio p. 249 B), which states: "The Domus Dei, in the great monastery of Glastonbury, called the Secret of the Lord. This Glastonbury Church possesses, in its own Villa, XII hides of land which never paid taxes."[10]

The Staff of Saint Joseph

After leaving the court of Arviragus, St. Joseph and his followers journeyed through the marshes and forests, coming at last to an elevated place called Weary-all Hill. They arrived at this dreary place precisely on Christmas Day and paused to rest and survey the region. Joseph is said to have thrust the long staff which he had carried on his journey into the earth and then led his companions in prayer, asking for divine blessing and guidance. (Joseph's staff, a symbol of power, could be compared to the miraculous staff of Moses and Aaron and the Caduceus of Hermes.)

While Joseph and his followers were praying, a group of savage people clad in the skins of animals and carrying crude weapons came out of the gloomy forest. Seeing that the strangers were kneeling in some kind of devotion, the natives made no effort to injure them.

As the group arose from their prayers, they beheld a miracle.

The dried and withered staff Joseph had stuck into the earth sprang to life, budded, and put forth white blossoms—just as had Aaron's rod. The Glastonbury Thorn, an unusual variety of hawthorn which flourishes only in this area of England, is said to have descended from this legendary staff of Joseph.

Botanists have trouble identifying this plant. Some think it came from Morocco, while others believe it may have originated in Siberia. Certainly it was not indigenous to the South of England. The Glastonbury Thorn flowers twice a year, around Christmas time and again in May. The original thorn tree, which had blossomed forth from Joseph's staff, was cut down in 1653 by a fanatical soldier in the army of Oliver Cromwell. Before this time, many cuttings were taken from it and planted in the surrounding areas; these still blossom around the time of the Winter Solstice. It is thought the Glastonbury Thorn is of the same variety as that used in the wreath of thorns placed on the head of Christ. It is still believed to have mystical virtues, and many people visit the area to see this remarkable plant.

The budding of the staff on Weary-all Hill was regarded by Joseph of Arimathea as evidence that the new community should be built on this site. The disciples set about to build a church of "wattle and daub" using the natural building material of the area and the local method of construction. They also built twelve wattle huts, circling the church, for living quarters. It was no indication of poverty to build a church in this style. The church lasted until the fifth century, and was dedicated to St. Mary, the mother of Christ. It was later known as the Chapel of St. Joseph.

The ground plan of the church was chronicled by the early monks and is still preserved in the ruined Lady Chapel of the Abbey. The Wattle Church was not small; it was sixty feet in length and twenty-six feet in width, approximately the same dimensions as the Tabernacle of Jerusalem. The church was built about A.D. 37, as stated by Bligh Bond and Gildas, and could accommodate some 120 people. The grounds around the building were duly sanctified, and the portion of the churchyard where Mary (the mother of Christ) is buried is considered the "holiest ground in England." St. Joseph and many of the saints were later

Bligh Bond's reconstruction of St. Joseph's Church at Glastonbury with the cells of the original twelve missionaries (1919).

buried in this same churchyard. Here the twelve labored together, converting many local residents to the teachings of the Christ. The first among their converts were the Druids of Britain, who found no difficulty in reconciling the teachings of Christ with their own teaching of resurrection and the inheritance of eternal life or reincarnation.

Regarding this first church, William of Malmesbury, the historian of Glastonbury, wrote (probably in 1126) that these twelve saints served God with peculiar devotion to this place, making addresses to the Blessed Virgin. They spent their time in watching, fasting and prayer and were supported in their difficulties by the assistance and appearance of the Blessed Virgin (as it is reasonable to believe); Malmesbury goes on to report that vouching for the truth of this matter are St. Patrick's charter and the writings of the ancients.

In the most ancient writing about Glastonbury, Melchinus or Maelgwyn in 540 tells of the burial of St. Joseph close to St. Mary's Chapel. He describes the location as next to the south corner of the house of prayer, made of prepared wattles over the "adorable powerful Virgin by the aforesaid circle of thirteen inhabiting that place." Joseph came to Glastonbury with eleven disciples and himself, hence the twelve hides of land given them, but in this passage Maelgwyn speaks of "a circle of thirteen"; could the extra one be Jesus?

Regarding the burial of Joseph, Lionel Smithett Lewis states that after the moving of Joseph's burial place several times, he was placed, in 1928, in the ancient St. Katherine's Chapel, the north transept in St. John the Baptist Church in Glastonbury. The tomb was known as John Allen's Tomb, probably to protect it. But, most important, it bears the initials of Joseph of Arimathea (J.A.) and a *caduceus* between the initials. Lewis also states that to this day the Patriarchs of the Eastern Church carry a caduceus, usually before them, instead of a crozier. The caduceus was the symbol of Hermes, who brought the Ark of the Covenant to Western civilization. It was also carried by Joseph of Arimathea and it was the staff that budded.

Druids of Glastonbury

In *Isis Unveiled*, H. P. Blavatsky speaks of the Druids of Great Britain who practiced rites of moral and physical purity, and certain austerities, which developed the vital soul-power of self-illumination. This afforded man the control over his own immortal spirit, giving him truly magical powers over the elementary spirits inferior to himself. The magic of the West is as ancient as that to be found in the East—Japan, China, India and Tibet. The Druids of Great Britain practiced this magic in the silent crypts of their deep caves.

The Semothees—the Druids of the Gauls—were knowledgeable in the physical as well as the spiritual sciences. They taught the secrets of the universe, the harmonious progress of the heavenly bodies, the formation of the earth and, above all, the immortality of the soul.

The Druids met in their sacred groves, which became the natural academies built by the hand of the Invisible Architect. The initiates assembled at the hour of midnight to learn about what man once was, and what he would be. They needed no artificial illumination, nor life-drawing gas, to light up their temples, for the moon beamed her most silvery rays on their oak-crowned heads, and these white-robed sacred bards knew how to converse with the solitary queen of the starry vault.

It is thought that the Druids emigrated from Atlantis to Egypt, where they were instrumental in helping to build the Great Pyramid. They also emigrated to Crete, Phoenicia and the Holy Land, and a large number settled in the British Isles. The Druids are also thought to have built Stonehenge Circle which, when measured, is found to incorporate astronomical relationships using the "pyramid" inch, the name given the old British inch. Only the British and the Hebrews before them used the pyramid inch.

It is likely that this measurement was brought from Egypt to Israel by Moses, and from Egypt to the British Isles by the Druids. The Druids were initiates of the Mysteries and must have understood about sacred geometry and the study of the stars and planets in order to build such a great structure as Stonehenge.

The pyramid inch is an important factor in sacred geometry. It was used in the building of the Great Pyramid, Stonehenge, Solomon's Temple, Rennes-le-Chateau, and other sacred sites. The Pyramid of Giza in Egypt has a perimeter of 36,524.2 pyramid inches. One hundredth (1/100) of this figure is 365.242, which is the exact number of days in a solar year.

When Christ came to Glastonbury, it was quite evident to the "wise men of the oak trees" that He was a Druid. In the words of Taliesin, the famous Prince-Bard and Druid (550), "Christ the word from the beginning, was from the beginning our Teacher, and we never lost His Teachings." It is evident here that when Christ was in Glastonbury he did not shut Himself up like a hermit, but carried on his quiet work as a teacher.

Glastonbury was a leading Druid center. A likely scenario is that Jesus met with these Druids and told them of the principles of His own Jewish religion, comparing the two, and pointing out the similarities. Both religions looked forward to the coming of a Savior with essentially the same name—*Hesus* in the case of the Druids, and *Jesus* of the Jews. There was also a remarkable similarity between the dress of the Archdruid and that of the Jewish High Priest. It seems Jesus' life and teachings would have agreed exactly with the reports of their own initiates. The first Christian missionaries capitalized upon these real or apparent similarities.

Christianity was accepted when a local king of Glastonbury converted to the "new" religion and allowed a "missionary saint" to build a church or monastery on the site of the old Druid sanctuary, where formerly the Druid priests had officiated. From the Druids came the first monks and priests of the Christian sect. Many of these converts were former pupils from the Druid colleges, and most were sons of kings and noblemen. In these Druid colleges, astronomy, astrology, geometry, mathematics, music, science and philosophy were taught. And in Britain and Gaul the Druids were the Ministers of Education.

It seems that the embracing of Christianity brought little change to the social order of the times and even the forms of religion were not radically altered. The Druids, stemming from Atlantis, undoubtedly knew the teachings of the Ark of the Covenant, and this is what they taught their students. This they had in common with Jesus, who knew these teachings from the Temple of Jerusalem and his initiation in the Great Pyramid.

The Natural Ark and the Tor of Glastonbury

Why was Glastonbury chosen as the place to take the Ark of the Covenant from Jerusalem? It is probable that Christ, Joseph of Arimathea and others in the group, having previously traveled there, understood about the safety of the area. It had natural barriers for its defense, and all down the ages this sacred place had been preserved. It had been a sacred site of the Druids, who, having the Atlantean background and understanding the geometry of the Ark, created an area much like Rennes-le-Château—a natural ark. The man-made hills surrounding Glastonbury had been built in the sacred shape of a pentagon. Glastonbury's land and hills formed a natural ark with the Tor (which was also man-made) in the center. Christ's earlier studies with the Druids during his "lost years" likely provided the background which equipped him with the ability to recognize the land of Glastonbury as a natural ark and "Holy Place."

Dion Fortune, the highly respected English mystic and writer, was in accord with the idea that Glastonbury is a natural ark constructed by the Atlanteans. In her beautifully descriptive book, *Avalon of the Heart*, she writes: "The Atlanteans, old tradition tells us, were great navigators, ranging in trade from the Black Sea to the Pacific; they were also great colonizers, and wherever they planted their colonies they brought their priests and their altars. They were Sun-worshipers and adored the Lord and Giver of Life in open circular temples, paved with great flagstones of marble and basalt. . . .

"Those who have seen the five-hundred-feet-high Glastonbury Tor are always perplexed as to whether it is natural or artificial. Its pyramidal form, set in the center of a great plain, is almost too good to be true—too appropriate to be the unaided work of Nature. Viewed from near at hand, a terraced track can clearly be seen winding in three tiers round the cone of the Tor, and this is indisputably the work of man. . . .

"It is well known that the ancients delighted to build their colonial cities upon the same plan as the mother city in the land of their race. Is it possible that our strange pyramidal hill, with its truncated top and its inland side as steep as earth will stand, may have been wrought to that likeness by human hands in memory of the sacred mountains of the mother continent. . . . It would not be a difficult matter to take a mound of clay, and with no other tools than picks and baskets mold it to the desired shape."[11]

Glastonbury Tor is one of the glories of the west country of England. The Tor, which looks over a wide area, was used by the ancient British as a fortress and, before the advent of Christianity, it is said to have been dedicated to Tot He, the Sun God, in whose honor fires were kindled as a part of Druid religious ceremony. Researchers confirm that the Tor could have been a great religious center several thousand years before Christ. When the deluge submerged Atlantis, it also swept away much of the origins of Western culture. Here wise and learned men, having

escaped the deluge of their continent, founded a place for learning where they could keep truth alive.

The Tor has a very large labyrinth surrounding its base and ascending up to the top. This labyrinth shape that winds its way up the Tor goes back to very ancient times. If a person was properly prepared internally, and walked this particular labyrinth, the body and eyes would shift from one angle to another, allowing the influences of light, sight and proportion to play upon the subtle bodies of the individual.

It takes several hours to walk this labyrinth properly and it can still be walked today. It is said that in the past, in a couple of places, the labyrinth actually moved inside the Tor, into some subterranean chambers. These caverns or vaults would have been places of initiation. In fact, subterranean chambers are found located all over Glastonbury. Excavation has been done on the Tor to try to find some of these chambers through the use of sonar and radar.

It is interesting to note that the magnetic power of the area is found to be different every time it is tested, and quite unusual. If you walk in one direction at the base of the Tor, the pace is an easy one; if you turn in the other direction, you seem to be walking uphill.

At the end of the labyrinth, one comes to the top of the Tor. In ancient times, a circle of standing stones (you still find them in parts of England) was to be found there. Since different stone circles function in different ways, the precise nature of the Tor stones is not known. Often the standing stones were earth acupuncture or needles into the earth to manipulate the dragon currents, presently called ley lines. St. Michael's Church, built over the original ruins on the top of the Tor, is where one goes to master the Dragon current, or the Kundalini. The Christians took this to mean mastering the serpent; hence came the name St. Michael and the Dragon.

When the Christians came to Glastonbury, the original stones were taken down and in their place was built a chapel to St. Michael. Because it was difficult to bring heavy material up to the top of the Tor, some of these standing stones were broken up and used to build St. Michael's church, particularly the tower. There was an earthquake in 1275 which destroyed the church, but left the tower standing. It is interesting that the Druids still have their standing stones on top of the Tor.

In the words of Dion Fortune, "Tradition tells that the Tor was a high place of the ancient Sun-worship and that a circle of stones like a miniature Stonehenge once stood upon the crest. These standing stones were overthrown when the worship of the Son supplanted that of the Sun, but so strong were the forces generated in the spot sacred to the rites of the older race that a church dedicated to St. Michael had to be erected upon the spot in order to keep down the dark influences of the pagan worship."[12] There was a special power in these standing stones with their metallic and quartz content. They provided a channel of energy, much like a tree, from heaven to earth.

One recent discovery associated with the Tor is the existence of two major ley lines. One ley line is known as the Michael ley line (named for Archangel Michael). This is considered the masculine energy line, which crosses at the Tor the feminine ley line known as the Mary line. From ancient stories we hear of Gwyn ap Nudd, King of the fairies, who lived under the Tor where so many mystical happenings occurred. Could it be that the vortex energy of the Tor causes these mystical happenings?

Between the Tor and the town area is the moon-shaped dome of Chalice Hill. Chalice Hill has an unusually soft feminine energy. It is said to be where Joseph of Arimathea buried the Grail. At its base is a "holy well," which continually pumps some 25,000 gallons of slightly radioactive water per day. Chalice Well was sacred to the Goddess worshippers of ancient times. In its center is a shaft built of huge blocks (like the material of the standing circles) which penetrates the earth. Many miracle healings have taken place at this well.

Glastonbury is also called the Crystal Isle, since crystals have long been associated with visions, which are also affiliated with high vortex energy. The shape of the Tor indicates that it represents the male energy, while nearby Chalice Hill, in the shape of the moon, is associated with female energy. At the wellhead of Chalice Well is the ancient symbol of two interlocking circles (as seen in the following figure), which form the Vesica Piscis, the pre-Christian symbol representing the blending of masculine and feminine natures, the meeting place of spirit and matter where the conscious and unconscious worlds come together. In Christian times the symbol of the fish was derived from the crossing of these two interlocking circles.

Zodiacs of Glastonbury

The floor of the first Christian Church of England, the one built by Joseph of Arimathea and his disciples and known as the Wattle Church, was discovered in the 1900s by the Director of Excavations of Glastonbury, Frederick Bligh Bond. Bond claimed that the symbol on the floor of the church perpetuated the ancient Mysteries. The site of this circular church was later preserved by an abbot of the Abbey of Glastonbury. A floor was constructed on the site of the St. Mary Chapel and is said to be a duplicate of the ancient Wattle Church. An altar was built in its center where two major ley lines cross, and along the periphery of the circle the abbot marked the twelve signs of the zodiac. Subsequently, the floor was purposely destroyed and not long after, the Abbey was largely destroyed in the fire of 1184.

Was this floor destroyed because of the secret that it held? The original floor is described as red, in whose center was the Sun or Host in gold, and from the center were lines of black indicating paths to the cells of the Saints, which were marked by golden stars. The Sun in the middle stood for Christ and the stars represented the disciples or saints. Joseph had created a shrine that was round, with an altar in the middle. The form of the chapel was likewise circular, as were the twelve houses of the apostles. The twelvefold system of measures reflected an older tradition, such as that found in Egypt and brought forth from Atlantis. It was a symbol of the astronomical nature of the twelve signs of the zodiac.

The signs of the zodiac on the floor of the Wattle Church resonated with the signs of the heavens. In very early times people from Egypt, who were descendants of Atlantis, dispersed at various periods of time, leaving the same twelve symbols in the form of monuments of twelve standing stones, such as are found through much of southern Europe, the shores of the Mediterranean of Africa, Greece, and northward into the Scythian regions. The trend of these people was westward and to the northwest, coming to the islands of Britain.

As to the floor of St. Mary Chapel, it may be well to quote William of Malmesbury, whose records date from the twelfth century. This old chronicler says, speaking of the chapel, which was on the site of the oldest Christian Church: ". . . In the pavement may be seen on every side stones designedly inlaid in triangles and squares, and figured with lead, under which, if I believe some sacred enigma to be contained . . ."[13]

The secret of the zodiac is explained with more clarity in another passage from Frederick Bligh Bond's book, *The Gate of Remembrance*, communicated in automatic (psychic) writing by the former monks of the Abbey to Bond: "When the Holy ones first came: round church in the midst: our Lord's body on Altar, and round it 12 cubics of apostles." In another section the monks give more information on Christ and the original church: "There was the Body of Christ, and round him would have been the Four Ways. Two were ye builded and no more. In ye floor of ye Mary Chapel was ye Zodiac, that all might see that understand the mystery. In ye midst of ye Chapel he was laid; and the Cross of Hym who was our Example and Exemplar."[14] There were several statements in this writing which indicate the literal presence of "the Lord" in Glastonbury including: (1) "Our Lord's body on Altar"; (2) "There was the body of Christ and round him would have been the four ways;" (3) "In ye midst of ye Chapel he was laid."

There is another zodiac in Glastonbury, a very large one in the form of a huge earthwork, which is circular and ten miles in diameter. It has only been rediscovered since the advent of the airplane because it is too large to see from any earthly vantage point. Much of this zodiac is natural and incorporates hills, lakes and so forth, but it has also been enhanced by man. This huge zodiac has symbols of each of the twelve signs carved out of the landscape in proper order. If one were to take a star map and scale it down so as to fit over that area of land mass, the correct stars would be in the correct locations within the correct astrological signs. Katherine Maltwood, who wrote *Guide to Glastonbury's Temple of the Stars*, rediscovered this geographical wonder in the 1920s. It is possible that when Joseph of Arimathea and his disciples came to Glastonbury and were given twelve hides of land, what they were actually given was custody of the twelve hides or signs of the zodiac.

The floor of the St. Mary Chapel is supposed to be an accurate depiction of the original Glastonbury zodiac, of which only a few small pieces still remain. Maltwood states: "The reason why we are able to trace the zodiacal creatures is that the land on which they lie was once the property of the first church of Britain, and up to the time of the Reformation the monks of Glastonbury were scrupulously careful to keep the ancient landmarks and waterways intact."[15] It is suggested in Maltwood's book that the originators of this zodiac were the Phoenicians in 2800 B.C.

John Michell reports that Keith Critchlow discovered: " . . . The dimensions of the St. Mary Chapel provide the inner figure of a geometric scheme on a larger scale in the dimensions of the Twelve Hides.."[16]

Catacombs and Underground Tunnels

Another author who gathered and wrote of mystical experiences about the area of Glastonbury was J. Foster Forbes, who, along with one of his psychometrist collaborators, Iris Campbell, wrote a book called *Giants, Myths and Megaliths*. When I saw this material quoted in John Michell's extraordinary book *New View Over Atlantis*, it reminded me of the catacombs of the Great Pyramid which Solon learned about from the Egyptian priests, and also of the Temple of Solomon, where the treasures were kept in the rooms under the Temple.

Forbes gives us this perspective: "Beneath the abbey are remains of vast catacombs caused by natural upheavals. These catacombs are very deep down, and it is through these underground channels that the magnetic currents of the world flowed. It was by this means that internal combustion was caused, known as the secret fires of the earth. . . . Now the Glastonbury Tor is raised over an epicenter of magnetism, and that which is located there is continually churning up underneath. . . . The contemplative order of monks drawn to this ancient site of Glaston— knowing as they did of these terrestrial-cum-celestial mysteries— made it their life's work to pray for the peace of the world. This they did by perfecting their thoughts to the seething underworld."[17]

Part of the planning of ancient "holy" temples or churches included placing the building over subterranean chambers, waterways, and often incorporated labyrinths. As has been noted earlier, ley lines, the earth's acupuncture system, follow a network around the globe on a mathematical pattern related to the heavens. Energy and power are carried on the ley lines and where the ley lines of the earth cross they create a particularly powerful vortex of energy. It was on sites such as these that the holy places of the earth were built in ancient times. These locations were chosen because they were centers where energy entered and exited the earth. This was all part of the "blueprint" designed to ensure that the area surrounding the sacred site was one that raised the consciousness of the people. This factor the Guilds or Masons used as part of their sacred mathematical formula to reconnect humanity to the Divine.

Metaphorically, one might say that these sites or buildings were built with the Ark of the Covenant as the cornerstone because the mathematics of the Ark were used to create these sacred centers. A single code of knowledge was used to establish these power places all over the world. Encoded in these great monuments are the spiritual laws of the universe.

Jerusalem, Glastonbury, Rennes-le-Château, the Great Pyramid and many other spiritual sites are built using these same principles. Cities which encompass these principles emanate energy and exert influence that heightens the perception and the consciousness of the people of the area. Certain sites of Egypt, Israel, and Alexandria—Delos and Delphi along with other places where shrines were built in the past but have now fallen into disrepair —still have this energy. In areas like ancient Greece, there are old ruins and monuments still emanating their energy and influence.

The Connection to King Arthur's Court

It was J. W. Taylor, author of *St. Joseph and Glastonbury* (1906), who made me realize the Hebrew lineage of the English kings. The companions and relatives of the settlers of Glastonbury are said to have intermarried with the families of the British kings or chieftains, and from them, by direct descent, in something like four hundred years, the great heroes of King Arthur's Court are said to have arisen. Taylor writes: "In the most readily accessible book of the 'Sangreal' (apart from the *Morte D' Arthur*), *The High History of the Holy Grail*, which was probably compiled about 1220 from the *Book of Josephes* in the Abbey Library at Glastonbury and has been translated by Dr. Sebastian Evans, it is impossible not to recognize the important and essential part played by this Hebrew lineage or descent. Every book bears witness to this, and the very names of many of the knights or their associates seem to imply their Jewish origin. Elinant of Escavalon, Joseph, Josephes, Lot, Joseus, Josuias, Galahad (?), Alain (?), Petrus, Brons or Hebron, Bruns Brundalis, Urien, Jonas, Pelles and Pelleas and Ban may be taken either as examples of Hebrew names or as indicating some special Hebrew association (from the Apocrypha, 1 Esdras 5:12, 37; 9:34)."[18]

Most interpreters of the Arthurian legend seem to assume that it was devised by bards and troubadours merely for the entertainment of high lords and ladies. Arthur ruled over a court of heroes and the King emerges as a type of culture hero. As Hercules performed twelve labors, Arthur fought twelve battles in the service of God and Britain. Unfortunately, he was betrayed by one of his own trusted knights and died with most of his knights at the battle of Camlan. The book *Morte D'Arthur* describes the death of the King and how his body was taken away to Avalon on a black ship. Arthur was crowned King of Britain in 516, and he died in his forty-first year. This story is a veiled account of the fall of the pagan Mysteries.

There is a great deal of speculation about the story of Arthur, his court, and Merlin. While still a small boy, Merlin was brought to the court of Vortigern, King of Britain, where he confused the priestly astrologers by making extraordinary predictions that later proved accurate. Merlin eventually served as counselor and magician for seven years of the reign of King Uther Pendragon. It is said that by enchantment, he made possible the birth of Arthur, the hero-king. The earliest historical records of King Arthur contain none of the mystical elements for which he is now known. There remains no mention of the Holy Grail, the Round Table, or the sword Excalibur. But legends claim that Merlin was with Arthur at his court at Caerleon-on-Usk, and guided the young King with his wise counsel.

The Merlin of myth is an adept whose biography is in symbolic form, but myths have secret meanings, and the seeker of the truth will examine them in the light of their origins.

Merlin, with his magic, caused to appear, before the high altar in the Cathedral Church of London, a large stone holding an anvil of steel in which was thrust a sword. Under the anvil, in letters of gold, was the inscription: "Who so pulleth out this sword of this stone and anvil, is rightwise king borne of England." As legend has it, only Arthur could draw the sword, which proved his kingship and right of succession. Esoteric traditions indicate that the test of the sword symbolizes initiation.

An order of spiritual descent, beginning with Merlin, passed to Arthur and was consummated in the knight Galahad. The knight Lancelot du Lac was the foster son of Vivienne, a nymph, who may be the same as the mysterious Lady of the Lake whose hand reached out for Arthur's sword when it was thrown into the lake. Lancelot, unable to accomplish his quest of the Grail because of his sin against the sanctity of marriage, fathers a spiritual hero, in this case Galahad. Galahad alone, of all the Round Table knights, attained the Grail, and is depicted as going to heaven without experiencing death. After the battle of Camlan, as the body of the dying Arthur is taken away, Sir Bedivere performs the last rites of the Round Table. He carries Excalibur to the shores of the lake and throws it far out over the water. A woman's hand rises from the deep and, grasping the sword, carries it beneath the waves. The poet Lord Tennyson writes that Sir Bedivere cried out: "But now the whole Round Table is dissolved which was an image of the mighty world."

A table top thought to be the Round Table of King Arthur is in the collection of the courthouse in the castle at Winchester, England, and is reproduced here from Hargrave Jennings' book *The Rosicrucians, Their Rites and Mysteries*. The middle of the Winchester table top is decorated with a large heraldic rose associated with the house of Tudor. There are seats for twenty-four knights arranged in pairs, and a double throne for the Grand Master and the unknown knight or adept, who was worthy to sit with the king in the "Siege Perilous."

Arthur's Round Table is a microcosm or mirror of the universe. The Winchester table seats twenty-six, but in old records the original table had space for thirty-two, which included the throne of the king and the seat of the Siege Perilous. Thirty-two chairs, plus the Grail throne in the center, present the significant number thirty-three, which is a possible Masonic reference to the

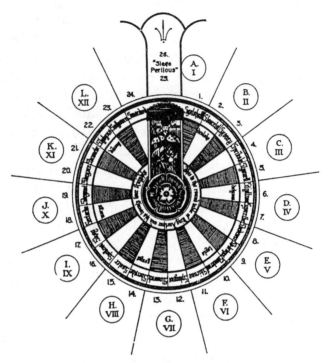

—from Jennings' *The Rosicrucians, Their Rites and Mysteries*

The Round Table of King Arthur

thirty-two degrees earned, plus one degree given by the "grace of God." Arthur's Round Table formed a zodiacal circle, formed by twelve knights, each representing zodiacal signs. King Arthur had set up the Round Table as a model of the divine cosmos.

An authentic account of the discovery of the grave of King Arthur is given by Giraldus Cambrensis, who was present on the occasion, and William of Malmesbury, who lived at the time. Later, when Henry II visited Wales, he was told by an ancient British bard that King Arthur had been buried at Glastonbury, and that strange pyramid monuments marked the grave. The monks of the abbey told Henry II that the remains of Arthur had been deeply interred, not in a stone tomb, but in a hollowed oak tree. (The oak tree of the Druids.)

An excavation took place between two pyramids or columns standing in the cemetery of the abbey. Under a stone was found a leaden cross which Giraldus claimed Arthur actually held in his hands. The cross was inscribed with the words: "Here lies buried the renowned King Arthur in the Island of Avallon." The remains of Guinevere were found on the same occasion, and also those of Modred, Arthur's son and slayer. The bones were removed to the church at Glastonbury and were placed before the high altar.

There is little reason to doubt that Merlin would have gained his great wisdom from the teachings of the Druids who were already connected to Glastonbury and also from the Rabbinical teachings passed down from Joseph of Arimathea's relatives who had intermarried and carried the mysteries with them. The mys-

—from *Two Glastonbury Legends*

The Leaden Cross Found in King Arthur's Grave

tical teachings of Christ were also passed down from Joseph of Arimathea's descendants and there is little doubt he also would have known the teachings of the Ark of the Covenant. This is likely the wisdom that Merlin taught Arthur and his knights.

Merlin would have known it would be necessary to recreate and repackage all the teachings for consumption by the people of Britain. So he brought forth the Grail teachings. Merlin created an empire and trained kings and queens and sons of noblemen to understand these teachings. He knew that if the teachings went out to the heads of the country, then they would rule with more intelligence and wisdom. In this way, humanity would continue to advance toward its ultimate goal of enlightenment.

It seems that not only are Arthur and Merlin connected to this story by the descendants of Joseph of Arimathea—but they are connected also through the Masons. Manly P. Hall connects Merlin and Arthur to the Masons in the following passage: "Arthur was the Grand Master of a secret Christian Masonic brotherhood of philosophic mystics who termed themselves *Knights*. Arthur received the exalted position of Grand Master of these Knights because he had faithfully accomplished the withdrawal of the sword (spirit) from the anvil of the base metals (his lower nature). As invariably happens, the historical Arthur soon was confused with the allegories and myths of his order until now the two are inseparable. . . . The medieval Rosicrucians were undoubtedly in possession of the true secret of the Arthurian cycle and the Grail legend, much of their symbolism having been incorporated into that order. . . ."[19]

The Discoveries of Frederick Bligh Bond

Frederick Bligh Bond (1864–1945), an honored and trusted authority on medieval architecture and church restoration, was hired by the Church of England to be the Director of Excavations for Glastonbury, after the Church of England acquired the site of the ruins of Glastonbury Abbey.

Bond was extraordinarily successful in his excavations and uncovered the foundations of previously unknown parts of the old Abbey. One such discovery was the foundation and the walls of

St. Edgar's Chapel to the east of the main body of the Abbey. It is Mr. Bond to whom we should be grateful for the information regarding Joseph's circular church. *Bond felt that Glastonbury Abbey embodied in stone a cosmic message,* and it was evidently the wish of the builders to record it in that manner. There is a passage in Bond's *The Gate of Remembrance,* in which the ancient monks of the Abbey, by means of automatic writing, referred to earlier, tell of the sacred geometry of the foundations and the distances or measurements which contain encoded messages in stone of their doctrines which had been lost in the latter days. One message states: "That which the brethren of old handed down to us, we followed, ever building on their plan. As we have said, our Abbey was a message in ye stones. In ye foundations and ye distances be a mystery—the mystery of our Faith, which ye have forgotten and we also in ye latter days. . . ."[20]

In 1921, Dean Armitage Robinson of Wells, who was Bond's supervisor, commissioned Bond to follow the directions given on a plaque found among the Abbey ruins and possibly discover the true position of the monument (pillar or pyramid) erected by

—from a print by A. Coney, 1817

View of the Abbey

—from *The Gate of Remembrance* by Bligh Bond

Conjectural Reconstruction of the Interior of the Abbey (drawn in 1908)

Sketch of Glastonbury Abbey Before Its Destruction in 1539

Saint David in the sixth century. A discovery of this nature
would serve to prove the true extent of the sacred site, then in
danger of being lost. Bond did discover the stone pyramid or pillar. It was about 29 feet to the north of the now standing Norman Chapel, and it proved to be exactly in line with its eastern
wall, thus showing that the builders of the later chapel had faithfully adhered to the measures of the original builders of the Wattle Church. He also discovered beneath the remnants of the
monument a circular platform or foundation seven feet in diameter, of apparently very ancient workmanship and likely dating from the earliest period.

Attached to the St. David Pillar was a brass plaque with Latin
text. The plaque was added about 1400, and gives reference to

The Remains of a Pillar (about 7 feet wide) Excavated by Bligh Bond

St. David and the significance of the pillar. This plaque, which was later found among the Abbey ruins, probably replaced an earlier one. In the sixteenth century a print was made directly from the plaque by Spelman and published in his *Concilia*. The inscription, which I found in John Michell's book *New Light on the Ancient Mystery of Glastonbury*, was translated by John Goodall. Since then the plaque has been lost. Because of its importance, it is most fortunate that it was copied. The plaque reads:

"The 31st year after the Passion of the Lord twelve saints, among whom Joseph of Arimathea was the first, came here. They built in this place that church, the first in this realm, which Christ in honour of his mother, and the place for their burial, presently dedicated. St. David, archbishop of Menevia [i.e., Wales] rested here. To whom the Lord (when he was disposed to dedicate that church), appeared in sleep and recalled him from his purpose, also in token that the same Lord had first dedicated that church with the cemetery: He pierced the bishop's hand with his finger, and thus pierced, it appeared in the sight of many on the morrow. Afterwards indeed the same bishop as the Lord revealed, and the number of the saints in the same grew: added a chancel to the eastern part of this church and consecrated it in honour of the Blessed Virgin. The altar whereof, of priceless sapphire, he marked the perpetual memory of these things. And lest the site or size of the earlier church should come to be forgotten because of such additions, he erected this column on a line drawn southwest through the two eastern angles of the same church, and cutting it off from the aforesaid chancel. And in length was 60 feet westward from that line, its breadth was truly 26 feet; the distance from the center of this pillar from the midpoint between the aforesaid angles, 48 feet."[21]

St. David's pyramid or pillar was not the only monument of this nature in the area of the central chapel. Others are on record. Two are thought to have been opposite the south door of the chapel, and the remains of these still existed in the eighteenth century. It was customary to have two pillars, representing the male and female polarities, in front of the tabernacle.

The Church of England authorities, owners of the Abbey ruins, were pleased with his progress, but because Bond's discoveries were made by "psychic methods," the excavations and discoveries he uncovered were drawing many mystically inclined visitors to Glastonbury, which irritated the authorities. In 1918, when Bond published *The Gate of Remembrance*, he unfortunately revealed that beginning in 1907 he and his friend Captain John Allen Bartlett had been in regular contact with the spirit world through the medium of automatic writing. Publication of his book created a scandal and, without warning, the executive officials of the Church of England ordered the excavations closed and covered up, in many cases before exact measurement could be taken.

At this time all the arrangements for research, which had been carried on for over fourteen years by the Somerset Archaeological Society, were ended. Later the Church authorities and other archaeologists condemned Bond for abusing his responsibilities. Even though he had been extremely successful in his excavations, Bond was discredited and released from his position. His excavations were covered over, and the Church authorities even went so far as to remove the excavation records of the Edgar Chapel and other of his discoveries from the official Abbey plans. His books were also removed from the Abbey bookstall. There is every possibility he was getting too close to the secrets and treasures which the Church of England and the Masons did not want exposed.

In 546 St. David built a channel to the Wattle Church. Until that time it had remained essentially unchanged. In 603 the church was enclosed in a wooden structure with a leaden roof. These ancient timbers sheltered the sacred foundation site until 1184, when a great fire consumed everything. In 1185 the remains of the Wattle Church were encased in a rectangular building using the construction plans of the existing Chapel of St. Mary, and the Zodiac circle was laid in the stone floor. This was called the Norman Chapel of St Mary.

The dimensions and measurements used to build the old church were meant to tell a story. The new Chapel of St. Mary told the same story. The measurements north and south are marked in English feet. Those running east and west are marked in Royal or Babylonian cubits. These are the relative measures of the double equilateral triangle or Vesica Piscis—the great Arcanum of the ancient guilds of Temple Builders, the Masons.

The Church of Glastonbury, which held many of the treasures brought from Jerusalem, was forced to close its doors in 1539 by Henry VIII, who was destroying monasteries all over England. Glastonbury Abbey was pulled down stone by stone and set on fire. It is thought that the severe treatment of Glastonbury Abbey was due to its being the most prestigious of all the abbeys, and an important place of pilgrimage for Roman Catholics, whom Henry opposed. Abbot Whiting of the Abbey had conceded to some of Henry's demands, like agreeing to his divorce from Catherine, but there were certain other points he would not concede. He would not tell where the treasure was hidden when Glastonbury was pulled down. Because of this the Abbot was hanged and quartered, and parts of his body displayed throughout England.

John Leland, an agent of Henry, spent twelve years going about the great monasteries and other libraries of England and Wales in order to search out their contents. When he reached Glastonbury, Abbot Whiting opened the library to him. Leland made a statement to the effect that he had been awestruck with what he had found in the Abbey library.

Regarding the Wattle Church, J. W. Taylor writes as follows: ". . . its dimensions correspond roughly with those of the Jewish tabernacle. . . . There reputedly built by Jewish builders stood the original wattled church or Lady Chapel, built as the Tabernacle was set up, and as the Temple was built with the House of God to the west of the sacred enclosure; and, opening out from it, directly continuous with it, toward the east where we are standing grew the great church—or what has been the great church—of St. Peter and St. Paul, one of the greatest, or perhaps the greatest, of all English churches."[22] Interestingly, the first Christian church of England was built by Jewish builders.

Masonic Connection

In 1897 the wattle and daub building became the property of the Church of England, which was made manifest during the Lambeth Conference in 1897. It was repored that a large number of bishops from all over the world, as well as from Britain and Ireland, assembled on August third on the Abbey grounds, where, during an address to the bishops, it was emphasized that Joseph's arrival and construction work in Glastonbury were actual facts of history. This address was given by Dr. G. F. Browne, then Bishop of Stepney. After the Lambeth Conference the whole of the Abbey grounds and the ruins were bought and made the property of the established Church of England.

This piece of information is particularly interesting to me because of my work with Marie and Manly P. Hall in connection with the Bruton Churchyard in Williamsburg, Virginia. Bruton was also owned by the Church of England. This is where many authorities believe an underground vault exists which once contained sacred treasures brought to America and buried by the Francis Bacon group. Once the contents of the vault were secretly moved from Williamsburg, the Church of England gave the property of Bruton Church to the United States government. (See chapter 12.) There seems to be a large link or connection between the Church of England and the Masonic Order, who are still guarding many secrets—among them that of the Ark of the Covenant and its various locations throughout the world.

On June 22, 1908, a Thanksgiving Service was held in the Glastonbury ruins. In attendance on behalf of the Crown were the Prince and Princess of Wales, later to become King George V and Queen Mary. The Archbishop of Canterbury and a large number of clergy also took part. Since that day an annual pilgrimage to Glastonbury takes place on the last Saturday of June and the ecclesiastical leaders of the Church of England rededicate themselves to Christ.

Sir Francis Bacon, Dr. John Dee and the Ark

In the seventeenth century, Sir Francis Bacon was the Lord High Chancellor of England under James I, the highest possible office next to the King. He was responsible for founding the Rosicrucian movement (part of the Philosophical Empire) and also produced a body of literature which included the Shakespeare writings (which are better explained in chapter 13), and was responsible for the King James version of the Bible.

Dr. John Dee was born in Wales in 1527, a physician, philosopher, scientist, astrologer, alchemist, cabalist, mathematician, as well as a diplomatic emissary of Queen Elizabeth I and her personal astrologer. Doctor Dee was absorbed in the metaphysics of the Hermetic tradition.

Sir Francis Bacon and Dr. John Dee were part of the adept group which were in process of forming the democracy of an enlightened Republic of America. This was part of the great plan:

—from *A True & Faithful Revelation, etc.* (London, 1659)

Dr. John Dee

the Republic of the Americas would be the Utopia, the Zion, the physical structure demonstrating the principles of the Ark of the Covenant. It was necessary for the physical Ark to reach America and the logical persons to carry out this plan were Sir Francis Bacon and Dr. John Dee.

—from *The Works of Jacob Cats* (Amsterdam, 1655)

Lampado Trado

The illustration above is taken from the Works of Jacob Cats. He was one of the Guild members and, as befitting the time, his illustration is filled with symbols. Remember, secrecy was necessary because at the time Cats' book was published, it was dangerous to one's good health to publish any philosophy that threatened the political power of church or state. One of the symbols Cats used is the extravagantly large Rose shown here on Bacon's shoe buckle, indicating the Rose Cross or the Rosicrucians. This particular kind of rose shoe buckle appears on the statue of Lord Bacon above his supposed tomb in St. Michael's Church at St. Albans. Dr. Dee, represented as the old man, is handing to Bacon a lamp, symbolizing the light of knowledge being passed from Dee the elder to Bacon the younger. Notice that the "light" is being passed over an underground vault, suggesting a knowledge about something buried.

It is known that the famous Dr. Dee visited Glastonbury on a number of occasions, one being in or around the year 1582. He was apparently drawn to Glastonbury along with his psychic companion Edward Kelley, and many visits are reported.

In his fascinating *New Light on the Ancient Mystery of Glastonbury*, John Michell makes an observation of Dr. John Dee that relates to the Ark: "In the 16th century, soon after the Abbey's dissolution, the sage John Dee sought the stone among its ruins, and is said to have learnt its secrets with the aid of his spirit medium, Edward Kelley. . . ."[23] This is the stone Dr. Dee was searching for and his instrument of finding it would have been the psychic Edward Kelley. The stone is also called The Philosopher's Stone or the Ark.

John Michell continues: "The average pilgrim would have known or cared nothing about number, geometry, sacred measures and the priestly arts. Yet the holy atmosphere which the pilgrims of the Abbey came to experience was sustained by these arts; and they in turn were derived from a traditional code of wisdom, transmitted through the Mystery schools and symbolized by the philosopher's stone. . . ."[24]

Underground tunnels around Glastonbury Abbey were investigated by Bligh Bond in his research, and it is reported that little research has been done since then. Bond thought there were four main tunnels attached to the Abbey. Three of these tunnels have been partially verified. When I was in Glastonbury in 1995, I talked with a woman at the front desk of the George and Pilgrims Hotel on High Street (built in 1475), and she told me there was indeed a tunnel which was partly open that still ran between the Abbey and this Hotel. The monks formerly used this hotel as the lodging place for their guests and pilgrims. In bad weather they would come and go through the tunnel. Because this area was once a marsh, it is reasonable to think that those same tunnels would now have become partly covered by marshy soil that had receded.

In addition to providing shelter from climate and weather, these tunnels would have provided a way for the monks to go undetected into the Abbey, its shrines and the crypt of the Lady Chapel. It is conceivable that this is the manner in which John Dee and Francis Bacon were able to take the Ark of the Covenant, have it in their possession for awhile, and recreate it. Then, when finished, replace it. There is also the possibility that other copies could have been made by Francis Bacon at this time, to be placed in other locations in Britain, America and other countries. Both Bacon and Dee would have had the authority to carry out this covert operation because of their high positions in the Freemasonic or Rosicrucian order.

I came across an intriguing article written by Patricia Villiers-Stuart called "Bend Me a Maze." She quotes a piece from an American magazine, the *East-West Journal*, by historian Andrew R. Rothovius titled "The Adams Family and the Grail Tradition: The Untold Chronicle of the Dragon Persecution." It seems that in 1823, three years before he died, John Adams, the second president of the United States, had a flat stone inscribed and put on the grave of his great-great-grandfather who had come to America as a settler in 1639. The inscription reads: "In memory of Henry Adams who took his flight from the Dragon persecution in Devonshire in England and alighted with eight sons near Mount Wollaston."[25]

The article goes on to explain that the Dragons were a group of people who looked forward to a more harmonious way of life which they wanted to establish in America. they derived their name from the Druids, who were also called "Dragons"—those who knew how to control the ley lines, often called the "Dragon lines" of the geodetic earth currents.

At the beginning of the seventeenth century, many famous names were associated with the Dragons, including Thomas Hariot, the mathematician; his pupil Sir Walter Raleigh, who wrote *History of the World*; Dr. John Dee; Christopher Mar-

lowe; and others. These men belonged to Francis Bacon's group
of Rosicrucians. While some Dragons lingered on in Devonshire
and remained a persecuted minority, others emigrated to the new
colonies which would eventually become the United States.

It is interesting to observe that Ms. Villiers-Stuart mentions in
her article that in the State of Vermont, in one of the earliest settled areas, is a town named Glastonbury. This American Glastonbury has a reputation for being a mysterious place. There
have been many disappearances over the years and numerous
UFO sightings. One U.S. correspondent described Glastonbury,
Vermont, as "a gateway to another dimension." This would
surely be an apt description of the British Glastonbury.

Glastonbury is the link between the old world and the new
world—the link between the ancient worlds of Egypt, Jerusalem,
Rome, Greece and the modern world of England and America.
Glastonbury exists as the blending of the old Mysteries with the
new, with the Christ consciousness—not Christ himself, but
Christ's message, which is the new covenant, the new way of being. It was in the "New World" of the Americas that the Masons
resolved to establish a country to be built upon the firm foundations of this new consciousness.

The New Jerusalem, Glastonbury, and the Old Jerusalem were
built upon a system of numbers patterned after the heavens. A
society ordered in such a manner upon these principles will spon-
taneously reflect order between nature and humankind.

There is a prophecy known to have existed in the Glastonbury
Abbey Library before the dissolution. It was written by Melkin,
who is commonly identified as a Welsh bard and chieftain who
lived at the time of King Arthur and Merlin. The prophecy was
lost during the dissolution of the Abbey, but was last quoted in
John of Glastonbury's book *Chronicle*, written in the fourteenth
century, which is now also lost. As it now stands, the prophecy
is incomplete. It has been translated, adapted and added to by
a succession of copyists. One of the fragments preserved indicates
that the tomb of St. Joseph of Arimathea, together with the Grail
talisman, will one day be discovered. It indicates the recovery of
the Grail and a Golden Age restored. (For more information on

this prophecy see John Michell's *New Light on the Ancient Mystery of Glastonbury*, page 161.)

An excellent channel, Victoria Ransom, who lives in Los Angeles, brought through from spirit the following prophecy, which was given to me while writing this book.

It is predicted that in the next ten to twenty years, the Ark in Glastonbury will be returned to Jerusalem, the Holy Land. When this happens, the Holy Land will be reconstituted and Jerusalem made a Holy City under a new enlightened United Nations. Because Jerusalem is claimed by all nationalities, Israel must allow the entire area around Jerusalem to become an international city in order for peace to come to the Middle East. It is inevitable that if Israel does this, war and aggression against the Jewish State will stop. Jerusalem is a holy spot.

Glastonbury was chosen to hold the Ark because it was known that Glastonbury would never be ravaged by war. This treasure was not returned to the Holy Land because the disturbances now happening were foreseen. It is predicted that when the Ark of Solomon's Temple returns to Jerusalem, it will be our second opportunity to raise our sights to the Christ Consciousness—the beginning of a golden age.

CHAPTER 12

THE MIDDLE AGES AND THE PHILOSOPHIC EMPIRE

efore we continue with how the Ark of the Covenant reached America, it is important to discuss the movement of the philosophical schools in Southern France during the Middle Ages. Each played an important role in bringing forth the Masonic Plan which culminated in the forming of the Republic of America. Included here are the stories of (1) the Catharists, who were largely responsible for starting the Puritan movement to America; (2) the Guilds, which brought forth through ciphers and codes the publication of books dealing with the projected reformation of the arts and sciences; (3) the Troubadours, whose stories and fables were taught through the power of the mind and heart, which required cultivation before a universal reformation could be brought about; and (4) the Knights Templars, whose teachings were accomplished through the construction of Cathedrals and Churches, the formations of which, on an energetic level, raised human consciousness to a new level and heralded the beginnings of the Renaissance.

The Catharists

The term *Catharists* or *Cathars* was used to apply to the pre-Reformation reformers whose stronghold stretched from Northern Spain across the southern provinces of France in the area termed the Languedoc.

There was considerable turmoil in southern France during the twelfth and thirteenth centuries. It is necessary to consider the fate of the Catharists (1200–1300) to appreciate the degree of organized resistance that developed against the remnants of the pagan philosophical schools still functioning at this time in southern France. So thoroughly were the Catharist doctrines destroyed by the Roman Church and its Inquisition, that it is almost impossible to reconstruct their total belief systems. They believed in the ultimate salvation of all people, and were devout Christians, but they rejected the workings of the Church. The Catharists baptized by the laying on of hands, and they taught reincarnation. Most importantly, their teachings were about love and compassion, much like the teachings of Christ.

The Gospel of John was quite early translated into Provencal, the language of the area of southern France where the Catharists resided. This gospel offered a theory of life that thousands understood and that they could apply to their own lives. It was a religion that was a spiritual interpretation of Christ himself. Montségur Castle, built by the Catharists high on a mountain top, so as to be near heaven, was one of the most extraordinary sites in the world. This was the Great Grail Castle that the Grail Questors searched for tirelessly—an initiation center known for the great spiritual treasure it held. Because of the Gospel of John, which centered on southern France, the worship of early Christians peaked in this area, where this new form of Christianity was referred to as *Catharism* (the word derives from the Greek *katharos*, or "pure"). After the Catharists were massacred by the Roman Catholic Church, the remaining Cathars, known as Puritans, fled to America where they were responsible for legislating religious tolerance.

By the year 1200, Rome was beginning to be alarmed that this renegade sect and its beliefs might threaten the Church. In addition, the rich barons and lords of Northern Europe coveted the rich cities and land in the south of France and were all too happy for an excuse to acquire this land for themselves. The Pope gave them the excuse they sought and enlisted them to act as "storm troopers" on behalf of the Church. In 1209 the Pope of Rome sent some 30,000 knights and foot soldiers from Northern Europe to war on the whole of southern France. The war lasted forty years.

In exchange for their faithful service, the Church of Rome promised the army remission of all their sins and an assured place in heaven. In addition, they were allowed to take all the loot they could steal. Towns, cities and crops of southern France were pillaged and destroyed. Whole populations were exterminated. In one town alone, Beziers, some 15,000 men, women, and children were slaughtered. The Church of Rome sanctioned and orchestrated a total blood-bath of the entire area of southern France— the first holocaust in Western History.

In March of 1244, near the end of the massacre, Montségur, the castle of the Catharists, was besieged for ten months. Before the Roman Catholic army descended upon Montségur for their final victory, four Catharist men and a guide descended the sheer western face of the mountain in the middle of the night in order to take their secret treasure to safety. It is likely that this treasure, so important to the Catharists, was hidden at Rennes-le-Château, the "Holy Sanctuary," about half-an-hour's ride from Montségur.

It is known that the Cathars were part of the community of Rennes-le-Château. During this time the Church of Rome preached against the heretical and sacrilegious "Grail Romances" which were then circulating. Is it possible that these Grail Romances were too close to the truth? Montségur was known as the Grail Castle. Otto Rohn, author of *Croisade contre la Graal*, claimed that the Grail Castle in the famous story of the Grail, *Munsalvaesche*, written by Wolfram von Enschenbach, is Montségur. It is also interesting to note that after World War II the Germans excavated in the area of the castle. What treasure were they looking for?

And so the question arises: what was the treasure that brought the Roman Catholic Church to southern France to murder the Catharists? It is most likely *the true story of Christ*, which undoubtedly would have endangered the myth created by the Ro-

—Picture taken by Glen Craney

The Castle of Montségur

man Catholic Church. Also, the only thing that could have been taken down the side of a very steep mountainside would have been something small like a book or manuscript.

The adepts of the Catharists and other Masonic Orders of this area did not perish with the fall of their schools. It is very likely that they chose to remain hidden in order to create new channels for the further teaching of their doctrines. These groups continually changed their appearances over the years to meet the new requirements. There has been no break in the esoteric teaching of truths handed down through the ages, even when the physical institutions have often been destroyed by the cruelty of an uneducated world.

The Guilds

Members of Guilds were craftsmen and artisans who used the language of their crafts to conceal the mysticism of the great movement of reformation that was in process as they enshrined the ancient teachings in the forms they created.

The persecution of the Catharists, Albigenses, Bogomiles and other groups of the Masonic Order scattered the adepts of the various sects over the entire continent of Europe. The higher initiates of the Order wandered about Europe disguised as troubadours, peddlers, merchants, and journeymen. These artisans and craftsmen established themselves in their chosen crafts and from them many distinguished printing establishments began.

In the late sixteenth and early seventeenth centuries, an unusual situation started with the great period of publication of books and tracts dealing with alchemy, cabalah, Rosicrucianism, and the improvement of the arts and sciences. Most of the books were published anonymously. In many cases it has been found that elaborate ciphers were incorporated into texts along with unusual emblems and symbolic figures. These elaborate programs involved printers in several countries operating with extreme secrecy.

In the face of bribery and persecution they kept the secrecy of the authors. We can assume the printers, typesetters and engravers joined the same invisible organization as the authors, philosophers, and scholars who wrote the material. Also the bookbinders, for they belonged to a Guild and were in a position to introduce many unusual emblems and figures on the covers of books.

An example is the famous jug watermark found in the paper on which most of the first editions of the writings of Lord Francis Bacon were printed. This jug is also found in many publications of the early Rosicrucians. The jug represents a vase or pitcher, often shown filled with fruit or grapes. The writer Harold Bayley believes that this vase is the symbol for the Holy Grail. He supports his view with examples which trace the vase directly to the Guild's papermakers.

With the invention of printing, the legends and fables of the Troubadours and Jongleurs gradually ended in their final published forms. The printers included secret marks in their books to indicate the presence of a cipher or double meaning. It is likely that the writers themselves were *bound into a secret society and were operating from a formal plan.*

—from the dedication page of the 1628 edition of
The Anatomy of Melancholy

Watermark Device
The heart with the crucified rose makes reference to Rosicrucian material.
Baconian ciphers were usually printed on paper bearing Rosicrucian
or Masonic watermarks

European public buildings, tombs, cathedrals and libraries were adorned with devices which were in no way part of the approved designs. Symbols and signatures were concealed in obscure places, but hardly a medieval structure has survived which does not include the symbols and signatures of the Secret Orders. The geometry of planets and stars was used and reproduced to the smallest level. The barely noticeable marks carved as Masonic signatures on individual stones were emblematical of the structure of the universe.

This amazing silent conspiracy extended through the entire world of the arts. The dissemination of the material was possible only because the Guilds and Unions were aware of the high purpose for which the Guild system had been organized.

The Guilds were composed of artisans and formed a link between the Troubadours and the trade unions. The secrets of their arts and crafts were carefully guarded by the Guild Masters,

MEDIEVAL SCOTTISH

SARACEN

EGYPTIAN

PERSIAN

MURISTANI

SYRIAN

JERUSALEM

MEDIEVAL ENGLAND

MEDIEVAL FRANCE

NINETEENTH CENTURY ENGLISH AND SCOTTISH

—from *Sacred Geometry* by Nigel Pennick

Masonic Signatures

whose crests dangled from hooks around the great Guild Cup, representing the Holy Grail, in the center of their Lodge.

Each Guild taught the universal teachings in the language of its own art. The Guild system was especially well rooted in Germany and England and was well established on the whole European continent. The world thought the Guilds were simple trade unions, but in reality they were influenced to some degree by Masonry.

The Guilds championed the human cause and honest practice. They protected their members and society from unreasonable exploitation. What better place could be found in which to plant the seeds for the formation of an enlightened democratic society than the Republic of the Americas!

The Troubadours

The Troubadours addressed the wrongs of Rome and took up the defense of the oppressed. They were celebrated as the true soldiers of the Christ. They were heretics banned by the Church because they attacked all forms of abuses of the Priesthood. Great numbers of the upper classes became Troubadours, and wandered to courts and castles spreading their doctrine.

The Troubadours were active in southern France, northern Spain, and Italy between the eleventh and fourteenth centuries. As wandering poets and minstrels, these singers of the Mysteries concealed profound spiritual truths in their songs, stories, myths and fables. These men and a few women, numbering about four hundred, were members of a secret society dedicated to uncovering the powers of the mind and heart that needed to be cultivated before it was possible to bring about a *universal reformation of mankind.*

The Troubadours, some of whom were kings, like Richard the Lion-Hearted, or queens, charmed listeners with their poetry, music, acting, and jesting. The teachings they disseminated in this way were principally the teachings of chivalry, which were to inspire others to become virtuous, good-mannered, kind and courageous. When individuals attained this state, they were ready to receive the higher teachings.

It was from the Troubadours that many of those myths and stories of the Age of Chivalry began, including the moral fables that right always conquers, and that the only true nobility is nobility of the spirit. Many children's fairy tales were originally sung by the Troubadours. These minstrels found ways to adapt the legends to their own purposes.

The teachings of the Troubadours were called "Courts of Love." Under the guise of romantic passion, the Troubadours preached the gospel of the divine love of God for humans, and that human love alone can unite humanity. They sang and wrote passionate ballads to the fair lady of their hearts. However, only the Troubadours knew that this lady was the Isis of Sais, the Sophia of the Gnosis, or other goddesses.

Minstrels concealed their knowledge from the profane, the Church and State. But the Church and State were aware that rebellion threatened if the Troubadours' teachings were successful in setting up their great Court of Love—world democracy; so they destroyed all that was structured by the singing sages.

The Inquisition was set up to preserve the social status. The members of the Philosophical Empire were convicted on some empty pretext, but the true reason for their destruction was their subversive political plotting against ecclesiastical and state authority. Once again the champions of the cause perished on the stake or the rack.

It is thought that the poet Dante Alighieri (1265–1321) was a Troubadour. Gabriele Rossetti (1783–1854), professor of Italian Language and Literature in King's College, London, was convinced that Dante was indeed a member of a *Secret Society*, and that his verses contained a hidden meaning. Rossetti explains that the rise of a new literature in the eleventh and twelfth centuries afforded the Secret Sects a weapon more powerful than any they had previously used. Rossetti explains that all paths of literature had been put into action by these secret assailants in poetry, romance, history, and science. Traces of their presence affected

—from *La Divina Commedia* (Firenze, 1892)

Dante Alighieri

all nations. The love poems and Love Courts of the Troubadours were vehicles for active political conspiracy.

In *Morals and Dogma*, Albert Pike points out that Dante's *Divine Comedy* contained the allegorical formula of the great secrets of the Society of the Roses-Croix (Rosicrucians). Although Dante's fame is derived principally from his *Divina Commedia*, his *Vita Nuova* links him most closely to the mystical speculation of the Troubadours.

The Knights Templars

The early Christine Church of the Apostles formed a militant organization for its preservation and protection. This organization included the Knights Templars, Knights of the Cross, the Knights Hospitalers and similar organizations. Eventually this whole movement became what we now know as the Renaissance and spread across Europe, culminating in England with the forming of the Rosicrucians.

In addition to the lost treasure of the Catharists from Montsegur, there also exists the vanished treasure of the Knights Templars in southern France. Members of this group claimed that they alone were in possession of the inner mysteries of Christ. One of the landmarks of the pentagon of Rennes-le-Château is the castle of Blanchefort. It was the Grand Master of the Templars, Bertrande de Blanchefort, who commissioned excavations in this area.

At present the secret of the Rennes Valley is known by the inner circle of the Masons or Templars known today as the Priors of Sion, who still keep this story hidden. Without a doubt one of the reasons for the persecution and final annihilation of the Templars was their holding of the secret of the early history of Christianity.

H. P. Blavatsky, in her book *Isis Unveiled*, refers to the Knights Templars as "the last European secret organization which, as a body, had in its possession some of the Mysteries of the East." Blavatsky informs us that the Templars "reverenced the doctrines of alchemy, astrology, magic, cabalistic talismans, and adhered to the secret teaching of their chiefs in the East." The chiefs in the East are the Adepts or Mahatmas of the hierarchy who have formed the order of Masonic tradition which bears witness to the Divine, organized, predetermined plan.

In their first nine years, the Templars lived in poverty. Hugh de Payen and Geoffrey of St. Omer had one war horse between them. This is symbolized on the great seal of the Templars, which shows two knights seated on one horse. The influence of the Order grew rapidly. It appealed to the concept of chivalry which dominated many minds of the time. In 1128, the Council of Troyes acknowledged the principles of the Knights Templars. At this time, St. Bernard prepared a code for their spiritual and temporal guidance.

Candidates for initiation gave their property to the Order, so while each member was individually poor, the Templars as a group became enormously wealthy. The Grand Master of the Templars ranked as a prince in all the courts of Europe.

One thing that set the Templars apart from others was their

Seal of the Knights Templars

high level of literacy. During the Middle Ages, royalty, Templars, and knights were about the only people who could read and write. The Templars embraced knights and noblemen, architects, bankers and true Masons in their ranks. The most highly educated noblemen of the time were the Templars, many of whom could read Greek and Latin; some knew of the Mystical Cabalah through their connection to the Cabalah centers of Spain and France. Much of the knowledge they used to build their Gothic cathedrals, using sacred geometry, came from ancient cabalistic texts.

There is every reason to believe that the Templars were connected to these esoteric centers and that the purpose of their Crusade to Jerusalem was to gather information of a similar nature. Before Christ died, many groups in the Holy Land were already studying sacred geometry, Pythagorean theories and the Cabalah. Wherever there was a Cabalah center, one could find information concerning the contents of the Ark of the Covenant.

The Knights Templars were founded in 1118 by Hugh de Payen and Geoffrey of St. Omer. These two, together with seven other

French knights, went to Jerusalem with the intention to guard the roads leading to the Holy Land. Giving this some thought, how could just nine men guard all the roads to Jerusalem and make them safe? Nevertheless, they were determined to guard the roads of Christian pilgrimage to the shrine of the Holy Land.

I think the Templars already knew what they were looking for when they went to the Holy Land, and that their covert operation had something to do with the esoteric brotherhood movement that was gaining ground throughout Europe. The secret mission of the Templars was probably formulated in France and spearheaded by St. Bernard, one of the driving forces behind the Crusades.

When these nine Templars presented themselves to King Baudouin II of Jerusalem, he gave them the privilege of the use of a building very close to the site of the original Temple of Solomon. The covert operation was the search for buried treasure rumored to be hidden below the old stable of Solomon's Temple. Tradition has it that the Templars found the hidden relics of Solomon's Temple and took them back to Europe.

Gothic Cathedrals; Labyrinths

The Templars made good use of the knowledge they had gained in Jerusalem. In a relatively short time, about 150 years after their visit to Jerusalem, an extraordinary transformation began to take place in Europe. This was the use of sacred architecture or sacred geometry in the building of the Gothic cathedrals. This period of Gothic architecture, construction in its esoteric form, marked a subtle yet significant change in consciousness and creative vision.

An influx of several different sciences was necessary in order to design and construct these buildings. They were built using forms of geometry sometimes called trivium and quadrivium. The study of quadrivium consisted of combining the knowledge of arithmetic, geometry, music and astronomy. These studies trained the mind to comprehend divine truths, for these disciplines were linked to the sacred numbers found in all things. *Be-*

cause Gothic cathedrals were built upon these principles, they would serve as models that would lead the mind to its sacred source. The Master Masons who built these buildings had to be knowledgeable in the basic sciences mentioned and the science of frequency, or the sound within the stone that they were using. They also needed to know the science of the human body—anatomy, physiology, psychology, and alchemy.

Another important factor in the building of these cathedrals was an understanding of the system of geomancy, or earth science, which has to do with the ley lines, or energy lines, that run within the earth. These earthly meridians consist of a dodecahedral energy network that underlies the whole of the earth, and can be considered as God's acupuncture system for our planet.

The human and earthly ley lines are interconnected with the planets to create an interlocking structural pattern operating between heaven and earth. Like the meridians in the human body, the earth ley lines contain subtle electrical currents that run through the earth and are carried by land, water and air. An energy vortex is created at the various places where these currents meet or cross, and it is on these power spots that the ancient pagans (Druids, Celts, Mithraic and other groups) built their temples. These locations are known as sacred sites of the earth, and they are actually part of the inner workings of the planet itself.

Very often new temples or cathedrals were built on top of the ruins of ancient temple sites. The art and science of geomancy was used to place these structures in special physical alignment with the earth. There are two major astronomical seasons a year when sacred buildings were laid out and oriented using the position of the sun in its relation to the earth at the equinoxes and solstices.

Some of the major cathedrals of France—like Chartres, Reims and Amiens—are consecrated to the Great Mother, and for this reason were given such names as Notre Dame (or Mary). When visiting these cathedrals, one was expected to visit them in progression at certain seasons or festivals of the year. This ritual was important to follow because Gothic cathedrals were built over certain energy or vortex spots within the earth and were designed so that the ley lines were used as amplifiers to create a specific effect upon the bodies of the visitors as they progressed from one cathedral to the next.

Gothic architecture appeared on the scene almost overnight. The Templars, we must remember, were rich and had the means of funding and hiring the artisans needed. The Masonic Guild was also probably partly responsible for funding these spiritual monuments.

In ordinary architecture, gravity is relied upon to maintain support of the structure through its weight. Gothic architecture is quite different. Here we find a system of flying buttresses, sweeping external structures invented in 1180, very much like the pillars of Stonehenge where the upward push on the stone combines with the pull of gravity. This produces a resonance within the stone itself. This resonance can then be keyed to certain musical notes. Each cathedral was designed with a particular key or tuning that involved certain notes. And each cathedral was tuned in a particular way. This is one of the reasons they were walked in a certain progressive order. Some of this tuning remains, but our modern world has created a great deal of interference. The wide open spaces that once surrounded the cathedrals are no longer there. Such spaces were purposely left open to act as resonating cavities.

There were also other kinds of esoteric symbology built into the cathedrals. As mentioned earlier, these buildings were often laid out on the sites of earlier pagan temples and usually constructed on a hill. Often they were built over an underground well or spring traditionally associated with healing. In the crypt of the Gothic cathedrals, a cross pattern was laid out. Underneath the building where the two arms of the cross meet was the area of the sacred crypts. These sacred crypts, called the "Royal Arches," were copied after the Temple of Solomon. If the Master Mason in charge of building the cathedral was knowledgeable, he designed the Royal Arches under the building.

The Templars became great teachers through the architecture of their buildings. The experience of going to church in a Gothic cathedral was special because it was the single place where one could be exposed to art, music, literature and, as a result, be elevated out of one's usual daily experience into the realm of spirit. These were great temples of mass initiation, and they were established all over Europe.

The cathedrals themselves were designed to have a specific effect on the people who visited them. Candidates for initiation were prepared esoterically with regard to the symbology of the cathedrals, and their consciousness was raised in many subtle ways. An example of this is the stained glass windows in which each color generates a certain frequency as light passes through it.

As the initiates or candidates for initiation entered the several doors of the cathedral at certain times of the year, they observed various works of art, tapestries and sculptures, each of which was designed to affect the subconscious mind and the subtle bodies of the initiates, who would turn at particular levels and pay homage to the different altars. At those times, the colored lights of the stained glass windows would play upon the face and body of the initiate. In addition to the visual effects created by the stained glass and art work, certain Gregorian chants would be sung in the cathedrals during certain times of the year, which built up a resonance within the stones.

The vaults of the ceiling were constructed in such a way as to create a four-dimensional volume of space that would act as an acceleration chamber (similar to those created in the Great Pyramid). Not all of these chambers were constructed using the dimensions of the pyramids; there were other geometries involved. As one stands on the floor of a Gothic cathedral in France, for example, the energy might only be slightly felt, if at all. But, if one were able to raise oneself half-way between the ceiling and the floor, one would feel an immense power. The top part of the cathedral, where vaults are often 120 feet high, is the focal point of the sacred geometry. Chartres Cathedral is an example of an attempt to reconstruct some of the energy chambers found in the Great Pyramid and the Temple of Solomon.

Labyrinths were inscribed on many cathedral floors. The labyrinth serves as a symbol of the spiritual pilgrimage, of the progression from the outer veils of matter to the inner light and revelation of God. The labyrinth's proportional matrix might also be seen to represent those harmonic laws which could lead one to realization and unity. The prepared candidate would walk the labyrinth and, in the shifting of the body and eyes from one angle to the other, allow the various qualities of light, sound, and proportion to play upon his or her subtle body. In this way, certain things could be seen within the architecture or the tapestries and art. In other words, walking the labyrinth produced a psychological as well as an etheric effect upon the body of whoever was consciously walking that particular path.

This goes back to ancient traditions when dance was the first form of prayer and a process of physical alignment. All these patterns had an effect upon the brain. The labyrinths had their part in tuning not only the body but also the circuitry within the brain itself, which was an initiation at a certain level. Townspeople and peasants alike went to church on a regular basis at this time, so we could say that the subtle bodies and the subconscious of the masses were being prepared for receiving greater light. This was, indeed, a great gift the Templars brought to Europe.

During initiations in ancient times, labyrinths were designed as an underground temple, which was nothing but the copy of a spiral or maze pattern. Traveling the labyrinth took the initiate from the outer world to the inner world of consciousness and then back out again. The labyrinth was the journey that the initiate took from the microcosm (earth) to the macrocosm (heaven) and back out to the microcosm. The word "labyrinth" symbolizes "finding the path of God."

Remains of these labyrinths have been found among American Indians, Hindus, Persians, Egyptians, Greeks, and in the cathedrals of Europe. Some labyrinths were merely involved pathways lined with stones or some part of a garden; others were literally miles of gloomy caverns under temples or hollowed out from the sides of mountains. Always, they were used as part of the initiation ceremony into the ancient Mysteries.

Labyrinths were also symbolic of the involvements or illusions of the lower world through which wanders the soul of humanity in search of truth. In the labyrinth dwells the lower animal man (with the head of the bull), who seeks to destroy the soul entangled in the maze of worldly ignorance. In this relation, the bull-man, who represents the Minotaur-like Egyptian Serapis, is the adversary who tests the souls of those who dare to seek union with the gods. The labyrinth was also used to represent the solar system, with the bull-man representing the sun dwelling in the mystic maze of its planets, moons, and asteroids. The reason one became tuned to a higher consciousness in walking the labyrinth was that one received the rhythms of the universe which the planets projected.

Today some cathedrals can be seen just as they were seven hundred years ago, with most of the stained glass and even their original sculpture intact. In Chartres the original choir stall with its gold, brass, and precious stones, which once added to the subtle vibrations and made the cathedral a bright spectacle, are gone.

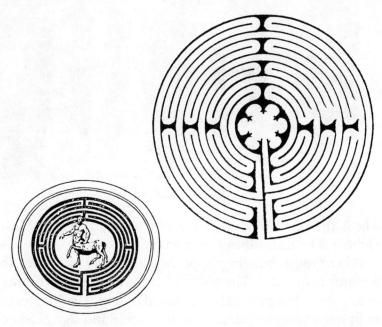

—from Montfaucon's *Antiquities*

Examples of Labyrinths

Chartres Cathedral

The National Cathedral in Washington D.C. was the last great cathedral to be built in this manner.

When Gothic buildings appeared, humanity was going through a major transition. The hidden Mysteries were becoming more available to the populace. As noted before, the Mysteries were built into these cathedrals, and the subtle and significant change the atmosphere of these buildings produced in people raised the consciousness of the masses.

CHAPTER 13

AMERICA AND THE ARK OF THE COVENANT

n this section I hope to convey the story of the Great Schools of initiates during that time of transition which led directly to the great social experiment, the founding of America in the Western Hemisphere. There was an uninhabited continent available in which people might build a nation according to the will of the Great Architect of the universe. The time of secrecy was ending. The "Invisible Empire," so often subtly suggested by the initiates could now build its house in the physical world.

The plans which had been held in readiness for centuries were put in motion. The Esoteric Orders of Asia, the Near East, and Europe were called to their assigned tasks. The conspiracy was to begin unfolding, and the initiates gathered to carry it out.

Up until this time, the Philosophical Empire was concerned mainly with the survival of knowledge. When the power of the Church to destroy all nonconformists had diminished, the Esoteric Orders began their emergence. The essential beliefs remained the same, but because both the Church and the State did everything possible to stop the progress of liberalism, it was necessary to maintain some secrecy.

Sir Francis Bacon, Shakespeare and the Rosicrucians

In the formation of the American Republic, it was the Rosicrucians who spearheaded the intellectual revolution. They believed in the existence of a secret doctrine (the Ark of the Covenant), pre-Christian in origin, handed down from great antiquity. They dedicated their program to the restoration of ancient philosophical systems in which human beings could reach a state of mutual understanding and spiritual integrity.

In 1660 a book was published in London titled: *New Atlantis*, begun by Sr. Francis Bacon, Lord Verulam, Viscount St. Alban's and completed by R. H. Esquire. Several authors have written that the *New Atlantis* provided a description of an existing Secret Society, with Bacon as founder. No student of Bacon's *New Atlantis* will fail to recognize the Masonic symbolism contained in this book. Francis Bacon's plan as laid out in the *New Atlantis* was to re-create and build a united brotherhood of the earth. The "New Atlantis" is the American continent, set apart for the great experiment of enlightened self-government. The explorers who opened the "New World" understood that they operated from a master plan.

Research confirms Sir Francis Bacon was the rightful heir to the throne of England, although history tells us that he was never acknowledged as such by his mother, Queen Elizabeth I, or his father, the Earl of Leicester. The infant Francis was given over to Sir Nicholas Bacon, Lord Keeper of the Great Seal of England and his wife Lady Ann Bacon. Elizabeth was known as the Virgin Queen. Even her marriage to Leicester was kept a secret. Elizabeth did, however, arrange for the young Francis Bacon to be given the highest education possible befitting an heir to the throne. Francis was a genius and he had a higher mission to fulfill.

Bacon was the founder of democracy and the true genius behind the colonization of America. The modern Freemasonic Order was profoundly influenced by, if not an actual outgrowth of, Francis Bacon's secret Society of Rosicrusse Freemasons, the symbols of which are permeated with Bacon's two great ideals: universal education and universal democracy.

Bacon brought education to the New World. He knew that without education personal belief systems lacked the conviction that would keep the individual free from domination by others. The fatal enemies of universal education are ignorance, superstition, and fear, the elements of the mind that keep the human soul in bondage. The Great Work was the perfect union of human purpose with the divine plan through understanding and working in harmony with the laws of Nature. Bacon set out to found a nation built on personal freedom of government and freedom of religion. Through the secret convening of the higher order of Masons and Rosicrucians, this vision of things to come was gradually introduced to a surprised world unaccustomed to thinking beyond the emergencies of the moment.

The greatest minds of England and Europe came together for his plan. A major element of the plan was to perpetuate the secrecy within an inner group of Initiates, while keeping the true purpose and plan unknown to the outer Order at large.

Francis Bacon, Baron of Verulam, Viscount St. Albans

Bacon became Lord Chancellor of England under King James I, and colonized the states of Virginia and the Carolinas in America. On the flag of the State of Virginia, we still see the goddess Pallas Athena, spear in hand, verifying for us what happened in the not-too-distant past. Athena also appears on many of the headings of Bacon's literature and on the headings of the Shakespeare plays and sonnets. This symbol was one of many codes and ciphers used by Bacon and his group to secretly tell about the history of the seventeenth century.

In a sense, Bacon exemplified the powers of the goddess by channeling this feminine energy into that of the masculine, which then allowed itself to be opened up and to merge with this feminine energy, transforming the heart of the nation. Bacon was an extraordinarily brilliant man. He knew that mankind, as a whole, sought to raise itself above the pigsty of materiality. He knew that all humans consciously or unconsciously aspired toward God. Bacon and his group set out ways to exemplify this aspiration and to show how it could be more easily attained. These educated and enlightened individuals must have realized that when one lives life according to higher values and tenets, one automatically becomes more sensitive to the feminine, nurturing side of creation

The Flag of Virginia

Pallas Athena, Goddess of Wisdom, known as the "Spear Shaker"
crowns the top of the Library of Congress in Washington, DC.

which, when combined with the masculine creative urge, assists in merging with the Divine.

Why, we might wonder, did Bacon (and his group) use Athena as his goddess representative? Athena represents the female side of intelligence—love, wisdom and truth. So Pallas Athena became Francis Bacon's symbol. Athena was considered the most important goddess of the enlightened democracies, which included Atlantis, Athens, and now the Republic of America.

Francis Bacon won the greatest minds of the British Isles and the European continent for co-workers in his stupendous task. Under his guidance, the "great plan" was incorporated and began showing up in innumerable writings by this secret group. The men who formed the nucleus of this group were initiated into the plan and sworn to absolute secrecy. They were poets and authors, and because they had gathered for the purpose of "shaking a lance at ignorance," they chose Athena, Goddess of the Muse, who was also called "The Spear-Shaker." They were known as the "Shakespeare Group."

The Supreme Council of the 33rd degree Scottish Rite of Freemasonry published an official paper called *The New Age*. In their April 1948 issue appeared an interesting article by A. Ueland, entitled "William Shakespear." While the author avoids any mention of the "Shakespear controversy," he does present indisputable evidence linking Masonry with the Shakespear works.[1]

It was Bacon's mission to bring enlightenment to human beings by appealing to their rational, scientific minds. He did this through poetry, literature, essays, the Bible, and government influence. Bacon wrote many books, some under his name and some under the name of poets and writers in his group. Included in this esteemed group were Lancelot Andrews, the great Anglican Archbishop, Toby Mathews, John Donne, Ben Jonson, Edmund Spenser, Sir Walter Raleigh, Francis Drake, George Withers, and many others. Nevertheless, Bacon was the guiding genius and mastermind behind the great plan.

Through Bacon and his group of writers, the Shakespeare writings were brought forth to explain the history of the period.

—Segment from Gustavi Seleni, *Cryptomenytices et Cryptographiae,* title page, 1624

Bacon, identified by his high hat of the Knights of the Helmet, is handing written matter to an actor identified by his Spear as Shakespear.

These historical facts had to be preserved to vindicate the shield of honor for the future generations and give a true and accurate account of the inception of the tremendous undertaking. This information could only be recorded in codes and ciphers for the safety of the group and to protect the messages. The man from Stratford, William Shakespeare, who could not even spell or write his name, was simply used as a guise.

The insightful and famed American writer Mark Twain, in his little booklet *Is Shakespeare Dead?* published in 1909, conveys to us that the man from Stratford, William Shakespeare, could not read or write and was too illiterate to be responsible for the wisdom and knowledge it took to write the plays. Ben Jonson summed it up in an incisive manner when he says of Sir Francis

Bacon: "Of greatness he could not want." Of the plays and of the man Shakespeare he says: "The most learned of works could not have been written by the least learned of men."

Shakespeare's Great Folio of 1623 is filled with Masonic symbolism and lore, and consideration for it is long overdue. A considerable segment of the first thirty-two degrees of Freemasonic ritualism is hidden in the text of the first Shakespeare folio. Masonic emblems are on the title pages of the folios, as well as on almost every book published by Bacon and his group. It has been said that the Freemasonry rituals are incorporated in Shakespearean works.

After the death of Queen Elizabeth, Sir Francis Bacon became Chancellor of England under King James I and headed the group responsible for editing and revising the King James version of the Bible. Bacon assembled men of great talents for this enormous undertaking—men of wide learning so that the Bible could be translated into many languages, just as the Ark of the Covenant had been translated into many languages by Dee and Bacon.

In the first edition of the King James Version of the Bible are one of those cryptic Baconian headpieces. It is thought by many scholars that Bacon cryptographically concealed in the Authorized Bible that which he dared not literally reveal in the text.

It is interesting to note that in the 46th Psalm of the King James Version of the Bible, the 46th word down from the first verse is the word SHAKE, and the 46th word up from the end is the word SPEAR. William T. Smedley writes in his book *Mystery of Francis Bacon*: "It will eventually be proved that the whole scheme of the Authorized [King James] Version of the Bible was Francis Bacon's."[2]

The original manuscripts of the Bible were given to Bacon by James I to check and edit, but the whereabouts of these original papers have never been found, nor have the originals of the Shakespeare writings. And yet it is reasonable to suppose that manuscripts of such importance would have been preserved. Some believe they could be and are in the vault of Bruton Church in America.

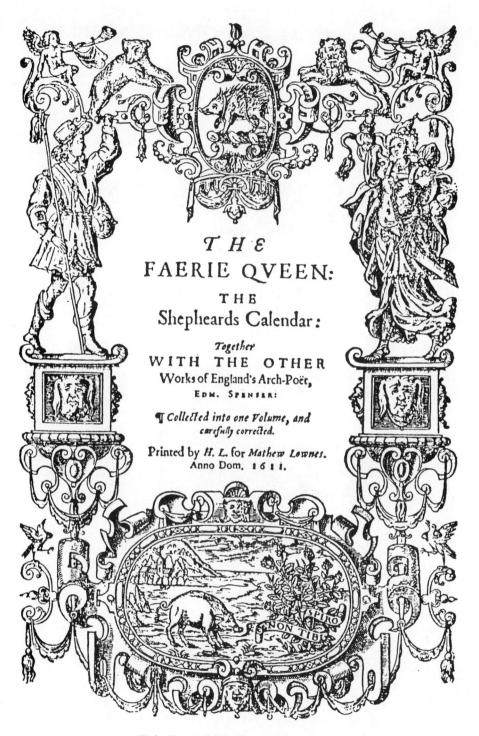

THE
FAERIE QVEEN:
THE
Shepheards Calendar :

Together
WITH THE OTHER
Works of England's Arch-Poët,
EDM. SPENSER:

¶ *Collected into one Volume, and*
carefully corrected.

Printed by *H. L.* for *Mathew Lownes.*
Anno Dom. 1611.

Title Page of *The Faerie Queene*
(1611 edition)

The first book of *The Faerie Queene*, by Edmond Spenser, showing Athena in the illustration.

—from the binding of a presentation copy of
Novum Organum, 1620

Francis Bacon's Boar Crest

—from *Alciati Emblemata*

A Baconian signature. Note the hog in the foreground.

As Chancellor of England and the genius behind the English colonization of America, Bacon was honored by many. Newfoundland issued a commemorative stamp honoring Bacon as the guiding spirit of the colonization scheme. Bacon and a select group of idealists built the foundations for a better world where truth could prevail and there could be an end to conflict, and delinquencies could be corrected. These principles are put forth in Bacon's book *New Atlantis*.

The first permanent English settlement in North America was established in Virginia in honor of Queen Elizabeth, the Virgin Queen. Sir George Sommers was appointed governor, in 1609, of the Colony of Virginia. When he sailed for the New World, his arrival was delayed when his ship foundered on the Hog Islands, so named because of the wild swine that infested the islands. Later, these islands were named the Bermudas.

Lord Bacon on a Stamp of Newfoundland

In 1609, James I granted a charter to the Bermuda Company. In 1612 Richard More and sixty colonists from Virginia settled on one of these islands. In that same year, coins were struck for use in the Bermudas named "hog money." The obverse of the shilling of this issue bears the legend "Sommer Islands" surrounding the figure of a wild boar. A ship under full sail is pictured on the reverse of the coin.

The boar is identical to the drawing of the crest of Lord Bacon, even to the curl of its porcine tail. The *Encyclopedia Britannica* (1946) states "the coins were struck in America, but numismatic catalogs describe them as being made for America." It would seem that the hog money was a clue bearing witness to the process of Bacon and the secret society directing the early colonization of America. (Also, a hog is certainly related to bacon.) The story is set forth in the Shakespeare play *The Tempest*.

To use Walter Raleigh's expression about Bacon: "And thy great genius in being concealed, is revealed." It is believed by some that Bacon feigned his death in 1626, disappeared from England, spent some time in European countries and later was deeply involved in the formation of the enlightened democracy of the Republic of America.

The Somers Islands Shilling

The Ark and Jamestown, Virginia

The logical place for the concealment of the Ark of the Covenant would be Virginia, America's first English colony. It is believed that Henry Blount, a true descendant of Sir Francis Bacon, who adopted the name Nathaniel Bacon after arriving in America, brought the records and a copy of the Ark to Jamestown, under great difficulties, and buried them under the Jamestown Church Tower in 1635. It is not possible to restore the exact pattern of the activities of this period because historical records were few and subject to destruction. It is thought that between 1610 and 1660 a great deal of material concerned with the development of the great plan for America was transferred for preservation and future use from Europe to the Western continent. The secret societies that were operating in Europe, like the Freemasons, Rosicrucians, and the Fellows of the Royal Society, had representatives in the colonies.

Reverend M. F. Carey, associate of the Philosophical Society of Great Britain, suggests, in his book *Freemasonry in All Ages*, that there is no documentary evidence of the introduction of Freemasonry into the United States, but it appears that it had an existence in America as early as the year 1606. Charles H. Merz gives credence to the belief that certain "Masonic" activities in America took place in the years between 1600 and 1620. He comments in his book *Guild Masonry in the Making* that there is much to indicate that the period of Bacon was the beginning of a secret Freemasonry "floor work," in America.

Once the Jamestown settlement had gained some order and permanence, descendants of the men who formed the original Baconian Society left England and settled in Jamestown. It was through this connection that the Great Plan began to evolve in America. There were marriages between the families of the original custodians of the philosophical heritage. The mingling of the blood of these settlers like the Bacons, produced many of America's prominent citizens.

Bacon's family was well represented in Virginia. They can be traced from Robert Bacon of Drinkstone, Suffolk, who was the father of Sir Nicholas Bacon, Lord Keeper of the Great Seal for Queen Elizabeth of England, to Nathaniel Bacon, who was the rebel who led Bacon's Rebellion in Virginia in 1676. There were many of the Bacon family who came to Virginia and were the channels for the transference of Lord Bacon's philosophy and projects.

When the Governor of Jamestown refused to protect the colonists from the neighboring Indian tribes, young Nathaniel Bacon defied the Governor, and a feud approaching revolution resulted. This feud ended by Nathaniel Bacon and his followers setting fire to the Jamestown settlement. This episode in history is referred to as "Bacon's Rebellion." It played an important part in the formation of the American national consciousness. Young Bacon's rebellion lasted about twenty weeks. It is said that he died of poison or malaria on October 1, 1676, while campaigning.

Bacon's Rebellion took place one hundred years before 1776, the date when the colonies of America declared themselves to be an independent nation. The causes of Bacon's Rebellion and the American Revolution were thought to be alike. According to John Fiske, in his book *Old Virginia and Her Neighbors*, Nathaniel Bacon the rebel gave a speech in 1676 to plead the cause of the oppressed.[3]

America's founders chose as their motto E PLURIBUS UNUM (MANY INTO ONE). Their purpose was to create a safe and secure land where people of all nations could come freely and combine into one human family. The plan for America is clearly stated in the Preamble of the Constitution, which proclaimed that we the people, of the United States of America would live lives that would benefit the entire global human family.

The Ark and Williamsburg, Virginia

In 1676 the Ark and its treasure were secretly moved from the Jamestown Church and laid to rest in a ten-foot-square chamber, or vault, buried twenty feet deep in the earth directly beneath the tower center of the first and original brick church in Bruton Parish. This was in the first Virginia capital, Middletown Plantation, eventually to be known as Williamsburg. The transfer of the treasure occurred in connection with Bacon's Rebellion, exactly one century before the birth of the American Republic in 1776.

In a manner of speaking, a second Bacon's Rebellion occurred in Williamsburg in 1938 when Marie Bauer Hall decided to dig up the vault. Her story is well documented in her small book titled *Foundations Unearthed*, first published in 1940, with a foreword written by Harold V. B. Voorhis, P.M., an outstanding Masonic author and scholar.

Before setting out on her Williamsburg quest, Marie Hall discovered in the Philosophical Research Society's Library the *George Wither Book of Emblems*, written in 1635. George Wither was known to be one of the inner group of Rosicrucians, and this book is a collection of emblems, both ancient and, at the time of publication, modern. Upon first opening the volume, she was confronted with what supposedly was a portrait of the author, George Wither, but which she recognized as that of Shakespeare. As she tells it, her eye was caught by a little shield in the background of the picture containing three crescent moons (Sir Francis Bacon is termed, in history, Hom Lunar or The Moon Man). The moons are divided by the tower shape of a broken bar, known as a "bar sinister," which had been agreed upon by the Bacon group as a sign of illegitimacy. Therefore, the picture purporting to be of George Wither was instead a picture of the "illegitimate moon-man" (Francis Bacon) wearing the mask of Shakespeare.

Although the George Wither book was written in England in

—from Wither's *A Collection of Emblemes Ancient and Moderne*

Picture of George Wither

1635, over a hundred years before most of the original buildings were ever erected in Williamsburg, there are pictures of these very same buildings in the Wither book. Marie Hall said that the capitol building depicted in the Wither book was recognized by a Rockefeller Restoration official when she showed it to him before she recognized it herself! She was also able to discover from Wither's Book many verifications of the Bruton Vault, including its existence, the location, size and depth of the vault, as well as its contents, and the circumstances attending its burial. Reiteration of this information was later extracted, by decoding methods, from tombstone inscriptions in the Bruton Churchyard.

The Wither book can be seen as one more proof that American history, including the story of the Bruton vault, was predetermined, and that certain events were carried out in almost minute accordance with a Great Plan, the plan of Francis Bacon and his illustrious group in Elizabethan England.

Capitol Building, Williamsburg

Marie Hall continued to find other strange circumstances. The Wither book was written in 1635, the same year that the vault records are thought to have been carried from England to Jamestown, Virginia, by Henry Blount. Blount, upon his arrival in America, took the name Nathaniel Bacon for protection. The valuable treasure was transferred from Jamestown to Williamsburg in 1676, shortly before Bacon's Rebellion, led by Nathaniel Bacon.

On Mrs. Hall's first visit to Bruton Churchyard in 1938, she was able to determine—from anagrams, cryptograms and codes deciphered from the tombstones in the churchyard—the exact location of the original brick church where the Bacon vault was supposed to have been buried nearly 300 years earlier. She found that the first tombstone near the entrance gate had a stone engraving with the very same coat of arms, showing the three crescents of the moon and a shield, that she had seen in the George Wither book. Later disclosures through her ciphers indicated that this was the tomb of Nathaniel Bacon.

Mrs. Hall soon realized that her goal of uncovering the vault could be accomplished only with the information from the tombstones. She found, for example, that the Edward Nott tomb, which rests on the southeast end of the old foundations, was inscribed with anagrams also found in the Wither book. With this information she hoped to convince the local authorities to give her permission to excavate.

From a Masonic record she found in Williamsburg, Marie Hall was further encouraged in her confidence that the vault was located in Bruton Churchyard. These Masonic records stated: "Under the first brick church in Bruton Parish, Williamsburg, Virginia, lies Francis Bacon's Vault." Based on her years of study, and an understanding of Bacon's work, she came to the conclusion that invaluable records and material that would be most important for the future use of society and its overall improvement, would be found in "Bacon's Vault!"

The present structure of Bruton Church does not stand on the same site as the earlier church. The original brick Old Bruton Church, built about the time of Bacon's Rebellion of 1676, was

—an early copy of a drawing made by Franz Ludwig Michel in 1702

The First Brick Church of Bruton Parish

demolished and all the records are missing. Misleading maps were originated and signed by men whose names were recognized by Marie as connected with the original undertaking of burying the vault, presumably another level of secrecy, simply for better protection of the vault and its contents. Annals of the Williamsburg Masonic Lodge are also as completely and mysteriously missing for the identical time period as are the Vestry records of Bruton Parish and its first brick church. Interestingly enough, the undaunted Marie found ancient Williamsburg city records and memorabilia in the Library of William and Mary College which verified the existence of a "brick church" in Bruton Parish built before the present church. An early book on colonial architecture mentions that the size of the original church was 60 feet by 24 feet internally, approximately the same size as the tabernacle and the original Wattle Church of Glastonbury.

The "proof" of the vault's existence in Williamsburg, and the nature of its importance, has been provided time and time again by Marie Hall and is recorded with the United States Government in Washington, D.C. While she was digging in Williamsburg, two Masons came to talk to her—one the owner of the London *Times* and the other a descendant of Sir Walter Raleigh. She called these men "Masons of the Inner Group," part of a small group of men indoctrinated in the noble scheme. They were carefully watching her work. She had opened a treasure chest which the Masons wanted suppressed.

In the 1920's the Rockefeller Foundation bought up nearly all of Williamsburg for its restoration project. They were unable to buy Bruton Churchyard because it belonged to the Church of England. Current U.S. records reveal that the Bruton Churchyard subsequently became the property of the United States Government. The question here is why did the Rockefeller Foundation want to buy Williamsburg and restore it in the first place? Were they hoping to discover the vault and its contents? It is interesting to note that at the time when Marie Hall discovered the location of the vault in Williamsburg, the Rockefellers bought Stratford on Avon in England so as to strengthen and perpetuate the myth of Shakespeare.

It seems that the Great Plan was on schedule, because soon after the vault was moved to Williamsburg from Jamestown, a secret group of colonists from the thirteen colonies used Freemasons to organize the military to overthrow the King of England.

Mr. and Mrs. Hall often talked with me about what was in the vault in Virginia. I believe Mr. Hall knew that the Ark had been taken out because he said to me on two different occasions that he thought the Williamsburg vault was empty.

In 1938, during Marie Hall's search for the vault, she employed up-dated scientific instruments whose surveys proved the location of the vault, and that it contained material enclosed in copper cylinders. On April Fool's Day in 1985, another survey was done and the copper cylinders, as Marie put it, "no longer talked back" to her. She knew the contents of the vault had been removed. In her book *Quest for Bruton Vault* (pp. 6 and 10), which records her story of finding the vault, she states: ". . . Once Bruton Vault in Williamsburg had been properly located—as confirmed by scientific instruments—its New Age content was immediately moved to a *safer location.*"[4]

Freemason and Rosicrucian data reveal that secret knowledge was passed on through veiled means far back in American history. In his book *America's Assignment with Destiny*, Manly P. Hall points to the fact that "Thomas Jefferson examined the 'repositories' of the Bacon group in colonial America, checked their contents and caused them to be resealed for future ages."[5]

Thomas Jefferson must have examined the repositories by way of the tunnels under Williamsburg. Marie Hall has written about these tunnels, which she discovered in 1938 when she first visited the city. She had heard about the tunnels from many of the elderly residents of the area.

Lyon Gardner Tyler was the nephew of U.S. President Tyler and at one time the prominent Chancellor of the University of William and Mary College in the Williamsburg area. He wrote of tunnels starting under the corner of the George Wythe house, located next to Bruton Church, and going across the churchyard. I have heard from another source that the tunnels come out at the James River, which borders Williamsburg.

An interesting note to this is that not only is the George Wythe house next door to Bruton Church, but George Wythe was one of the Founding Fathers of America. He also was one of the signers of the Declaration of Independence (written by Thomas Jefferson). Wythe was the teacher of Jefferson, who had examined the vault. It was known that Jefferson came to the Wythe house to study law from George Wythe. George Washington also stayed at the Wythe house when traveling through the city.

These tunnels are important and were hidden well. They were probably used by the inner group of Masons to move the Ark of the Covenant to the new capital of America (Washington D.C.) from Williamsburg. I have been told that the tunnels are now deteriorating and not in good condition.

These were some of the interesting circumstances that made me realize the Williamsburg vault had not been totally emptied. I believe it is probable that the vault still contains Bacon's books, which had been lost, and manuscripts like those of the Shakespeare writings and the King James Version of the Bible. It is not unlikely that an autobiography of Sir Francis Bacon, the Lord High Chancellor of England and Viscount of St. Albans, also remains in the Williamsburg vault. In Sir Francis Bacon's time it was common to build a vault. Bacon was a scholar, a teacher, historian, and writer, so he would no doubt have had his own vault for depiction of his own history.

The records were preserved to be opened one day to give concrete proof of the founding of America and its purpose. (Or as Marie Hall says, "to give concrete proof to concrete minds.") In all probability, there was no need to take the personal records of Bacon out of Williamsburg; however, the Ark was removed because the building planned in Washington, the new capitol, was being made ready to house the Ark.

The Ark and Washington, D.C.

The Masons left many clues in the national capitol that refer to Bacon and Athena. In Washington, D.C. there is a bronze statue of Chief Justice John Marshall sitting on a large chair. The base of this statue, which is approximately three feet high by five feet long has an embossed relief of Minerva, the Roman name for the goddess Athena, and it reads: "Minerva dictating the Constitution to young America." I found it interesting that it was signed "W. W. Story." Was this the cryptic name the Masons used for "Western World Story"?

The statue was situated in front of the Capitol Building (on the side facing the mall) until some time after 1960, when it was moved to the Supreme Court Building, where it now stands. The base of the statue, the embossed relief, was removed and is now housed in the National Archives.

On a recent trip to Washington, I found in the Library of Congress a mosaic picture of Minerva/Athena, approximately 30 feet high, located halfway up the staircase leading to the second floor balcony inside the library. She is depicted as a guardian of civilization and promoter of the arts and sciences. In the same building there is a painting of a woman wearing a helmet and carrying a sword and shield, which are symbols of Athena. This painting flanks the window at the east end of the Great Hall's second-floor north corridor. Also at the bottom of the staircase in the Great Hall of the Library is a statue of Minerva/Athena holding a light.

During the 1950s, a friend told me that he saw the original Constitution of the United States, then displayed in a case on the same second-floor balcony of the Library of Congress. Below the case was an inscription indicating that the architect of the enclosure was one Francis Bacon from Boston. Attempted correspondence proved the address provided for the designer with the interesting name did not exist. Another cryptic Masonic message?

Athena seemed to turn up in many places in Washington. In the exhibition area of the National Archives Building where the Constitution is now located, I looked at the original Constitution of the United States, which is covered and guarded in a heavy glass, framed in a metal that looked like bronze. Then, as I was

The embossed relief reads, "Minerva [Athena] dictating the Constitution to Young America." MARIE HALL IN FOREGROUND

Mosaic of Minerva/Athena in the Library of Congress, Washington D.C.

looking at the Constitution, there on the lower left corner of the frame I found her—a small head of Athena wearing her helmet.

Another interesting note: Athena also appears on the first flag of the first English colony to be established in the New World. Even the seal of California depicts Athena. It seems that Bacon and the Founding Fathers left their influence for all to see.

While visiting a bookstore in Los Angeles, I chanced across a book called *The Talisman of the United States: The Mysterious Street Lines of Washington D.C.* written by Charles L. Westbrook, Jr. This book appealed to me because of my background and study of the history of the United States and the Masonic Founding Fathers, who laid out the streets of our Capital city.

The book demonstrates that some of the streets of Washington are laid out in geometric patterns. The Capital's important buildings are placed in golden triangles, pentagrams and other geometric symbols and patterns.

Charles Westbrook uncovered three pentagrams in the street design of Washington D.C. One pentagram points directly to the Capitol Building, another has a point directed to the White House, and the third pentagram extends from the Washington Monument. The first two pentagrams also have one point in direct alignment with the Washington Monument. The question here is why is the Washington Monument given so much attention? What made it so special or important to the Founding Fathers that these pentagrams all point in the direction of that megalithic obelisk?

The Washington monument is known as the world's tallest obelisk (555 feet). There are many obelisks located in key cities

all over the world, mostly taken from ancient Egypt. Freemasons were responsible for bringing these ancient artifacts to such important cities as Buenos Aries, London, Paris, Vatican City, Rome and Boston. Unlike any other, the Washington obelisk was constructed under Masonic supervision.

In his epic book *The Magic of Obelisks*, Peter Tompkins refers to the Masons moving the Alexandrian Obelisk to New York in 1880: "A very important historical discovery was made relating to the order of Freemasons, confirming its claim of ancient origin. A discovery was made beneath the foundations of a granite block, the upper part of which had been cut in the form of a Mason's square. Embedded in the mortar was also a Mason's trowel of iron or steel, and two granite blocks, one polished, the other unfinished, the perfect and the rough ashlars of Masonry."[6] Since the Alexandrian Obelisk goes back to the time of ancient Egypt, it gives us further proof of how far back in time the Masons were active.

There have been many theories about these giant obelisks. One theory is that they act as an antenna focusing solar energy or etheric rays from the sun to the ground and fill the ground with energy and power. My belief is that the Washington Monument acts as an antenna which focuses the etheric energy into the grid system of Washington, D.C. and gives the city added power. It acts like a solar focusing needle.

I had discovered that when an Ark was hidden, part of the material was often buried in an obelisk for safekeeping against theft, fire, weather, water and other disasters. The stone of the obelisk serves as a protective. There is a possibility that this is why the Founding Fathers pointed so carefully to the Washington Monument with street symbols as their code. There is no doubt that the city was deliberately laid out with the knowledge that at some time the Ark would rest in this great city and give it added power and strength for America's secret destiny.

I had heard about the symbols of the streets of Washington, but there was nothing I could find in our history books about them. These symbols can only be viewed from an airplane or the top of a high building such as the Capitol or the Washington Monument. In his book, Mr. Westbrook quotes a story about Charles Dickens' first visit to the new Capital. He climbed to the top of the Capitol Building so he could see the whole city, and wrote afterwards about the city: "It is sometimes called the City of Magnificent Distances, but it might with greater propriety be termed the City of Magnificent Intentions; for it is only on taking a bird's eye view of it from the top of the Capitol that one can at all comprehend the vast designs of its projector, an aspiring Frenchman."[7]

History tells us that a Frenchman named Major Pierre Charles L'Enfant was the city planner for Washington. It also tells us that L'Enfant was merely the middleman working from a set of plans developed by George Washington and Thomas Jefferson. Washington and L'Enfant served in the War of Independence and both were members of the newly formed Society of Cincinnati. In a letter from Jefferson to L'Enfant dated August 18, 1791, Jefferson communicates his ideas for the map of the city of Washington.

It is interesting to note that three years of George Washington's diary have mysteriously disappeared, along with Jefferson's correspondence concerning the development of our nation's Capital. It seems that these hidden treasures were important enough that secrecy needed to be maintained concerning them.

Additionally, both Washington and Jefferson have been linked to organizations of Freemasonry. During the time of the American Revolution those same Masonic orders included such notable members as Benjamin Franklin, James Monroe, Alexander Hamilton, Paul Revere, John Paul Jones. Interestingly, the Marquis de Lafayette and Benedict Arnold were also Freemasons. Other revolutions against state and church were led by Freemasons, such as Simon Bolivar, Benito Juarez, Giuseppe Garibaldi, and Sam Houston.

Many illustrious Presidents of the United States are also claimed by Masonic historians to be Masons. This list includes in addition to Washington and Jefferson, James Monroe, John Quincy Adams, Andrew Jackson, James K. Polk, James Buchanan, Andrew Johnson, James A. Garfield, William McKinley, Theodore Roosevelt, William Howard Taft, Warren G. Harding, Franklin D. Roosevelt, Harry S. Truman, Lyndon B. Johnson, Gerald R. Ford and an "honorary brother," Ronald Reagan.

George Washington's affiliation to the Masonic organization is demonstrated by the many portraits of him that include Masonic symbols hanging in our Capitol building. The official White House portrait of George Washington is on display and shows the double eagle on the leg of the table next to Washington. This double eagle is the symbol of the Scottish Rite of Masonry. The same double eagle is found on the flag in a second portrait of Washington.

One of the last Gothic cathedrals to be built is in Washington. The Washington National Cathedral was built much like its medieval French and English predecessors. Stonemasons were brought from Europe in order to build this magnificent edifice along the earlier lines of ancient and true architecture using sacred geometry. This church, along with the boulevards, buildings, and monuments of the new Capital, was envisioned by Washington, Jefferson, and Pierre L'Enfant in 1791.

—Engraving by Currier and Ives, 1868
George Washington in Masonic Regalia

The Masons laid the Cathedral's foundation stone in 1907, making the Washington Cathedral one of the last buildings to be laid out in true Masonic fashion. The charter for the building of the cathedral was granted by Congress in 1893. Because of inadequate finances, however, it took a great amount of time to finish construction. Sections were added gradually over the years, and the debt was finally retired in 1989–1990. The completed cathedral was dedicated in 1990 after 83 years of construction

Having just written the chapter of this book on Glastonbury, I was privileged to hear at the Philosophical Research Society an outstanding lecture by Georgia Lambert about Glastonbury. Ms. Lambert told how the Washington National Cathedral had in its garden a cutting of the thorn tree from Glastonbury. She also discussed the fact that the cathedral had a chair from the Abbey of Glastonbury. The Washington Cathedral was the last great Gothic Church built in the style of the early Templars Churches of Europe.

I began to think—what were the Masons going to do with this building where so many artifacts from Glastonbury were installed? What story were they carrying all the way from England?

I checked the alignment of the National Cathedral using a map of the city and examined the mathematics of the building with my friend William Dotson, a talented astrologer well versed in sacred geometry. We discovered that the Masons planned it so one of the points of the three pentagrams in the street lines of Washington pointed directly to the altar of the cathedral. The line, as we measured it using the mathematics of Phi, one of the principles of sacred geometry, went straight through the altar of the cathedral.

For the Ark to be in Washington seems logical since it is the present capital of America, and the Ark had been hidden in the previous capital, Williamsburg, Virginia. This is why Manly P. Hall had told me the vault at Williamsburg was empty—the Ark had been moved to the building that had been built to house it. Only Mr. Hall would have known this as one of the inner-group Masons. The capital of the United States is the appropriate location for this powerful Ark and, like Solomon's Temple, it can affect in a positive manner all of the surrounding area.

Map of Washington D.C.

The manner in which Washington National Cathedral is laid out is not found in the guidebooks and not likely pointed out to tourists. There is an underground crypt at a place where the two arms of the cathedral cross, which is dedicated to Joseph of Arimathea, the uncle of Jesus. It is from Joseph of Arimathea and his settlement at Glastonbury, that mystic Christianity descends. Next to the crypt area of Joseph of Arimathea, in the National Cathedral, is a small chapel called Glastonbury Cathedral. Here stands a throne chair carved out of stone taken from Glastonbury Abbey. Also, on the grounds of the Cathedral can be found a thorn tree grown from a cutting of the sacred thorn tree of Glastonbury, which is said to have grown from Joseph's staff.

The cathedral is built on 53 acres on Mount St. Albans, which is another interesting connection to the Masons and Francis Bacon, whose full title is: Sir Francis Bacon, Lord Verulam, Viscount St. Albans. There is also a landscaped approach from Wisconsin Avenue to the cathedral, anchored to the south by *St. Albans* Parish Church. And on the south portal of the cathedral, between two massive sets of doors, is a statue of *St. Alban*. The thorn tree from Glastonbury grows in its own plot of ground in front of *St. Albans* School for Boys.

The cathedral's central tower, "Gloria in Excelcis," was finished in 1964 and is the highest point in Washington D.C. The marble flooring is intricately designed with an inlaid Jerusalem Cross; the insignias of St. Peter (the keys of the kingdom) and of St. Paul; and the book and sword. Some of the decorative features include statues of Abraham Lincoln and George Washington.

The symbols and artwork portrayed in the cathedral tell a multitude of stories, all based on the Judeo-Christian beliefs that have come down to us over the centuries. On the third highest level of windows on the north side, Noah and the flood are depicted. The portrayals of the stories underlying the foundations of Christianity are laid out in the Hebrew tradition, which helps to focus our attention on the continuing story from Creation to Christ at the Last Judgment. In the nave is a window that describes the lineage of Jesus, showing the long passage of time as the history of the Hebrew people unfolded. From left to right, we see Abraham, David the King, and the defeat and captivity of the Jews. This takes us to the fourth panel, where Mary and Joseph with the infant Christ represent the birth of Christianity.

The Children's Chapel, in which all the furnishings are child-size, features windows portraying the child Samuel, the boy David, and the young Jesus in the Temple. Noah's Ark is depicted in needlepoint on the altar kneeler.

The cathedral is administered by the Episcopal Church, the same church that oversees Bruton Parish Church in Williamsburg. Its pulpit is frequently graced by the Archbishop of Canterbury, worldwide titular head of the Anglican Church, or Church of England, of which the Episcopal Church is the American counterpart. The cathedral is "a House of Prayer for All People." Entry is free and open to all. Within its walls the Jewish Ram's Horn has been heard as well as the Muslim call to prayer. People of all faiths come to this cathedral. Dr. Martin Luther King, Jr. preached his last Sunday sermon from the pulpit of Washington National Cathedral.

The American Founding Fathers

The following quotation is from Sir Francis Bacon's *Instauratio Magna*: "The Glory of God is to conceal a thing, but the glory of the King [man] is to find it out: As if the divine nature, according to the innocent and sweet play of children, which hide themselves to the end that they may be found, took delight to hide his works to the end that they may be found out; and of his indulgence and goodness to mankind has chosen the soul of man to be his play-fellow in this game."

Francis Bacon's hope and aspiration was the creation of a Utopia across the Atlantic in the New World; the realization of his "New Atlantis" in the form of a free society in which Freemasonic principles would govern the social, political and economic life of the nation and its people. It is for these reasons that the Lord Chancellor of England took such an active interest in the colonization of America, sending members of his family to settle and help organize the early colony of Virginia. In America, through men like George Washington, Thomas Jefferson and Benjamin

Franklin, as well as through the revolutionary activities of his many Rosicrucian and Freemasonic followers, Bacon hoped to create a new nation dedicated to his political philosophy as given from the divine plan.

A little insight into the plan for America is given in the book *The Ultimate Frontier* by Eklal Kueshana: "The United States of America was designed as an important stepping-stone toward the evolution of the kind of citizens and civilization conducive to a balanced society. During the revolutionary era of the 1770's when the colonists were persuaded to separate from England, there were men of greatness on hand to guide the budding nation. Several students of the Brotherhoods—notably Franklin, Jefferson, Madison, and Washington—managed to establish the political machinery most conducive to a society based on the high ideals of their time. The dominant philosophic atmosphere of the period was based on the doctrines of Reasonable Man, Rationalism, separation of church and state, the fallacy of the divine right of kings, human equality, democracy, John Locke's treatises on property rights, and the mysteries of a resurgent Freemasonry in France. . . . The Declaration of Independence, the Constitution of the United States and the Bill of Rights have now come to be regarded as mileposts of human achievement. Our founding fathers had difficulty in persuading the colonies to remain united and to accept their untried theories, but the continuing success of the United States is evidence their ideas were sound.

"The faith, vision, and fortitude of these founders were the result of their training. They guided the new nation in accordance with instructions and had foreknowledge that they would succeed. As students of the Brotherhoods, they knew the nation they were forming was planned about six thousand years before. The sub rosa influence throughout the world prepared the way for the founding of the United States of America; yet the Brothers worked so inconspicuously and adroitly that nobody sensed the fitting together of a detailed grand design begun six millennia before."[8]

The adepts or inner group of Masons which helped form the Americas showed themselves on a couple of special occasions in the formation of the country. One such event is described in *Our Flag, or The Evolution of the Stars and Stripes*, published in 1890 by Robert Allen Campbell. The account, taken from chapter 2, titled "The Colonial Flag," gives the details of an important, obscure episode of American history—the designing of the Colonial flag in 1775 which took place in Cambridge, Massachusetts. It involves a mysterious man concerning whom no information is available other than that he was on familiar terms with both General Washington and Benjamin Franklin. The following is an abbreviated description of this mysterious stranger and how he influenced the design of the flag of America.

It seems little had been known concerning this old gentleman. In the materials from which this account is compiled, his name is not mentioned, but he is referred to as "the Professor." He was evidently far beyond seventy years of age. He often referred to historical events of more than a century previous just as if he had been a living witness to their occurrence. He was erect, vigorous and active—hale, hearty and clear-minded, as strong and energetic in every way as in the prime of life. He was tall, of fine figure, perfectly easy, very dignified in his manner, courteous, gracious and commanding. He was for those times, considering the customs of the colonists, very peculiar in his method of living; for he ate no flesh, fowl or fish; he never used for food any "green thing," any root or anything unripe; he drank no liquor, wine or ale. He confined his diet to cereals and their products, fruits that were ripened on the stem in the sun, nuts, mild tea and the sweet of honey, sugar and molasses.

He was well educated and highly cultivated and very studious. He spent his time in the patient and persistent scanning of a number of very rare old books and ancient manuscripts which he seemed to be deciphering, translating or rewriting. These books and manuscripts, together with his own writings, he never showed to anyone; and he did not even mention them in his conversations with the family, except in the most casual way; and he always locked them up carefully in a large, old-fashioned, cubically shaped, iron-bound, heavy oaken chest, whenever he left his room, even for his meals. He was a quiet, though a very genial and very interesting, member of the family; and he was seemingly at home with any and every topic coming up in conversation. He was, in short, one whom everyone would notice and respect, but few felt acquainted with; one whom no one would question as to where he came from, or where he journeyed.

The committee appointed by the Colonial Congress to design a flag accepted an invitation to be guests of the family with whom the Professor was staying at Cambridge. General Washington joined them for the purpose of deciding upon an emblem for the flag. By the signs that passed between them, it was evident that General Washington and Benjamin Franklin recognized the Professor. By unanimous approval, he was invited to become a member of the committee. The Professor was treated with the most profound respect and all his suggestions immediately acted upon. He submitted a pattern which he considered symbolically appropriate for the new flag of America. This was unhesitatingly accepted by the six other members of the committee. The Professor then vanished and nothing further is known concerning him.

Another of these mysterious episodes occurred during the evening of July 4, 1776 at the signing of the Declaration of Independence. It seems that in the old State House in Philadelphia, a group of men were gathered for the monumental task of breaking the tie between the old country and the new and claiming liberty for the colonies as a free nation. It was a difficult moment, and many of those present feared that their lives would be forfeit for their boldness.

In the middle of the debate a voice rang out. The debaters stopped and turned to look upon a stranger who had suddenly appeared in their midst, awakening them with his oratory. No one present had ever seen this stranger and none knew how he had entered the room. Nevertheless, his tall form and pale face filled each man present with awe. The stranger's voice stirred them to their very soul. His closing words rang through the building, "God has given America to be free!" And then a wild enthusiasm burst forth and name after name, the men signed the Declaration of Independence.

But then the man who had accomplished this immortal task and lifted the veil from the eyes of the assemblage, and revealed to them a part of the great purpose for which America was conceived, disappeared; he was never seen again and his identity was never established.

There are other episodes of a similar kind recorded by historians upon the founding of every new nation. Are they coincidence, or are the Secret Societies still present in the world, serving mankind as they did of old? I often wonder what connection these mysterious strangers had to Francis Bacon.

From the letters of Thomas Jefferson, which are preserved in the Library of Congress, considerable data concerning the session about the signing of the Declaration of Independence has been gathered. This speech is also thought to be in a rare old volume of early American speeches of an earlier date than those preserved in the first of the volumes of the Congressional Record, which can be found in the Theosophical Society Library in Adyar, India. This speech is recorded in the May 1938 issue of *The Theosophist Magazine*, the official publication of the Theosophical Society.

The Masons closely supervised the Great Plan. Masonic lodges were introduced into the American colonies very early. By the time of the Revolutionary War, there were lodges in each of the thirteen colonies. Boston Masons were responsible for organizing the "Boston Tea Party." Paul Revere was a Master Mason, as was every general officer in the Revolutionary army. There were two thousand Masons among the other officers, including men of Jewish, Catholic, and Protestant persuasion.

When peace came it was Robert Livingston, a Mason, who administered the oath of office to George Washington as first President of the United States. When the cornerstone of the Capitol was laid in Washington, D.C. in September 1793, the ceremony was performed by members of the Grand Lodge of Maryland and several other lodges under the jurisdiction of the Washington Lodge #22. President Washington himself was clothed in the Masonic Apron and other Masonic regalia.

The Great Plan was made not only for North America but for

Notice the Ark of the Covenant under the wings of the cherubim in these Masonic crests.

Latin America as well, with the same philosophy of liberty, equality and fraternity.

Sir Walter Raleigh, a well-known member of the Baconian circle, confided his private plans for his South American expedition to King James I, who then told the Spanish Count Gondomar of Raleigh's plans. The Spanish, not wanting the English to disturb their colonial holdings, were waiting with a strong force for Raleigh. In the fighting, Raleigh's son was killed. King James promised Gondomar that Raleigh would be publicly executed for the action he had taken against Spain.

Bacon is known to have visited Sir Walter Raleigh during his imprisonment in the Tower of London. The first edition of *The History of the World*, which Raleigh is thought to have written during his imprisonment, contains emblems and devices belonging to the Baconian group. Ben Jonson, another member of the Baconian group, said, referring to Raleigh and his book: "The best wits in England were employed in making his history."

One hundred and seventy-five years after Walter Raleigh laid down his life for America, the citizens of Carolina remembered the man to whose courage they owed their existence as a state. They named the capital of their colony *Raleigh*.

The turbulent republics of South America also had their Masonic Lodges, which in many cases were disguised as political clubs. The Grand Lodge of Mexico was started in 1825, but prior to that date there was known Masonic activity in that country. Many outstanding Latin Americans of the French revolution period were educated in Europe and returned to their homeland indoctrinated with the knowledge of the French revolutionists.

One of the important political reformers was Miguel Hidalgo (1753–1811), who was called "the Father of Mexican Independence." His career emphasized liberal principles imported from the Secret Societies of Spain. Under various protective names of political clubs such as Liberty Circles, and Social Enterprises, the spirit of liberty extended its influence from the European Masonic Lodges of liberation to the country of Mexico.

Benito Pablo Juarez, who was born in 1806 in a little Zapotecan Indian village of some twenty families, became the emancipator of Mexico. It is said his God was Freedom, served by a priesthood of liberators. Juarez became a Mason at a very young age. After the dethroning of the Maximilian Empire, Mexican Freemasonry consolidated in 1868. Benito Juarez was one of its highest ranking officials.

General Francisco Javier Mina, a Freemason, was another martyr to Mexican liberty. Ignacio Comonfort, also a member of the Freemason Fraternity, acted as Secretary of War under President Alvarez and later was appointed acting President of the Republic. General Porfirio Diaz, an early supporter of Juarez, became a member of the Masonic Fraternity. Diaz attained the 33rd degree and acted as Sovereign Grand Commander of the Supreme Council of Mexico for many years. He was succeeded in 1880 by General Manuel Gonzales, also a 33rd degree Mason. Diaz, elected President of Mexico in 1884, remained in office until his resignation in 1911. General Mariano Escobedo, a friend of Juarez and Diaz, was also a Mason and a member of the Supreme Council of Mexico.[9]

There are reports identifying many of the political reformers of the Latin American countries with the Fraternities and Societies of the Indian tribes. Pancho Villa and Benito Juarez were thought to have such affiliations.

A name familiar to most of us is Simon Bolivar, the liberator of Latin America (1783–1830). He was in direct contact with European Secret Societies. It is evident that Bolivar was not only a great statesman, but also a brilliant and liberal intellectual. He read extensively authors like Rousseau, Hume, and Spinoza. It is said that Bolivar was strongly inclined toward mysticism, and turned to philosophy for inspiration and guidance. He was a devout Catholic, but he refused to accept the reactionary tendencies of his church.

Simon Bolivar, when visiting Italy and France, contacted the various Masonic Fraternity groups. He was converted by the democratic ideology. Bolivar and his tutor, Simon Rodriguez, were standing on the summit of the holy hill in Rome when the young Bolivar fell on his knees and cried out to Rodriguez: "I swear before you, I swear by the God of my forefathers, I swear by my native country, that I shall never allow my hands to be idle nor my soul to rest until I have broken the shackles which chain us to Spain." During his European travel Bolivar joined the Masonic Order, and later, in Paris, he was raised to Master of the Lodge of the Nine Sisters.

Several years ago I was privileged to see a marble monument of Bolivar in the principal square of Caracas, his birthplace, which carries the bold words: "Simon Bolivar, Liberator of Venezuela, New Granada, Ecuador and Peru, and Founder of Bolivia."

The United States had great sympathy for the struggles of the Latin American Countries. George Washington's stepson sent to Bolivar, as a token of esteem, a small picture of Washington and a medallion which included a lock of Washington's hair.

The vision that the Liberator Bolivar left to his people can be understood from a few quotations taken from the book *Simon Bolivar*, by Gefard Masur: "America," said Bolivar in 1823, "is not a problem; neither is it a fact. It is the highest and most irrefutable assignment of Destiny." In a document dated 1829, the Liberator wrote: "I have achieved no other good than independence. That was my mission. The nations I have founded will, after prolonged and bitter agony, go into an eclipse, but will later emerge as states of the one great republic, AMERICA."[10]

America is important because of what its civilization is contributing to the evolutionary consciousness of all human beings. Each epoch of history makes its own contribution to the evolution of humanity. America stands for the idea that Enlightened Democracy is a major philosophical thought form and will be important for many centuries to come—until Enlightened Democracy is fully ingrained in all thought patterns of humanity.

CHAPTER 14

THE ALCHEMICAL MARRIAGE

hen we read about initiation procedures both in the mystical and the psychic worlds, there is still a veil of secrecy left over from the ancient past, as if people should not be allowed free access or were not trained enough to know the truth! I believe people are overly trained and overly ready. Their need to know is now vast and desperate. People are now having many of these so-called "secret rites" and initiation procedures (the psychic experiences encountered in the initiation schools) in their everyday lives. People are taking major initiations almost casually. This may seem to trivialize the process, but it really has the opposite effect. It takes ordinary reality to a more profound level. People now take for granted what is happening to them psychologically, when in ancient times they would have spent many years preparing for such initiations in a temple. This is a great evolutionary movement for humankind.

The "Alchemical Marriage" is the most important initiation process which all the "mysteries" taught. Charles Leadbeater, a Masonic scholar, describes in *The Hidden Life of Freemasonry* how the process of self-transformation, or the Alchemical Marriage, is presented in the inner fabric of the first three degrees of Masonry. He refers to certain currents of etheric force that flow through and around the spine of every human being. It is part of the plan of Freemasonry to stimulate the activity of these forces in the human body in order that evolution may be quickened.

The "Ida" or feminine aspect of the force is taught in the first degree, thereby making it easier for the candidate to control passion and emotion. The second degree, the "Pingala" or masculine aspect, is strengthened in order to facilitate the control of the mind; but in the third degree the central energy itself, "Sushumna," is aroused, thereby opening the way for the influence of pure Spirit. It is by passing up and through this channel, the Sushumna, that a yogi leaves his physical body at will in such a manner that he can retain full consciousness on higher planes and bring back a clear memory of his experiences.

Because this self-transformation process is so extremely important, I would like to expand on the concept. The following material is taken from *The Crone Oracles*, which I co-authored with Victoria Ransom: "In the Hindu energy system of the body, the body's energy is divided into two polarities: the *ida*, which is the female polarity, and the *pingala*, which is the male polarity. These polarities are contained in 'channels' running vertically through the center of the body. . . . These polarities represent a certain way in which energy moves, and with certain qualities and characteristics. There are actual physical attributes to the energies and there are also different applications. When you really look at the two channels within the 'Sushumna' (the central core, the main holding vessel of the two channels) you begin to see the differences of those energies and their effects. These energies determine how people relate to the outer world, to their mind, their bodies, and their sexuality as well as their gender identity in the body.

"When we utilize the male channel of energy we often use it to do one of three things: (1) the primary use is to keep the life-force energy operating on the physical plane; specifically to regulate the amount and the intensity of that energy in the physical body. It does not mean that it is the source of it, only that the male side seems to regulate it. The male channel regulates energy in the body as it interacts with the outer world. This, of course, leads us immediately to the next function, (2) which is energy for the mind, because the energy in the spinal channel maintains the brain. Most of all it maintains the rational conscious mind, the waking mind. (3) The third function of the male channel is as an energy connection into the soul through the mental aspects creating energy that can be expressed or directed by the body.

"In the female channel, there are some aspects in common and some differences: (1) The first function of the feminine is to connect into the unconscious—the sleep state, the dream state, and the higher modes of consciousness beyond physical reality. (2) The second function of the feminine (like the male) serves the soul so that the soul may express through the feminine polarity through feeling or intuition. (3) The third function of the female channel maintains the etheric and other electrical systems of the physical body's health and function. You can see that many metaphysical theories and techniques (meditation, acupuncture, homeopathic medicine and the science of electromagnetics) influence the feminine polarity of the life-force energy (often called 'shakti' or 'kundalini').

"If as a culture or as a planet, we are busy validating only the male side of the energy system, then the female can atrophy or go awry. The seeds of disease or dysfunction on any plane of consciousness always begin in the unconscious. Disease always begins in that which is not seen, accounted for, owned, or acknowledged. Many forms of consciousness training (as well as holistic medicine and ecology) reflect a philosophy that we are all connected. This is a movement toward the validation, recognition, and acknowledgment of the existence of the feminine polarity of energy and consciousness."[1]

One important resolve of Masonry is to achieve the ALCHEMICAL MARRIAGE. This is a term "that encompasses a tradition of alchemy (chemistry), hermetic wisdom (the Cabalistic Mysteries) and Tantra (the science of coscmic fire). What is created in this fusion of the male and the female polarities (or kundalini) is a oneness of the divine vibration. When the alchemical marriage within a person's consciousness is achieved, it is achieved by the opening of the heart center where the male and female energies of consciousness unite in the heart, become divine within the heart, causing the human to become not only divine within but to merge into the Divine without.

"The Alchemical Marriage is the first step toward union with the Divine—union with god/goddess. First the male and female within the self must fuse, which then allows people to connect to their own divinity. Then from that connection they can connect or communicate to the Divine in all Creation."[2]

The sacred geometry which has been discussed in this book was incorporated in the Ark of the Covenant to help us achieve this goal. When structures are designed in the sacred geometry of the universe, or when we listen to the sounds of sacred music or have the experience of looking at art and poetry constructed in sacred sounds and geometry, we can naturally come into balance because we become as one with the universe. The ancients understood and designed their temples and cities so they acted as catalysts to enable the individual to harmonize with the heavens.

Sacred geometry can be used to build the structures and found the sciences which will energetically open up the world, but there are other answers to how we reach or obtain the Alchemical Marriage. It can be accomplished with unconditional love, compassion, understanding as taught by Christ and many other Christ-like teachers. Meditation is a good tool to accomplish this goal.

The phrase "unconditional love," as taught by Christ, may require a little explaining. When we say someone is compassionate, it is because in our minds that person has no personal reason to love or bond with anyone; but they do anyway, unconditionally. They love without conditions. They are constantly emitting vibrations of love. This we know as compassion. By practicing love, compassion and wisdom through the heart we keep the gateway to the soul open. To carry the key of compassion is to achieve the highest in human evolution, which ultimately is enlightenment.

The pathway to soul enlightenment is through the heart; it is not enough to simply search the depth of the mind. It is important to use the mind and the heart together to resolve conflicts within. We talk about using the heart, which means expressing love and compassion (loving unconditionally). After having used this method of solving conflicts within, self-knowledge begins to automatically connect into the core self or soul. In our outer life we will find many circumstances that lead to this point. Often it is pain, loss, crisis or illness which conspire externally or internally to provide the catalyst for this eternal quest.

Francis Bacon taught that the greatest handicap to the advancement of learning is the human mind. As long as the individual is in captivity to the tyranny of mind, mind will hold the individual to the conditions with which it is familiar. The key phrase here is to break this tyranny with "love and compassion." This is the feminine path which Christ and the Secret Societies taught. Once we polarize to the feminine aspects of ourselves, we can manifest the duality of both the male and female in our body, which allows us to merge and transcend—to join together in the union of the Alchemical Marriage.

—Woodcut from Johannes Sambucus, *Emblemata*, Antwerp, 1564

Male and Female Yearning for Unity

The Secret Societies and Their Emphasis on the Feminine

Secret Societies throughout the Ages have emphasized the female side of learning. *Christ taught these feminine principles, which are love and compassion.* These are qualities of every human being. Most religions, including conventional Christianity, tread a masculine path. The early part of the Bible is based on the Ten Commandments, a masculine orientation of adherence to a rigorous code. Christ spoke of the Ten Commandments, yet he represented the feminine path. He did not call for the obedience that comes from the Old Testament; instead, Christ called for the surrender and opening of the heart. The act of surrendering shifts the heart to the feminine polarity. To surrender to this concept requires a feminine polarity because one can only "create" through the love principle. The difference between the feminine and the masculine approach to finding God is that on the feminine path we seek a direct experience of the Divine in our own time and in our own way; on the masculine path, we must adhere to certain tenets or dogmas.

It is likely that Christ chose twelve male apostles because these men needed to be initiated into the feminine; there would then be more icons than himself to serve as models for humanity.

Unfortunately, the medieval era understood Christ's choice of male apostles to mean that only men could become like Christ. If you carefully review history and read of the women who followed Christ, you will see that Christ honored them; He treated Mary Magdalene as an equal to Himself. The Masons founded America on these feminine teachings.

Feminine Aspects of America's Constitution

Thomas Jefferson, one of the great Founding Fathers of America, was the author and engineer of the Constitution. He fashioned the Constitution of this new Republic on the feminine principles of a fully American democratic system strongly influenced by a model that the Founding Fathers witnessed for themselves on the Western continent. It was the Iroquois Indians whose rule of law Jefferson integrated into the American Constitution. The roots of American democracy and its feminine aspects were embodied in the manner in which the Iroquois nation ruled itself.

When the new inhabitants landed on the Atlantic seaboard of America, they found a Native American civilization that has been called the "Great League of the American Iroquois." This was already an established American democracy on the American continent. The Iroquois on the eastern seaboard spread out the great white carpet of peace to the new inhabitants. They had a great reverence for integrity.

This Great League of the American Iroquois had a full Senate. They had previously visited England and had been accepted in the court of England, as they were leaders of the Indian people—the wise ones. What was different and particular about these people was that in the election of their senators and officers, only the WOMEN could cast the ballot; the men could not elect Senators or officers. The women did not serve in the jobs, but decided who was going to get them. Women were the electors of all the ruling people, all the heads of all the departments and the heads of the Iroquois nation.

The Iroquois had certain important laws. The congressmen of each of the different states had meetings at the Great White Lodge to carry on the business of the Great Five Nations, later known as Six Nations, of the Iroquois people. When the time came for legislation, the senators could ballot on every problem that came up except that which affected their own tribe. Another tribe was assigned that task. Nor could an Indian vote for the advancement of his own people. Everyone was required to consider the greater good for all.

Three hundred years ago, the ideas and political systems of the Iroquois and other confederations were so appealing that William Penn described the Native confederations of eastern America as political societies with sachemships (chiefs of confederations) inherited through the FEMALE SIDE. Penn was also familiar with the Condolence Ceremony of the Iroquois, which was crucial for an understanding of their confederacy. He stated that "when someone kills a woman they pay double [the wampum] 'since

. . . she breeds children which men cannot. . . .' After exposure to American Indian forms of government and unity, William Penn proposed a 'Plan for a Union of the Colonies in America.' Although it was just an outline, Penn seemed inspired by his observations of American Indian Political policies."[3] (*Indian Roots of American Democracy*, edited by Jose Barreiro).

Benjamin Franklin borrowed heavily from the Iroquois League in his early proposals for the structure of the new government. A couple of generations later, Franklin formulated another plan of colonial union which would even more closely reflect Iroquois influences. Franklin, familiar with the ways of the Iroquois, published a series of Indian treaties. He attended a Condolence Ceremony in 1753, less than a year before his authorship of the Albany Plan for the Union. Without the example of the Iroquois Nation and their open-hearted acceptance of the new settlers, the American republic would likely have taken on a very different form. Jefferson, Adams, Madison and Franklin, the architects of the Constitution, had experienced the ways of the Native Americans, knew their ideas of government were important, and incorporated many of their precepts into the cornerstone of American government, the United States Constitution.

The Statue of Liberty

It is no coincidence that Freemasonry was linked so closely to the American Republic that it used its key monuments as symbols. At the heart of these symbols are linked the Masons as preservers of the wisdom of the ages. The Statue of Liberty unfolds the highest purpose of the American nations—Liberty, the giver of Light.

Auguste Bartholdi, the sculptor of the Statue of Liberty, originally named his creation "Liberty Enlightening the World." The outward purpose of the statue was to rekindle democracy in France by acknowledging America as the home of liberty. Bartholdi and many of his supporters were Freemasons and understood the deeper meaning of the statue.

It was the Frenchman Edouard Leboulaye who, because of his pro-American feeling, proposed a monument to French and

American friendship incorporating the ideals of American democracy. This happened after the American Civil War and France's war with Prussia, both of which had devastating effects on the people and their countries. Inspired by Leboulaye, Auguste Bartholdi, one of France's leading sculptors, resolved to create a statue representing the ideals of liberty. In 1870, Bartholdi came to America to promote the "Liberty project." He was so inspired he decided the correct place for the statue would be Bedloe's Island in the midst of New York Harbor.

When Bartholdi returned to France, he met with Henri Martin, a prominent Freemason and Lodge Master, who would become an important patron of the project. Bartholdi was initiated into the Masonic Lodge of Alsace-Lorraine in Paris and the project came under the influence of the Freemasons.

Bartholdi originally modeled Liberty with a torch in her right hand and a broken chain in her left. Through the urging of Leboulaye and the Freemasons the chain was replaced with the TABLETS OF THE LAW dated July 4, 1776. The tablet stated the concept that "all men are created equal, and . . . endowed by their Creator with certain unalienable rights, that among these are life, liberty, and the pursuit of happiness." The concept of Liberty as portrayed by this magnificent statue would forever be identified with truth, justice and peace.

The Masonic influence on the statue is pictorially represented on the covers of two popular Masonic publications of the time. Printed between 1860 and 1870, these covers depict images of a female standing on top of the world. In one, she is shown with her right hand lifting a flame-radiating candle, while holding an UNROLLED SCROLL (THE LAW) in her left hand. The other cover shows this same image with the female figure holding a triangle in the left hand, symbolizing justice, and a mirror, the Masonic symbol for truth, in her right hand. Both the mirror and the flame are, in Masonic symbology, givers of light.

The Masons also use a ritual which contains the phrase: "The Great Architect of the Universe has given the Sun to the world to enlighten it, and Liberty to sustain it." Notice also how Bartholdi gave Liberty a crown of seven rays as if the sun were radiating from her.

On August 5, 1884, the Masons laid the cornerstone of the pedestal for the Statue of Liberty. The ceremony was led by the Grand Masonic Lodge of New York State. (Some of the foregoing material was taken from the excellent treatise "Liberty Enlightening the World" by Paul Zamarian).

A friend of mine, who is an Indian Shaman, gave me this beautiful explanation of the statue: "The Statue of Liberty represents the World Mother of the universe, carrying the victory torch of the eternal living flame of God, the Supreme Father of the universe. Therefore it symbolizes the Father, Mother and God. Her flame is consuming all darkness in America. She resides on a spiritual vortex to which people of all nations gravitate. She declares oneness and unity through the sacred flame for America and for all the nations of the earth. This consuming fire transcends all consciousness and creeds. When you take the I AM out of AMERICA you have the I AM RACE. Therefore, spelling AMERICA is a code, and when RACE is released in this freedom flame, the world will be liberated into the oneness. What Miss Liberty actually symbolizes is the releasing of the New Age of Unity all over the world to be realized in the Aquarian Age. She symbolizes the Declaration of Independence and freedom for all her children.

"She is the Mother which carries in her womb all the elements on which she resides. As a statue she resides on a spiritual vortex that has been planned by the ascended masters eons ago. She stands in victory over darkness with the torch of FIRE held high into the AIR, giving reverence to God. She stands over WATER, representing the cleansing and purification of EARTH. Therefore, as the Statue of Liberty she stands victorious over all the elements of fire, air, water, and earth. She also wears a corona or crown of the sun, which refers us to the earliest form of pagan religious expression—God identified as the Sun."

My Shaman friend gave me more information regarding the spiritual ties between North and South America: "The statue of Liberty is known to the Great White Brotherhood as the 'Goddess of Liberty.' What a wonderful symbol she is, and how few ever stop to realize what it means. It is really a focus of spiritual power, guarding the shores of America. The Torch held high

represents the light of the mighty 'I Am' presence, which reveals the way and sends its rays of love and peace into humankind, who truly seek the 'Light.'

"It is through the spirit of North America that the light is held high in silent greeting to the figure of the Christ that stands high on the towering Andes in South America. Little is known of the mighty power that caused the Statue of Liberty to be placed where it is, or why the figure of Jesus occupies its high pinnacle in the Southern Hemisphere. The majesty and power of these figures are a marvelous expression of the 'Great Presence' which carries the 'Light' and guards and sustains America and all of humankind. These are not accidents or the results of blind chance for there is no such thing anywhere in the universe. You may be sure that these figures, placed at these particular points, give indication of service which both continents will give to the rest of the world."

Several years ago, when visiting Brazil, I saw the spectacular sculptured figure of Jesus, towering high above Rio de Janeiro. It is awesome to think about these sculptures as part of the spiritual tie between North and South America. The Masons who designed and placed these statues were truly inspired. It is also of great interest that we now have a balance of male and female energies.

From the time of Atlantis, secret societies have worked to create the background of knowledge necessary for the establishment of an enlightened democracy among nations of the world. Many peoples of the world today are striving toward enlightened democracy. *However, what is missing in American democracy is the feminine element of love and compassion.* It is the prayer of many that all nations will align and, within each nation, attain the "Alchemical Marriage."

Christ the Redeemer
The statue of Christ on Corcovado Mountain (Hunchback Mountain) located above
modern Rio de Janeiro.

CHAPTER 15

THE MASONIC CONNECTION TO THE HOLY GRAIL

rail stories and Grail Romances are written and told in a cloaked and secret manner. *They are actually stories used to cover up what the Masonic Secret Societies have been hiding for eons of time.* They express the truth about: (1) The Ark of the Covenant given to us on the Emerald Tablet, (2) The life of Christ and the Royal Family, (3) The Alchemical Marriage of spirit and matter.

Much of what has been revealed about the Grail has been selected storytelling because humans have needed a physical image on which to build a tradition of ritual and services of initiation in order to communicate with the Divine within and without. So, the Grail became chameleon-like in nature. The quest for the Grail ultimately leads one from ignorance to enlightenment.

The Holy Grail is thought to be a number of things. The Ark of the Covenant was one of the first images—the first physical object that had Grail-like qualities. The Grail is to some a divine cup guarded by the angels, like the Sangreal, or Holy Grail, for which King Arthur's brave knights so valiantly searched. It can be many other things, like the crown jewel of archangel Lucifer which fell from heaven.

An example of the secret manner in which the Holy Grail is

presented is demonstrated in Manly P. Hall's book *The Secret Teachings of All Ages*. A section on the Holy Grail reads: "Like the sapphire Schethiya, the *Lapis Exilis*, crown jewel of the Archangel Lucifer, fell from heaven. Michael, archangel of the sun and the Hidden God of Israel, at the head of the angelic hosts swooped down upon Lucifer and his legions of rebellious spirits. During the conflict, Michael with his flaming sword struck the flashing *Lapis Exilis* from the coronet of his adversary, and the GREEN STONE fell through all the celestial rings into the dark and immeasurable Abyss. Out of Lucifer's radiant gem was fashioned the Sangreal or Holy Grail, from which Christ is said to have drunk at the Last Supper. . . . the Holy Grail is undoubtedly a type of the *ark* or *vessel* in which the life of the world is preserved and therefore is significant of the body of the Great Mother—Nature. . . ."[1]

This story is veiled in allegory. When Mr. Hall writes that "the GREEN STONE fell through all the celestial rings into the dark abyss," he is indicating that the ARK OF THE COVENANT, which was originally given to us on an EMERALD TABLET, fell from the CELESTIAL RINGS meaning HEAVEN to the ABYSS meaning EARTH. In the statement "Out of Lucifer's radiant gem was fashioned the SANGREAL or HOLY GRAIL, from which Christ is said to have drunk at the Last Supper," it is meant that Christ drank from the VESSEL OF KNOWLEDGE which was the ARK OF THE COVENANT.

In a small booklet by Manly P. Hall called *Legends of Glastonbury Abbey*, I found this statement: "The earliest references [to the Grail] are 'to the book which is called the HOLY GRAIL.' This seems to imply that a sacred manuscript rather than a cup was intended."[2] In this booklet it is also noted that the Grail speaks, giving oracles and words of holy consolation. Certain early works on magical philosophy hint that the "Ark of the Covenant" was oracular in character because of specially prepared chambers in its interior. By their shape and arrangement they were so attuned to the vibrations of the invisible world that they caught and amplified the voices of the ages.

The Grail came to Glastonbury with Christ, Joseph of Arimathea and Joseph's disciples. After the destruction of Solomon's Temple in Jerusalem and the feigned death of Jesus, Joseph brought the Ark of the Covenant and many other artifacts belonging to Jesus, including the ritual dinnerware of the Last Supper or Passover Seder—a chalice, a plate, and a bowl to Glastonbury. All of this, which was taken out of Jerusalem, was the legacy of Jesus and Mary, his mother, the living descendants of the house of David. The famous Grail writer Wolfram von Eschenbach traces the Holy Grail in his Grail Romances to King Solomon's Temple in Jerusalem.

So the Holy Grail is thought to be many different things. There are those who believe it was also the book or script which Joseph of Arimathea wrote at Glastonbury containing the life story and secret teachings of the royal family of Christ, a genetic history, a genealogy, a history of the house of Christ and the house of David and Solomon.

In England the Grail Quest became the central object of the Knights of the Round Table. Toward the end of the twelfth century, the first so-called Grail Romances appeared in Europe. The Grail Cycle, as it has descended to us, originated in the thirteenth century among the Troubadours, the Jongleurs and the Jesters, all part of the Philosophic Empire. All of these groups are part of the secret Masonic societies, and their stories, fables, and myths told of the Grail, which carried the secret traditions of the truth they knew and understood. These stories were always told or sung in fables, symbol, allegory. Later the Guilds such as the printers and trade unions hid the Grail stories cleverly in their writing and circulated them to disseminate their convictions.

The skill of the medieval storytellers and poets was so great that their stories came to be accepted as part of history. An example of this is that several ancient communities claimed to possess the Holy Grail. It was supposed to have been in the keeping of the patriarch of Jerusalem during the thirteenth century, and the Christians of Constantinople claimed it at the same time. In the cathedral at Genoa, a green cup was kept which, according to the Genoese, was the "sacred cup." The Emperor Napoleon I took this green cup to Paris, where he had it tested chemically and found it to be green glass. With these stories our admiration for the inventions of the Troubadours is increased.

The legends of chivalry, usually presented in a veiled manner, are parts of a well-organized plan. The hero tales are sacred rituals belonging to secret fraternities and their way of perpetuating the esoteric doctrines. It is the grand plan of the Mystery Schools to free humanity from the bondage of ignorance, fear, and superstition. The orders of chivalry were dedicated to restoring the primitive or pagan Christian Church as it existed at the time of Christ and the apostles.

The legends of the Holy Grail developed around the rituals, symbols, and emblems of King Arthur's Order of the Round Table. The gathering of the knights about the Round Table was thought to represent Jesus and his apostles at the Last Supper and also represented a model of the divine cosmos. The Knights Templars, the Knights Hospitalers and the Teutonic Knights have been called "the military apostles of the religion of love."

The Holy Grail Quest was the most mysterious of the legends of the Orders of Chivalry. The Knights of the Quest were, in allegory, seeking a cup guarded by angels, which usually appeared to the pure of heart in a circle of splendid light, veiled with a silken cloth (which meant veiled teachings). The blood of Christ, flowing in the Grail cup (meaning the bloodline of Christ) signified Christ's true teachings, and the cup or chalice that contained his blood was his Esoteric School. The search for the Grail by the knights was the spiritual adventure of regeneration and was concealed, under veiled language about initiation into the spiritual teachings of Christ.

The mystical sects refused to accept the exoteric or outer religion of the Roman Catholic Church, which claimed infallibility. The esoteric or hidden church of the Grail believed that the search for truth was possible without benefit of clergy or church. These initiates dedicated themselves to the perpetuation of a universal religion. They were driven into obscurity by the prevailing religious and political factions of the times, but the Grail Church existed secretly for many centuries after its disappearance from history. Persecution could not destroy these secret societies;

instead, it scattered them and in this manner spread the very teachings which it tried to obliterate.

The Grail Romances

Grail Romances are again a method of selective storytelling, often written in metaphors and allegories discreetly revealing mysteries that the Masons or Secret Orders were protecting. The Grail Romances told the story of ancient rituals having for their ultimate goal initiation into the secret sciences of life. These Mysteries were taught as high spiritual teachings concerning the Alchemical Marriage of humans to the Divine, or the union of heaven and earth. At the time these stories were circulated, they had to be given in metaphors and allegories because the church authorities in Europe condemned them and severe punishment could befall the storytellers. So they went under cover; but the medieval Grail Romances were carefully and cleverly adapted to the age of Christianity.

There are three Grail story traditions that have descended to us: the *Titurel* tradition which originated in Asia, the *Parsifal* tradition originating in France, and the *Lohengrin* tradition, which began in Belgium. To demonstrate how these Grail Romances were written and concealed in elaborate dramative formats, following are parts of the story of *Parzival*, perhaps the greatest and most important of all the Grail stories.

Parzival was written between 1190 and 1220 by Wolfram von Eschenbach, a Knight Templar. It is said he received his facts from Guiot de Provence (Provence was a cabalah center in Southern France) who in turn received his information from an Eastern astrologer, Flegetanis, who compiled an account while studying in Arab colleges in Toledo, and from the writings of Mazadan, which he discovered in Anjou. Guiot was a Jongleur, one of the divisions of the Troubadours which provides a link with the French Troubadours and the Minnesingers, the German Troubadours—all part of the Masonic order.

In the Arthurian legend, one of the most famous Knights of the Round Table was Percival (*Parzival* in German), who figured prominently in the Quest for the Grail. Percival's first appearance in literature is in the French poem *Percival ou le conte du Graal*, written in 1175 by Chretien de Troyes. Eschenbach adapted his epic verse from the *Percival* of Chretien de Troyes.

In the story of *Parzival*, Eschenbach tells readers where the Grail originated, which follows a similar pattern of other Grail writers: "The Grail was brought down by angels from the stars to the earth and left there. Since it has been on earth, it has had to be guarded. That band of dedicated knights who swore to guard themselves from defilement have since that time undertaken custody of the Grail. Researchers later found similar records in the chronicles of Anjou, France, and the lineage of the Angevin Dynasty (which then governed Britain, large parts of France, Provence, Occitania, and had formed alliances in Spain and the Holy Land)."[3] This story is similar to Manly P. Hall's story of the Green Stone which fell from Archangel Lucifer's crown, on which the Ark of the Covenant was written.

The "band of dedicated knights who swore to guard themselves from defilement" and took custody of the Grail are without doubt part of the Secret Societies formed to protect these Mysteries. Because Eschenbach was a Knight Templar, it is likely he is describing the Templars as the band of dedicated knights.

In *Parzival* the relic of the Grail is depicted as a Stone. Eschenbach conveys to us that however ill a mortal may be, from the day on which he sees the Stone he cannot die for that week, nor does he lose his color, and if anyone, man or maid, were to look at the Grail, his color would be as fresh as in his early prime for two hundred years. In other words, the Stone confers on mortal men such power that their flesh and bones are soon made young again. This Stone is called the Grail. In Eschenbach's cryptic prose of *Parzival*, the Grail also served as an oracle, which agrees with what Manly P. Hall expressed in his writing about the Holy Grail. Mr. Hall's account of Wolfram von Eschenbach ties this story to the Ark of the Covenant: "This account is all the more remarkable when the same mystic-poet states that the Grail was not a cup or vessel, but a Stone. We may, then, think again of the Philosophers' Stone and the Hermetic Emerald. These stories are fragments of one concept, and must be so considered."[4]

Later Eschenbach's Grail story associates Parzival with Prester John and Asia. Parzival took the sacred cup to Asia, where he received the name of Prester John. In 1144 the Bishop of Gabala reported that a certain John governed as priest-king in an inaccessible region of the Far East. This Bishop also reported that this John belonged to the race of Magi or Adepts, and was so wealthy that he carried a scepter of pure emeralds.

In this manner a rumor spread throughout Europe that a mysterious Christian monk had become the supreme ruler over the nations of Asia. Here we begin to see the Secret Orders of Europe involved in the perpetuation of the fable of the Asiatic Lord. In the Catholic Encyclopedia, the article on Prester John places the country of John the Prester in the area of Tibet. The following description appears therein: "This is the land of the good King and lord, known as Prester John, lord of all Eastern and Southern India, lord of all the kings of India, in whose mountains are found all kinds of precious stones."

We may ask why Parsifal took the Grail to the Far East. Manly P. Hall answers this question by informing us that the Grail cover-up story is also about the adepts and mahatmas who are the Invisible Government of the World and the true spiritual governors of the mundane sphere. "The original location," he writes, "given for the empire of Prester John was the area of the Gobi Desert, where he lived in an enchanted palace in the mountains. If you ask Eastern initiates to describe the Northern Paradise, called Dejung or Shambhala, the mysterious city of the adepts, they will tell you that it is in the heart of the Gobi Desert. In the old sand of Shamo, the Ancient Mother, stands the Temple of the Invisible Government of the World. High in the etheric atmosphere of the planet it floats, supported upon an outcropping of azoic rock, called the Sacred or Imperishable Island.

"The fabled mahatmas of Asia should not be regarded as isolated initiates but as members of an exalted Fraternity, which has been called the Trans-Himalayan Brotherhood. This order of exalted men, servants of the Lord of the World, are the spiritual governors of the mundane sphere. They gather at prescribed intervals in the Temple of Shambhala on the Sacred Island and give allegiance to the Lord of Lords, the King of Kings, Regent of the Sun and Master of the World."[5]

In Eschenbach's myth the true story is hidden in the writing. *The Masons have been continually directed and inspired by a group of enlightened adepts or mahatmas.* Wolfram von Eschenbach realized this, and his Order of the Holy Grail, with its temple and its knights, is a veiled reference to the spiritual center of Shambhala where these adepts or mahatmas resided.

During a lecture on "The Holy Grail," Mr. Hall explained: "The Church of the 'Holy Grail' was not on the earth plane. You could not become part of a physical church called the Holy Grail. It never occurred to the Christian historians that the Sacred City of the gods could be anything except an Asiatic version of Rome. Beneath the name and legend of Prester John is concealed the identity of the unknown name of one of the highest adepts of the Philosophic Empire. Naturally he could not be found, but the Golden City was the same abode of the god-men that Lao-tse was seeking when he departed alone into the sands of Shamo, riding on his green ox."[6]

With the writing of the Grail Romances, while the tradition may be obscure and sometimes confusing, it becomes evident that we have a description of the descent of a Secret Society which existed before the beginning of the Christian era, and formed an

Esoteric Empire. This empire, known as the Kingdom of the Grail, functioned as a political force in Europe even as late as the rise of Napoleon.

The early drawing of the "Ship of Fools," executed in 1500, is from *The Shyppe of Fooles*, Paris. This drawing expresses a parody of the quest for the Grail, which is a voyage toward enlightenment and everlasting life. The Grail stories abound in these mysterious vessels carrying the Grail-seekers in their adventures. (Notice the hog on the flag.)

CHAPTER 16

CONCLUSION

n today's society many would find hard to believe the important role that the Masons have played in history. Many of us view them only as fun-loving social groups. The members of these groups no doubt feel a connection to the past which many of them are unable to express or even understand. I hope this book makes them proud of just how dedicated their past history has been. The purpose of the Masons of antiquity and today is to teach the doctrine of one God, the resurrection of man to eternal life (or the proof of immortality), the dignity of the human soul, and to lead the people to see the reflection of the Deity in the beauty, magnificence and splendor of the universe—this is the divine plan.

The history told in this book goes as far back as Atlantis and deals with a period of time known in Masonry as the "Orders of the Holy Grail." The inner group of Masons—an order of adepts, often called The Philosophic Empire, The Great School, The Invisible Government of the World, and the Secret Societies—has always protected the mysteries of the Ark of the Covenant, the Alchemical Marriage, and later in history, the true story of Christ. When the secrets of the ARK OF THE COVENANT and the ALCHEMICAL MARRIAGE are understood in their entirety, the world we live in will be transformed into a place of true harmony.

The Ark was brought from Egypt to Israel by Moses, and the Temple to house the Ark was built by Solomon. There are Arks hidden all over the world in various places, of which this book traces a few. To hide the secrets of these Mysteries, the Secret Societies wrote and talked in symbolism, parable and allegory. These camouflaged forms of cryptic speech gradually evolved into what was known as the poetical language, seen today in the writings of Dante, Shakespeare, and the Grail Romances.

With the invention of printing, the myths, legends and fables of the Bards, Troubadours and Jongleurs escalated to their final published forms dealing with alchemy, cabalah, and the Rosicrucian documents. Much of the material was published anonymously. The secrets were jealously guarded, elaborate ciphers were incorporated into the text, and symbolical emblems were introduced. Many remain today to give us clues about this great body of work. This massive conspiracy involved historians, writers, artists, printers and trade union members operating in several countries under extreme secrecy. These groups were known as Guilds; they formed a link with the Troubadours, who verbalized and sang about the Mysteries.

Organized religion has kept us ignorant of the fact that we have our own personal connection to the Divine as taught in the Alchemical Marriage. The current cycle gives people permission to be their own spiritual lotus flowers, as opposed to attaching to an organization or dogma to become enlightened. This is the time when the power of the priest class is being given to the hearts of humankind. We are now realizing that *we* are the Ark—we are constructed in the sacred geometry of the universe—in the same dimensions as the Ark, and we can be personally activated as an Ark if we decide to do so. We are the microcosmic materialization of the macrocosm.

The symbol of the Star of David, also called the Seal of Solomon, has always given us the message that we are created in the same manner as the universe ("as above, so below"), one triangle pointing up and the other pointing down. In this new evolution of time, we will realize that we can connect to the Divine as did our ancient ancestors before us. We have lost the ability to

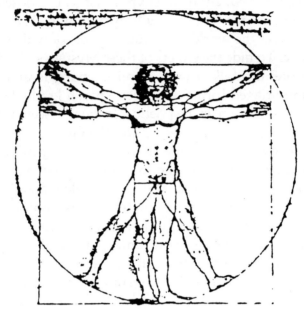

Leonardo da Vinci demonstrates that the circumference of the circle is the same as the perimeter of the square, thereby "Squaring the Circle." The circle is indicative of wholeness or Godlikeness, and the square of humanness. The theme, again, is "As Above, So Below."

make our personal connections to God and have, as a result, let ourselves be directed by others. One of the first teachings of Francis Bacon, when founding the Republic of America, was the promotion of education for all human beings. He did this so that we would learn to discern for ourselves the difference between truth and falsehood.

Before the year 2000 B.C. the power flowed to women; they had the divine right of power. This was the period of the goddess or matriarchal society and is said to have lasted for a cycle of many thousands of years. Then the cycle changed to a patriarchal one, which has lasted approximately 4000 years. We are now coming to the end of that cycle. We are now arriving at the cycle characterized by the ancient philosophers and sages as the

Alchemical Marriage of the Universe. This has been foretold in prophecy. It is said that the Alchemical Marriage will be achieved with the balancing of the two energies called "male" and "female." Each of these energies functions in a different way, and the balancing of the male and female energies within each of us will cause a third phase to come into manifestation. This third phase is often characterized by the word *Divine*.

Christ, Joseph of Arimathea, and his group of disciples brought to Glastonbury the Ark of the Covenant, the teachings of Christ and the sacred dishes of the Last Supper (or Seder) of Christ and his disciples—all part of the Holy Grail. These treasures were brought from the Temple of Solomon in Jerusalem and were passed on to the care of Merlin and Arthur by the descendants of Joseph of Arimathea and his group who, through marriage, became relatives of the Knights of Arthur. Merlin learned the teachings of Christ, the Druids, and the Ark of the Covenant and taught them to King Arthur and his Knights. Through Merlin's schools these teachings were passed to heads of nations.

It is from this period that the Grail legends begin. They are stories steeped in allegory about the Ark of the Covenant, the Alchemical Marriage and the life and teachings of Jesus. These Grail legends could only be told and written in allegorical form by knowledgeable Masons like Robert de Boron, or the celebrated Troubadour and Knight Templar Wolfram von Eschenbach and others. The quest for the Grail is ultimately the quest which leads from ignorance to enlightenment.

My friend the Indian Shaman quoted earlier has said to me: "THERE IS THE ONE AND THERE ARE THE MANY. THE MYSTERY OF THE ONE IS THAT IT HAS BECOME MANY. THE DESTINY OF THE MANY IS THAT THEY MUST RETURN TO THE ONE." This book clearly points to the conclusion that all religion started from the same source. Religion itself has only one beginning; it is we mortals who have misunderstood and separated ourselves from the "oneness."

It is not possible to ignore the current evidence of identical systems of number and measure appearing in spiritual sites throughout the world. Inevitably, mankind will come to the realization that there is a single code of knowledge, philosophy, science and religion and that this knowledge once flourished universally. The Ark of the Covenant is a copy of the Code of the Law for the whole of the universe and is the unifying link in our civilization.

CHAPTER NOTES

CHAPTER 1: THE INVISIBLE AND VISIBLE MASONS

1.   Manly P. Hall: *The Secret Teachings of All Ages*, p. CXL

2.   Albert Pike: *Morals and Dogma*, p. 206

3.   Manly P. Hall: *America's Assignment with Destiny*, pp. 49–50

4.   Grace A. Fendler: *New Truths about Columbus*, p. 11

CHAPTER 2: THE ARK OF THE COVENANT, ITS PURPOSE AND CONTENT

1.   *Masonic Manuscripts*, Harleian, Sloan, Edinburgh-Kilwinning, Lansdowne. Ref: See *Encyclopedia of Freemasonry* by Albert Mackey, M.D. These manuscripts are found in the British Museum. The Harleian manuscript is an old record of the constitution of Freemasonry, originally collected by Robert Harley, Earl of Oxford, the celebrated Prime Minister of Queen Anne. Sloan manuscript was once the property of Sir Hans Sloan. The Edinburgh-Kilwinning is inserted into the unpublished records of the Craft by Bro. D. Murrey Lyon.

2.   Albert Pike: *Morals and Dogma of the Ancient and Accepted Scottish Rite of Freemasonry*

3.   H. P. Blavatsky: *The Secret Doctrine*, vol. 3, p. 147

4.   Manly P. Hall: *Old Testament Wisdom*, p. 130

5.   Lazarus Bendavid quoted in Erich Von Daniken: *Signs of the Gods*, pp. 15–16

6.   *Signs of the Gods,* pp. 15–16

7.   Christian D. Ginsburg: *The Essenes—The Kabbalah,* p. 86

8.   Albert Pike: *Morals and Dogma,* p. 841

9.   *Morals and Dogma,* p. 843

10.   *Morals and Dogma,* p. 839

11.   H. P. Blavatsky: *The Secret Doctrine,* vol. 5, p. 177

12.   Christian D. Ginsburg: *The Essenes—The Kabbalah,* p. 127

13.   S. L. MacGregor Mathers: *The Kabbalah Unveiled,* Preface by his wife, M. MacGregor Mathers, page xiii

CHAPTER 3: ATLANTIS AND THE ARK OF THE COVENANT

1.   Manly P. Hall: *The Secret Destiny of America,* pp. 53–55

2.   John Michell: *The Dimensions of Paradise*

3.   Rudolf Steiner: *Submerged Continents of Atlantis and Lemuria*

4.   Ignatius Donnelly: *Atlantis, the Antediluvian World*

5.   Augustus Le Plongeon: *Queen Moo and the Egyptian Sphinx,* quoted by W. P. Phelon: *Our Story of Atlantis,* p. 25

CHAPTER 4: EGYPT AND THE ARK OF THE COVENANT

1.   I am indebted for much of the material in this chapter to William Eisen's book *Agasha, Master of Wisdom*

2.   Peter Tompkins: *Secrets of the Great Pyramid,* p. 1

3.   William Eisen: *Agasha, Master of Wisdom,* pp. 136–151

4.   Mark Lehner: *The Egyptian Heritage,* p. 88

CHAPTER 5: MOSES' EXODUS FROM EGYPT WITH THE ARK OF THE COVENANT

1.   John Michell and Christine Rhone: *Twelve Tribe Nations,* p. 155

2.   *Twelve Tribe Nations,* p. 150

CHAPTER 6: KING SOLOMON'S TEMPLE AND THE ARK OF THE COVENANT

1. Albert Pike: *Morals and Dogma of the Ancient and Accepted Scottish Rite of Freemasonry*

2. Albert G. Mackey, M.D.: *Encyclopedia of Freemasonry and Its Kindred Sciences*, p. 971

3. Hippolyto Joseph Da Costa: *Dionysian Artificers*

4. H. P. Blavatsky: *The Secret Doctrine*, vol. 4, p. 32. Anthropogenesis, parts 2 and 3

5. C. W. Leadbeater: *Ancient Mystic Rites*, pp. 75, 77

CHAPTER 8: ALEXANDRIA AND THE ARK OF THE COVENANT

1. H. P. Blavatsky: *Isis Unveiled*, vol. 2, p. 29

2. Edward Gibbon: *The Decline and Fall of the Roman Empire*, vol. 5, p. 229

3. Milton Terry (translator): *The Sibylline Oracles*, p. 12

4. Albert Pike: *Morals and Dogma*, p. 774

5. Dr. Sigismund Bacstrom quoted in Manly P. Hall: *The Secret Teachings of All Ages*, p. CLVIII

6. H. P. Blavatsky: *Isis Unveiled*, vol. 2, p. 444

7. Professor A. Wilder, *New Platonism and Alchemy* (Albany 1869), p. 6, quoted in Blavatsky: *Isis Unveiled*, vol. 2, p. 444

8. Frances Yates: *Giordano Bruno and the Hermetic Tradition*

CHAPTER 9: CHRIST AND THE ARK OF THE COVENANT

1. Barbara Thiering: *Jesus and the Riddle of the Dead Sea Scrolls*, pp. 41–42

2. Manly P. Hall: *The Secret Teachings of All Ages*, p. CLXXVII

3. *The Secret Teachings of All Ages*, p. CLXXVII

4. Christian D. Ginsburg: *The Essenes—The Kabbalah*, p. 14

5. H. Spencer Lewis: *The Mystical Life of Jesus*, p. 27

6. Edmond Bordeaux Szekely: *From Enoch to the Dead Sea Scrolls*, p. 14

7. Edouard Schuré: *The Great Initiates*, p. 425

8. Manly P. Hall: *The Mystical Christ*, p. 63

9. Hone, *The Arabic Gospel of the Infancy*, Chs. XX and XI, quoted in Blavatsky: *Isis Unveiled*, vol. 2, p. 154

10. Manly P. Hall: *The Mystical Christ*, p. 66

11. Manly P. Hall: "The Unrecorded Years in the Life of Christ," Lecture Notes #273, pp. 6, 7

12. Manly P. Hall: *The Mystical Christ*, p. 8

13. John Allegro: *The Dead Sea Scrolls and the Christian Myth*, p. 12

14. Michael Baigent, Richard Leigh, and Henry Lincoln: *The Messianic Legacy*, p. 88

15. John Dominic Crossan: *Who Killed Jesus?* quotation taken from the front and back cover

16. Jerry Snider, review of Robert Funk: *Honest to Jesus*, in "Magical Blend" (March, 1997)

17. H. Spencer Lewis: *The Mystical Life of Jesus*, pp. 273, 288–95

18. *The Mystical Life of Jesus*, p. 289

19. *The Mystical Life of Jesus* pp. 291–294

20. It is interesting to note this story that appeared November 1, 1997, in the Los Angeles *Times*: "In the Vatican's strongest condemnation of moral passivity during the Holocaust, Pope John Paul II said Friday that anti-Semitic prejudices based on 'wrong and unjust interpretations' of the New Testament deadened the 'spiritual resistance' of many Christians to the Nazi persecutions of Jews. . . ."

CHAPTER 10: FRANCE AND THE ARK OF THE COVENANT

1. The quotation of *Perceval Continuation*, Mons, MS. V.33, 755 ff., Armand Hoog ed. (1949, 1974), quoted in Norma Goodrich: *The Holy Grail*, p. 53–54

2.   Clement of Alexandria: *Stromata*, vol. 3, 6:52

3.   The quotation of William Caxton of Legenda Aurea (Golden Legend), published in 1275, is from *Genisis*, by David Wood, p. 48

4.   H. P. Blavatsky: *Isis Unveiled*, vol. 2, p. 154

5.   Manly P. Hall: *The Secret Teachings of All Ages*, p. XXVI

CHAPTER 11: GLASTONBURY AND THE ARK OF THE COVENANT

1.   Lionel Smithett Lewis: *St. Joseph of Arimathea at Glastonbury*, p. 144

2.   Gildas, the Wise Albanicus (A.D. 425–512): *De excidio Britanniae*, Sec. 8, p. 25

3.   Bligh Bond: *The Mystery of Glaston*, quoted in Lionel Smithett Lewis: *Joseph of Arimathea at Glastonbury*, p. 166

4.   Rev. C. C. Dobson: *Did Our Lord Visit Britain as They Say in Cornwall and Somerset?* p. 30

5.   The quotation of A. H. Lewis: *Christ in Cornwall*, quoted in John Matthews (ed.): *A Glastonbury Reader*, p. 184

6.   Isabel Hill Elder: *Joseph of Arimathea*, pp. 13, 14

7.   William Malmesbury quoted in E. Raymond Capt: *Traditions of Glastonbury*, pp. 55–56

8.   C. C. Dobson: *Did Our Lord Visit Britain as They Say in Cornwall and Sommerset?* p. 43

9.   *Grand-Saint-Graal*, Incident 31 ff., Nutt p. 60 ("History of the Holy Grail"), vol. 2, ch. 41, quoted in Norma Lorre Goodrich: *The Holy Grail*, pp. 78–80

10.   *Domesday Book*, written 1086 A.D., Glastonbury Domesday Survey, Folio p. 249 B

11.   Dion Fortune: *Avalon of the Heart*, quoted in John Matthews (ed.): *A Glastonbury Reader*, pp. 219–221

12.   *Avalon of the Heart* in *A Glastonbury Reader*, p. 221

13. William of Malmesbury quoted in Frederick Bligh Bond: *Gate of Remembrance*, p. 148

14. *Gate of Remembrance*, p. 147

15. Katherine Maltwood: *Guide to Glastonbury's Temple of the Stars*, p. 6

16. John Michell: *The New View over Atlantis*, p. 172

17. *The New View over Atlantis*, p. 171

18. J. W. Taylor: *St. Joseph and Glastonbury* quoted in John Matthews (ed.): *A Glastonbury Reader*, pp. 111–13

19. Manly P. Hall: *The Secret Teachings of All Ages*, p. CLXXX

20. Frederick Bligh Bond: *The Gate of Remembrance*, p. 147

21. John Michell: *New Light on the Ancient Mystery of Glastonbury*, p. 122

22. J. W. Taylor: *St. Joseph and Glastonbury* quoted in Matthews (ed.): *A Glastonbury Reader*, p. 101

23. John Michell: *New Light on the Ancient Mystery of Glastonbury*, pp. 158–59

24. *New Light on the Ancient Mystery of Glastonbury*, p. 159

25. Patricia Villiers-Stuart: "Bend Me a Maze," quoted in Anthony Roberts (ed.): *Glastonbury, Ancient Avalon, New Jerusalem*, p. 166

CHAPTER 13: AMERICA AND THE ARK OF THE COVENANT

1. *Baconian Magazine*, vol. XXXV, #140 (July 1951)

2. William Smedley: *The Mystery of Francis Bacon*, p. 138

3. For the text of this speech, see: Manly P. Hall: *America's Assignment with Destiny*, p. 75

4. Marie Bauer Hall: *Quest for Bruton Vault*, pp. 6, 10

5. Manly P. Hall: *America's Assignment with Destiny*, p. 64

6. Peter Tompkins: *The Magic of Obelisks*, p. 339

7. Charles L. Westbrook, Jr.: *The Talisman of the United States*, p. 22

8. Eklal Kueshana: *The Ultimate Frontier*, pp. 73–74

9. *The Montana Mason*, article "Masonry in Mexico," February 1922

10. Gefard Masur quoted in Manly P. Hall: *America's Assignment with Destiny*, p. 103

CHAPTER 14: THE ALCHEMICAL MARRIAGE

1. Victoria Ransom and Henrietta Bernstein: *The Crone Oracles*, pp. 29–30

2. *The Crone Oracles*, p. 133

3. Jose Barreiro, editor: *Indian Roots of American Democracy*, p. 48

CHAPTER 15: THE MASONIC CONNECTION TO THE HOLY GRAIL

1. Manly P. Hall: *The Secret Teaching of All Ages*, p. XCIX

2. Manly P. Hall: *Legends of Glastonbury Abbey*, p. 10

3. Norma Lorre Goodrich: *The Holy Grail*, p. 23

4. Manly P. Hall: *Orders of the Quest: The Holy Grail*, p. 84

5. Manly P. Hall: *Orders of the Quest: The Holy Grail*, p. 100

6. Manly P. Hall: "The Holy Grail" (Lecture Audio Tape)

REFERENCES

Allegro, J. M.: *The Treasure of the Copper Scroll* (London, 1960)

—— *The Dead Sea Scrolls and the Christian Myth* (Westridge Books, 1979) (Prometheus Books, N.Y. 1992)

Ashe, Geoffrey: *The Glastonbury Tor Maze: At the Foot of the Tree* (Glastonbury, 1979)

Bacon, Sir Francis: *Advancement of Learning* (London, 1605, 1640; Amsterdam 1694)

—— *King James Revision of the Holy Bible* (London, 1611)

—— *New Atlantis*, Begun by Lord Verulam Viscount St. Albans and continued by R. H. Esquire (London, 1627)

—— *Novum Organum Scientiarum* (Amsterdam, 1695)

Bacstrom, Sigismund; *Collection of Alchemical Manuscripts* (18 vols.) manuscript copies from rare alchemical writing, with notes on the Emerald Tablet by Dr. Bacstrom (mentioned by A. E. Waite in his *Brotherhood of the Rosy Cross*)

Baigent, M., and Leigh, R.: *The Temple and the Lodge* (New York, 1989)

Baigent, M., Leigh, R., and Lincoln, H.: *Holy Blood, Holy Grail* (London, 1982, 1983; New York 1983)

—— *The Messianic legacy* (New York, 1987)

Baronius, Cardinal Caesar: *Ecclesiastical Annals*, ending A.D. 1198

244

Barreiro, Jose, editor: *Indian Roots of American Democracy* (Akwekon Press, Cornell University, Ithaca, New York, 1992)

Bayley, Harold: *The Lost Language of Symbolism* (2 vols., New York, 1912, 1951, 1952)

Benet's Third Edition Readers Encyclopedia (Harper and Row, New York, 1987)

Bernstein, Henrietta: *Cabalah Primer* (DeVorss & Co., Marina del Rey, Calif., 1984)

—— *The Crone Oracles*, co-authored with Victoria Ransom (Samuel Weiser Inc., Maine, 1994)

Blavatsky, H. P.: *Isis Unveiled* (Theosophical Publishing House, Adyar, India 1877 and 1882)

—— *The Secret Doctrine* (The Theosophical Society, Adyar, India, 1962)

Bond, Frederick Bligh: *Gates of Remembrance* (England, 1918, 1978)

—— *The Company of Avalon* (England, 1924)

Budge, Sir E. A. Wallis, (trans.): *The Book of the Glory of Kings, the Kebra Nagast* (London, c. 1920)

Carter, Mary Ellen, under the editorship of Hugh Lynn Cayce: *Edgar Cayce on Prophecy* (Warner Books, 1968)

Charpentier, Louis: *Les Mystères Templiers* (Paris, 1967)

Clement of Alexandria: *Stromata*, writings contained in *The Ante-Nicene Fathers* (New York, 1926).

Crossan, John Dominic: *Who Killed Jesus?* (Harper San Francisco, 1995)

Da Costa: *Dionysian Artificers* (Republished with Introduction by Manly P. Hall, Philosophical Research Society, Los Angeles, 1964, 1975)

Dante Alighieri: *La Divina Commedia* (Torino, 1891)

—— *La Vita Nuova and the Divina Commedia* (New York, 1901)

Deacon, Richard: *John Dee: Scientist, Geographer, Astrologer and Secret Agent to Elizabeth I* (London, 1968)

De Borron (or Boron), Robert: *Le Roman de l'Estoire dou Graal*, ed. by William Nitze (Paris, 1927)

De Troyes, Chretien: *Perceval ou le Roman du Graal* (Preface by Armond Hoog); trans. and notes by Jean-Pierre-Foucher and Andre Ortais (Paris, 1949, 1974)

Devereux, Paul: *Places of Power* (London, 1990)

Dobson, Rev. C. C.: *Did Our Lord Visit Britain as They Say in Cornwall and Somserset?* (The Avalon Press, England, 1936)

Dodd, Alfred: *The Secret History of Francis Bacon* (Rider, London, 1941)

Donnelly, Ignatius: *Atlantis, the Antediluvian World* (New York and London, 1882)

—— *The Great Cryptogram* (Chicago, New York, London, 1888)

Ebers, George: *Egypt: Descriptive, Historical, and Picturesque*, vol. I (London, Paris and New York, n.d.)

Evans, Sebastian (ed. and trans.): *The High History of the Holy Grail* (London, undated), translated from the old French, from the *Book of Josephes in the Glastonbury Abbey Library* (J. M. Dent 1899, London) (James Clarke 1969, London and New York)

Eisen, William: *Agasha: Master of Wisdom* (DeVorss & Co., Marina del Rey, Calif., 1977)

—— *The Agashan Discourses* (1978)

—— *The English Cabalah* Vol. 1 (1980)

—— *The English Cabalah* Vol. 2 (1982)

—— *The Essence of the Cabalah* (1984)

—— *The Cabalah of Astrology* (1986)

—— *The Universal Language of Cabalah* (1989)

Eisenman, R. H.: *Maccabees, Zadokites, Christians and Qumran* (Leiden, 1983)

Eschenbach, Wolfram von: *Parzival*, trans. by A. T. Hatto (London and New York, 1980). Another translation by Charles E. Passage (New York, 1961)

Fanthorpe, Lionel and Patricia: *Secrets of Rennes-le-Château* (Samuel Weiser, Inc., Maine, 1992)

Fendler, Grace: *New Truths about Columbus* (Los Angeles, 1934)

Fiske, John: *Old Virginia and Her Neighbors*, vol. 2 (Boston, 1897)

Forbes, J. Foster: *Giants of Britain* (Thomas Publications, Birmingham, 1945)

Fortune, Dion: *Avalon of the Heart* (The Aquarian Press, London, 1936, revised 1986)

Franklin, Benjamin: *Poor Richard's Almanac*. Published under the name of Richard Saunders (1733–1758)

—— *Anderson's Constitution of Freemasonry* (Peter Pauper Press, Mt. Vernon, New York)

French, Peter: *John Dee, The World of an Elizabethan Magus* (London, 1972, 1984)

Funk, Robert W.: *Honest to Jesus* (Harper San Francisco, 1996)

Geoffrey of Monmouth: *Histories of the Kings of England* (London, J. M. Deat, 1934; also trans. by L. Thorpe, 1988)

Gibbon, Edward: *The Decline and Fall of the Roman Empire*, vol. 5 (New York, 1899)

Gibbs, Ray: *The Legendary XII Hides of Glastonbury* (Llanerch Enterprises, Wales, 1988)

Ginsburg, Christian D.: *The Essenes, Their History and Doctrine: The Kabbalah, Its Doctrines, Development and Literature* (Green and Co., London, 1862, 1920; Samuel Weiser Inc., Maine, 1972)

Goodrich, Norma Lorre: *The Holy Grail* (New York, 1992)

Gospel of Nicodemus, See *The Lost Books of the Bible and the Forgotten Books of Eden*. Introduction by Franke Crane (New York, Newfoundland, London, Ontario, 1974)

Grand-Saint-Graal, See Kempe, Dorothy

Gurteen, Dr. S. Humphreys: *The Arthurian Epic* (New York and London, 1895)

Hall, Marie Bauer: *Foundations Unearthed, Quest for Bruton Vault* (Veritas Press, Los Angeles, California 1940, 1974)

Hall, Manly P.: (works published by the Philosophical Research Society, Los Angeles, California):

—— *America's Assignment with Destiny* (1931)

—— *The Secret Destiny of America* (1944, 1972)

—— "Legends of Glastonbury Abbey" (article from *P.R.S. Journal*, vol. 18, no. 2)

—— *Masonic Orders of Fraternity* (1950, 1976)

—— *Orders of the Quest, The Holy Grail* (1949, 1976)

—— *Old Testament Wisdom* (1957)

—— *The Secret Teachings of All Ages, An Encyclopedic Outline of Masonic, Hermetic, Qabbalistic, and Rosicrucian Symbolical Philosophy* (1928)

—— *Twelve World Teachers* (1957)

—— *The Mystical Christ* (1951)

—— *The Lost Keys of Freemasonry* (1923, 1976)

—— *Mystics and Mysteries of Alexandria* (1988)

—— *Freemasonry of the Ancient Egyptians* (1937)

—— "The Unrecorded Years in the Life of Christ" (Lecture Notes #273)

—— "The Holy Grail" (Lecture Audio Tape) Copyright The Philosophical Research Society

Hallam, Arthur Henry: *Sullo Spirito* (London, 1832)

Hancock, Graham and Bauval, Robert: *The Message of the Sphinx* (Crown Publishers, Inc., New York, 1996)

Heckethorne, Charles William: *The Secret Societies of All Ages and Countries* (London, 1897, 1928, 1978)

Heline, Corinne: *Mystic Masonry and the Bible* (Santa Monica, Calif. 1989)

Hermes: *The Divine Pymander of Hermes Mercurius Trismegistus* (London, 1650) trans. from Arabic and Greek by Dr. Everard

—— *Hermetics*, edited by Walter Scott (Oxford, 1924)

Higgins, Godfrey: *Anacalypsis* (London, 1836, 1972)

—— *The Celtic Druids* (London, 1827)

Irenaeus, Bishop of Lyons: *Against Heresies* (Writings contained in *The Ante-Nicene Fathers*, New York, 1926)

Irving, Sir Henry, ed.: *The Complete Works of William Shakespeare* (New York and London, Funk and Wagnalls, 1927)

James, M. P., trans.: *Acts of Pilate and the Gospel of Nicodemus in The Apocryphal New Testament* (Oxford Unviersity Press, 1924)

Jennings, Hargrave: *The Rosicrucians, Their Rites and Mysteries* (First Edition, London, 1870) (Health Research, Calif., 1966)

Josephus, Flavius: *Antiquities of the Jews: A History of the Jewish Wars and Life of Flavius Josephus*, trans. W. Whiston (London, n.d.)

Justin, Martyr: Writings Contained in *The Ante-Nicene Fathers* (New York, 1926)

Kempe, Dorothy: *The Legends of The Holy Grail, Its Sources, Character and Development* (London, 1905)

Kueshana, Eklal: *The Ultimate Frontier* (The Adelphi Organization, Texas, 1963, 1986)

Lawrence, Msc.D., Shirley Blackwell: *Numerology and the English Cabalah* (Newcastle, California, 1994)

Leadbeater, C. W.: *The Hidden Life of Freemasonry* (Theosophical Publishing House, India, 1963)

Lehner, Mark: *The Egyptian Heritage* (A.R.E. Press, Virginia Beach, Virginia, 1974)

Le Plongeon, Dr. Augustus: *Queen Moo and the Egyptian Sphinx* (New York, 1900)

—— *Sacred Mysteries Among the Mayas and the Quiches* (New York, 1909)

249

—— *Our Story of Atlantis* (Philosophical Publishing Co., Quaker-town, Pa., 1937)

Lewis, H. Spencer: *The Mystical Life of Jesus* (The Rosicrucian Order, AMORC, Inc., San Jose, CA., 1977)

—— *The Secret Doctrines of Jesus* (The Rosicrucian Order, AMORC, 1957)

Lewis, Lionel Smithett: *St Joseph of Arimathea at Glastonbury, or The Apostolic Church of Britain* (Cambridge, 1922) (James Clarke, 1955, 1976)

Lincoln, Henry: *The Holy Place* (Little, Brown and Co., New York, 1991)

Lovelich, Henry: *History of the Holy Grail*, a translation of *Grand Seint Graal*, 1450. Written originally in French Prose at Glastonbury between 1191–1212. Also called *The High History of the Holy Grail*, ed. by Frederick J. Furnivall (London, 1925)

Maccoby, Haim: *Revolution in Judea* (New York, 1980)

Mackey, M.D., Albert G.: *Encyclopedia of Freemasonry and Its Kindred Sciences* (The Masonic History Co., Chicago, 1950)

MacNulty, W. Kirk: *Freemasonry, A Journey Through Ritual and Symbol* (England, 1991)

Malory, Sir Thomas: *Le Morte d'Arthur*, 2 vols. (London and New York, 1906, 1961) (First edition 1485)

Maltwood, Katherine E.: *The Enchantments of Britain* (Victoria, B.C., 1944)

—— *Guide to Glastonbury's Temple of the Stars* (London, 1934)

Masonic Manuscripts, Harleian, Sloan, Edinburgh-Kilwinning, Lans-downe. See *Encyclopedia of Freemasonry* by Albert Mackey.

Mathers, S. L. MacGregor: *The Kabbalah Unveiled* (London, 1888; Samuel Weiser, Inc., 1983)

Matthews, John: editor of *Glastonbury Reader* (London, 1991)

—— *The Household of the Grail* (England, 1990)

—— *The Grail, Quest for the Eternal* (England, 1981)

McKenzie, Kenneth, R. H.: *The Masonic Cyclopedia* (London, 1877)

Mead, G. R. S.: *Thrice-Greatest Hermes* (London, 1906)

Michell, John: *The New View over Atlantis* (New York, 1969, 1983)

—— *New Light on the Ancient Mystery of Glastonbury* (Somserset, 1990)

—— *The Dimensions of Paradise* (Harper & Row, San Francisco, 1988)

—— and Christine Rhone: *Twelve Tribe Nations and the Science of Enchanting the Landscape* (U.S.A., 1991)

Pagels, Elaine: *The Gnostic Gospels* (London, 1980)

Paine, Lauran: *Bolivar the Liberator* (New York, 1970)

Parker, Arthur C.: *American Indian Freemasonry* (New York, 1919)

Pearlman, M.: *The Dead Sea Scrolls in the Shrine of the Book* (Jerusalem, 1988)

Perlesvaus, or *Le Haut Levre du Graal*, Ed. by W. A. Nitze and T. A. Jenkins, 2 vols. (Chicago, 1932) (New York, 1972)

Phelon, W. P., M.D.: *Our Story of Atlantis, Written Down for the Hermetic Brotherhood and Future Rulers of America* (The Philosophical Publishing Co., Quakertown, Pa., 1937)

Pike, Albert: *Morals and Dogma of the Ancient and Accepted Scottish Rite of Freemasonry* (Washington, D.C., 1960)

Plato: *Timaeus and Critias*, translated with an introduction by Desmond Lee (London, 1971)

Pott, Mrs. Henry: *Francis Bacon and His Secret Society* (London, 1911)

Raleigh, Sir Walter: *The History of the World* (London, 1614)

Roberts, Anthony, ed.: *Glastonbury, Ancient Avalon, New Jerusalem* (London, Rider 1978, 1992)

Robinson, Joseph Armitage: *Two Glastonbury Legends: King Arthur and St. Joseph of Arimathea* (Cambridge, 1926)

Schuré, Edouard: *The Great Initiates, A Study of the Secret History of Religions* (France, 1889) (Steiner Books, New York, 1961)

—— *The Mysteries of Egypt* (Philadelphia, 1925)

Shakespeare, William: *The Tempest* (London, 1611)

Skinner, Ralston J.: *The Source of Measures* (San Diego, 1982)

Smedley, William T.: *The Mystery of Francis Bacon* (Health Research, U.S.A., 1967)

Spence, Lewis: *The Mysteries of Britain, Sacred Rites and Traditions of Ancient Britain Restored* (London, Rider, 1928)

Spong, John Shelby: *Born of Woman* (Harper, San Francisco, 1992)

Steiner, Rudolf: *Submerged Continents of Atlantis and Lemuria* (Rajput Press, 1911)

Szekely, Edmond Bordeaux: *From Enoch to the Dead Sea Scrolls* (Academy Books, San Diego, Calif. 1977)

Taylor, J. W.: *St. Joseph and Glastonbury*, orig. *Coming of the Saints* (London, 1906, 1969)

Taylor, Thomas: *Iamblichus, The Mysteries of the Egyptians, Chaldeans and Assyrians* (London, 1895)

Terry, Milton S. (trans.): *The Sibylline Oracles* (New York, 1890)

Thiering, Barbara: *Jesus and the Riddle of the Dead Sea Scrolls: Unlocking the Secrets of His Life Story* (Harper Collins, 1992)

Tompkins, Peter: *The Magic of Obelisks* (U.S.A., 1981)

—— *Secrets of the Great Pyramid* (Harper and Row, 1971)

Twain, Mark: *Essays and Sketches by Mark Twain* (New York, 1995)

Tyler, Lyon Gardner: *Williamsburg, the Old Colonial Capital* (Richmond, 1907)

Von Daniken, Erich: *Signs of the Gods* (New York, 1980)

Von Eschenbach, Wolfram: *Parzival*, trans. by A. T. Hatto (London and New York, 1981)

—— also trans. by Helen M. Mustard and Charles E. Passage (New York, 1961)

—— *Titurel*, trans. by Charles E. Passage (New York, 1984)

Voragine, Jacobus de: *The Golden Legend*, F. S. Ellis, ed. (London, 1900) Trans. and adapted from Latin by Granger Ryan and Helmest Ripperger (Arno Press, New York, 1969)

Waite, A. E.: *The Real History of the Rosicrucians* (London, 1887)

—— *The New Encyclopaedia of Freemasonry* (London, 1921)

Westbrook, Jr., Charles L.: *The Talisman of the United States: The Mysterious Street Lines of Washington D.C.* (The Westcom Press, North Carolina, 1990)

William of Malmesbury: *De Antiquitate Glastoniensis Ecctesiae, 1129–39*, trans. as *On the Antiquity of the Church of Glastonbury;* also *Gesta Regum,* or *De Gestis Regum Anglarium (Acts of Kings)* (London, 1887)

Wilson, R. M.: *The Gospel of Philip* (London, 1962)

Wither, George: *A collection of Emblemes, Ancient and Moderne* (England, 1634) (The Philosophical Research Society, Inc., Los Angeles, 1987)

Wood, David: *Genisis, The First Book of Revelations* (The Baton Press, Kent, England, 1985)

Yates, Frances Amelia: *The Rosicrucian Enlightenment* (London and Boston, 1972) (Paladin, Granada St. Albans, England, 1975)

—— *Giordano Bruno and the Hermetic Tradition* (University of Chicago Press, 1964, 1977)

Zamarian, Paul: *Liberty Enlightening the World* (Mt. Shasta, California, 1986)

ABOUT THE AUTHOR

Henrietta Bernstein writes and lectures on the ancient Mysteries. She has co-authored the book *The Crone Oracles: The Initiates Guide to the Ancient Mysteries* (Samuel Weiser, Inc., 1994), which has also been published in Germany. Her book *Cabalah Primer* (DeVorss, 1984) was the first book to be published by a woman on the esoteric subject of cabalah combined with sacred geometry, as given in the Ark of the Covenant.

Ms. Bernstein is president and director of the Cabalah Research Foundation established by the noted Cabalist William Eisen, with whose work she was closely associated before his death in 1989. Her background of research also includes many years of study of the ancient Mysteries with Manly P. Hall, a world-recognized authority on these subjects and founder of the Philosophical Research Society. During that time she also worked in Marie Bauer Hall's Veritat Foundation, a non-profit educational organization.

After receiving her degree from the University of Southern California, Ms. Bernstein undertook graduate studies in mathematics, physics, chemistry, and philosophy. She has organized and chaired conferences on Electric Magnetic Energy and Earth Energy and Electric Magnetic Medicine. In 1997, she was invited to Japan to give a series of lectures in various cities on East-West understanding. She is listed in WHO'S WHO IN AMERICA and WHO'S WHO OF AMERICAN WOMEN.